MIND AND CONSCIOUSNESS

Other interview books from Automatic Press ♦ V|P

Formal Philosophy
edited by Vincent F. Hendricks & John Symons
November 2005

Masses of Formal Philosophy
edited by Vincent F. Hendricks & John Symons
October 2006

Political Questions: 5 Questions for Political Philosophers
edited by Morten Ebbe Juul Nielsen
December 2006

Philosophy of Technology: 5 Questions
edited by Jan-Kyrre Berg Olsen & Evan Selinger
February 2007

Game Theory: 5 Questions
edited by Vincent F. Hendricks & Pelle Guldborg Hansen
April 2007

Legal Philosophy: 5 Questions
edited by Morten Ebbe Juul Nielsen
October 2007

Philosophy of Mathematics: 5 Questions
edited by Vincent F. Hendricks & Hannes Leitgeb
January 2008

Philosophy of Computing and Information: 5 Questions
edited by Luciano Floridi
Sepetmber 2008

Philosophy of the Social Sciences: 5 Questions
edited by Diego Ríos & Christoph Schmidt-Petri
September 2008

Epistemology: 5 Questions
edited by Vincent F. Hendricks & Duncan Pritchard
September 2008

Complexity: 5 Questions
Carlos Gershenson
November 2008

See all published and forthcoming books in the 5 Questions series at
www.vince-inc.com/automatic.html

MIND AND CONSCIOUSNESS

5 QUESTIONS

edited by

Patrick Grim

Automatic Press ◆ VIP

Automatic Press ♦ $\frac{V}{I}$P

Information on this title: www.vince-inc.com/automatic.html

© Automatic Press / VIP 2009

This publication is in copyright. Subject to statuary exception and to the provisions of relevant collective licensing agreements, no reproduction of any part may take place without the written permission of the publisher.

First published 2009

Printed in the United States of America
and the United Kingdom

ISBN-10 87-92130-10-0 paperback
ISBN-13 978-87-92130-10-5 paperback

The publisher has no responsibilities for
the persistence or accuracy of URLs for external or
third party Internet Web sites referred to in this publication
and does not guarantee that any content on such
Web sites is, or will remain, accurate or appropriate.

Typeset in $\LaTeX 2_\varepsilon$
Cover art by Chris Silverman
Graphic design by Vincent F. Hendricks

Contents

Preface   iii

Acknowledgements   v

1   Lynne Rudder Baker   1

2   David Chalmers   11

3   Daniel Dennett   25

4   Fred Dretske   31

5   Owen Flanagan   39

6   Samuel Guttenplan   47

7   Valerie Gray Hardcastle   59

8   John Heil   69

9   Douglas Hofstadter   79

10   Terence Horgan   105

11   Frank Jackson   107

12   Jaegwon Kim   117

13   William Lycan   123

14   Alva Noë   135

15   Hilary Putnam   145

16   David Rosenthal   155

17   John Searle   171

18 Stephen Stich	181
19 Galen Strawson	193
20 Michael Tye	209
About the Editor	217
Index	220

Preface

Debate in issues of mind is active and ongoing, with implications not only for philosophy but for psychology, artificial intelligence and the neurosciences. In this volume I've asked some of the foremost philosophers of mind to answer questions both substantive and personal about the field.

I've asked them about how they came to philosophy of mind and what they regard as their foremost contributions. I've asked them what philosophy's role is in relation to the complex of sciences and other disciplines now pursuing questions of mind. I've asked them what they view as the major open questions in the field, and what they consider the most promising prospects for future work.

The issue of consciousness is central to contemporary work, and is one of the areas in which debate rages most vociferously. I have asked participants to share their views as to whether a science of consciousness is possible.

A richer understanding of rival approaches often comes with an understanding of the personal histories behind those approaches. Academic writing, however, tends to submerge personality beneath a scholarly surface of positions and arguments. The interview format can compensate for these shortcomings by encouraging brevity, by allowing an less formal, less guarded, and more colloquial expression of views, and by fostering a personal touch. These interviews are intended to offer that richer glimpse of contemporary philosophy of mind through some of the people who make it what it is.

Patrick Grim
Stony Brook
October 2008

Acknowledgements

I would like to thank the series editor, Vincent F. Hendricks, my publisher Automatic Press ♦ $\frac{V}{I}$P, in particular senior publishing editor V.J. Menshy, for continuing to take on these 'rather unusual academic' projects.

Patrick Grim
Stony Brook
October 2008

WWW.VINCE-INC.COM

1
Lynne Rudder Baker

Distinguished Professor
University of Massachusetts, Amherst, USA

Why were you initially drawn to philosophy of mind?

After an undergraduate degree with a major in mathematics, I turned to philosophy—in part because philosophy had all the interest of math (and logic) plus an indefinitely wide range of subject matter. I began philosophy at an intersection of metaphysics and philosophy of science. My dissertation, *Ontological and Linguistic Aspects of Temporal Becoming*, was on the philosophy of time. A convinced physicalist, I defended the idea that past, present and future (the A-series) are merely "mind-dependent." I spent a year as a Mellon post-doctoral fellow at the University of Pittsburgh, working mainly with Adolf Grünbaum, who was very generous to me with his time. Other members of the philosophical community in Pittsburgh suggested that there was no philosophical interest in nowness; the word 'now' exhausted whatever there was of real interest concerning the status of the present. I therefore turned my attention from the status of the present (nowness) to the word 'now'.

The word 'now' threw me into studying indexical reference. It was a short step from there to interest in indexical belief, and more generally, to interest in *de re* belief. So, I found myself right in the middle of philosophy of mind. In 1979, I read Tyler Burge's ground-breaking "Individualism and the Mental" and, ever since, I've been an extreme social and physical externalist. My externalism extends to all mental states with conceptual content. I've argued against narrow content, against reductionism and eliminativism, and against the assumption that beliefs, desires, and intentions are some kind of mental entities. These latter arguments led me into the metaphysics of mind.

My interest in a nonreductive metaphysics of mind pushed me to conclude that minds (and thoughts, beliefs, etc.) are not entities. They are properties of entities. (The word 'belief' is just a nominalization of 'believes that'.) This conclusion led me to the question: What are beliefs, etc., properties of?

Ah, persons! Exemplification of properties requires a subject, an exemplifier. I am the subject of my attitudes; my brain provides the vehicle. I (a person) am the thinker; my brain is what I think with.

So, I turned to the metaphysics of persons and discovered what I think is the key to understanding the natural world: the idea of constitution. Persons are constituted by bodies (organisms); credit cards are constituted by pieces of plastic; pieces of gold are constituted by aggregates of Au atoms.

Constitution, I believe, is a basic relation among material things. Aggregates of hydrogen atoms and chlorine atoms constitute hydrogen chloride molecules. The relation between the molecules and the aggregate of atoms is not identity: The aggregate of atoms makes up molecules only when the atoms are chemically bonded; the same aggregate of atoms spatially dispersed would not make up molecules.

The metaphysical picture is this: Everything is of some primary kind essentially. Things of one primary kind (or aggregates of things of one or more primary kind) when in certain circumstances, *constitute* things of a higher-level primary kind. (Officially, I do not use the idea of 'higher-level primary kind' in my definition of 'constitution'; rather, I use the idea of constitution to define 'higher-level primary kind.') Everything that we encounter in the natural world—from molecules to persons—is constituted at each moment that it exists, at some level, by aggregates of physical particles. An entity (e.g., an animal or automobile) can be constituted by different things at different times.

Constitution is not identity (the top and legs of the table existed before the table did); it is not mereological composition (the aggregate of top and legs that constitutes the table at t is neither a proper nor an improper part of the table at t).

Constitution is a comprehensive vehicle of novelty: a biological cell is a different kind of thing from the aggregate of molecules that constitutes it. A world with organisms in it would have fundamentally different kinds of entities from a world that lacked organisms—even if the latter world had the same chemicals as, but a different enviroment from, the world that had organisms.

Constitution is nonreductive.

Applied to persons, the Constitution View holds that the relation between a person and her body (typically, a human organism after a certain stage of development) is constitution. Why is the relation between a person and her body constitution rather than identity (as Animalists hold)? Persons have first-person perspectives (whether rudimentary or robust) and they have them essentially. A body that constitutes a person has a first-person perspective only contingently, and only derivatively—in virtue of constituting something that has a first-person perspective nonderivatively. I have worked out a nonCartesian idea of a first-person perspective, both rudimentary and robust, in detail. An entity with a robust first-person perspective can conceive of itself as itself—from the first-person point of view, without any third-person name, description, or demonstrative. Attitudes that manifest robust first-person perspectives are expressed by, e.g., "I hope that I'll not get a speeding ticket," or "I wonder how I'll die." Realizing that an entity with a first-person perspective has numerous attitudes, I returned, with my Constitution View of persons in hand, to the philosophy of mind.

What makes the idea of constitution applicable to philosophy of mind is this: instances of mental properties (e.g., intending to signal a left turn) are constituted at t by instances of neural properties. And the important features of constitution that apply to entities are in place with respect to constitution of property instances. So, the (so-called token) 'intending to signal a left turn' is not identical with, and not reducible to, the neural properties that constitute it. However, intending to signal a left turn may well have causal efficacy independent of the neural properties that constitute my intention. (See my "Nonreductive Materialism" forthcoming in *The Oxford Handbook of the Philosophy of Mind*.)

When someone exemplifies a mental property—say, my intending to signal a left turn, she is in a contentful mental state. Such a state is often said to have two kinds of properties: properties represented in the content and properties of the "vehicles" that carry content. Here is my "take" on this distinction: Attitudes and other contentful mental states are individuated by their content. It is content that makes my intention an intention to signal a left turn, rather than an intention to turn off the radio. The vehicle, on my view, is what constitutes the attitude. Although 'vehicle' is a noun, the vehicle of my intention to signal a left turn comprises the exemplification of properties by my brain. I, the person, am the one with the intention; my brain has properties that provide the vehicle for the intention. When my brain exemplifies such-and-such properties in such-and-such circumstances (e.g., in circumstances where there are automobiles and laws and conventions about driving), then I have an intention to signal a left turn. So, constitution is a key to understanding mentality.

The attitude (individuated by its content) is at a personal level, and the vehicle that constitutes it is at a subpersonal level. The vehicle may have nonbiological parts that play essential roles in cognitive processing. Think of cochlear implants that allow biologically deaf people to hear and comprehend language. The neural processing is integrated with bionic processing as the vehicle for the person's understanding. (Keeping personal and subpersonal levels distinct is important to me because I do not believe that there are extended agents or extended persons; at best, there are extended vehicles.)

Many attitudes are properties that depend on our being situated in the physical and social environments that we are in. The dependence in question is not just causal, but is ontological: Nothing would *be* an instance of intending to signal a left turn in a world without conventions, laws, and machines similar to ours.

To sum up: I don't think that the mind/body distinction is basic; rather, a basic distinction is between persons—who exemplify all manner of mental and other properties—and bodies (typically, organisms). The relation of constitution is a ubiquitous relation that holds both between persons and bodies and also between mental properties and neural (or other constituting) properties.

What do you consider your most important contribution to the field?

I have consistently argued for nonreductive materialism. (Caveat: Nonreductive materialism in the natural world; if the natural world exhausts reality, then I'm committed to nonreductive materialism *tout court*.) I hope to have made a two-fold contribution by developing the idea of constitution-without-identity, and by arguing for the significance of a (nonCartesian) first-person perspective.

With respect to constitution: Constitution is a comprehensive relation that unites entities at different levels without identity; it is a relation distinct from mereological composition; it is nonreductive; it does not "privilege" a mind-independent/mind-dependent distinction. Extension of the idea of constitution from concrete entities to property-instances makes the idea of constitution applicable to philosophy of mind. Attitudes are non-entities, I have argued; rather, attitudes are properties exemplified by persons or organisms. Attitudes (personal-level) are constituted by (subpersonal-level) brain and bionic states.

With respect to the first-person perspective: I have tried to show the significance of the first-person perspective for rational and moral agency, as well as for personhood. I am working out a nonCartesian account of the first-person perspective that fits comfortably with a rather extreme form of externalism, according to which all of the attitudes that we can be aware of ontologically depend on the fact that we are language-users.

I also hope to make a methodological contribution by approaching standard metaphysical questions from the point of view of what I call 'Practical Realism.' According to Practical Realism, metaphysics should be responsive to reflection on successful cognitive practices, both scientific and nonscientific. Practical Realism is *realist* since it is concerned with reality and not just with levels of description, and since it allows that there may exist things beyond our ability to recognize them. Practical Realism is *practical* since it takes the everyday world—that part of reality that includes us, what we do, our language, and the things we interact with—to be no less ontologically significant than the microphysical parts of reality.

This approach has two consequences: First, Practical Realism unsettles the idea that there is a sharp distinction between language and "the world". If we consider language, not to be a formal system but to be a cognitive tool, then we cannot think of it in isolation from the world: to learn a language is to acquire a picture of the world. It is not that the world we encounter is independent of the concepts embedded in our language. We would never encounter, say, heavy traffic if we did not have a language that embeds a host of relevant concepts. Second, Practical Realism precludes the attempt to do metaphysics while restricting ourselves to what is mind-independent. We cannot take reality to be exhausted by what there would be if we didn't exist, that is, if there were no minds.

This point is underscored by use of the idea of constitution as a lever to pry open reality. Indeed, the comprehensiveness of the idea of constitution—which applies equally to molecules and to credit cards—displaces the mind-independent/mind-dependent distinction as a foundation for metaphysics. Various kinds of artifacts belong in basic ontology as much as electrons do. A microscope cannot be replaced by the aggregate of particles that constitutes it; still less can credit cards be replaced by "lower-level" objects. Since artifacts are real, nonredundant objects, they belong in ontology.

We persons, using our minds, contribute to reality. The physical particles out of which all particular entities in the natural world are made up are not the only items in ontology. Artifacts and artworks, irreducible to particles, could not exist in a world without minds. We are part of the natural world, and we change the natural world in fundamental ways. We add new kinds of entities to ontology: from spy satellites to landscape paintings to driver's licenses. Indeed, we can even intervene in the course of evolution.

Comprehensive use of the idea of constitution makes another contribution to philosophy. It shows how everyday things, whose existence we cannot in good faith deny, can be as ontologically significant as electrons. This idea stands in contrast to mereological theories, which are manifestly inadequate to account for ordinary objects as encountered. Constitutionalism simply by-passes the notion that entities can be understood in terms of their parts. It is better to approach entities in terms of what they can do, rather than in terms of what they are made of.

What is the proper role of philosophy in relation to psychology, artificial intelligence, and the neurosciences?

The neurosciences and much of psychology study the (subpersonal) mechanisms that make possible our mental phenomena. (Social psychology and some approaches to clinical psychology are exceptions. Even classical psychoanalysis, I think, is an exception: 'subconscious' does not imply 'subpersonal'.) Artificial intelligence provides models of intelligence that may or may not accurately reflect the mechanisms of human intelligence; my guess is that artificial intelligence will contribute many tools (especially prostheses) for us, whether it provides insights into neural mechanisms or not. I see three roles for philosophy vis à vis the neurosciences and some parts of psychology:

First, philosophers should function as critics—not of empirical results, but of interpretations of empirical results. So, when connectionist results are interpreted as implying that nobody ever believed anything, philosophers should step in and challenge the notion of 'believing' at issue. Philosophers should help us all keep straight the difference between us—persons, subjects of experience—and our brains.

Second, and relatedly, philosophers should consider framework issues (not to say there's a clear demarcation between framework and empirical results), by constructing larger pictures in which to situate scientific and technological findings. For example, we must find a place in our understanding of cognition for cochlear implants, which make bionic contributions to cognitive processing of spoken language.

Third, philosophers should call attention to, and discuss, ethical questions that arise with new technologies and that are overlooked by scientists' eagerness to make discoveries and to invent new devices. We have seen philosophers play this role in medical ethics and in biotechnology. I think that this role will only increase in the future with foreseeable (and nevertheless startling) technological changes.

Is a science of consciousness possible?

The discussions about a science of consciousness have focused on phenomenal consciousness—"raw feels," like the feel of velvet or the smell of garlic. I think that it is a fundamental error to erect a barrier between intentional psychology and phenomenal consciousness. Much of what we are conscious of is intentional. (Think of the TV ad, "I could've had a V8." Although the makers of the ad may be satisfied to have a subconscious influence on your behavior, the ad has induced in me an experience that is both conscious and intentional—expressed by "I could've had a V8.") Typically, conscious experience is intentional: the conscious experience of hearing the announcement that you won an election changes your mental state; so does the conscious realization that you have locked your keys in your car. (Speculation: Only entities with intentional states are conscious entities.)

No doubt there are neural states (perhaps oscillations of some sort; perhaps not localized but distributed) that make conscious experience possible. These states may be discovered and come to be understood in a way that would make it appropriate to say that we have a science of consciousness. On my view, it would be more accurate to say that we would have is a science of the mechanisms that make states conscious—that is, the mechanisms that *constitute* conscious states.

Neural mechanisms can be understood only in third-personal terms. So, the science of consciousness would not show us what consciousness is, or what significance it has for the person who is conscious, or what it's like to be conscious. But from an engineering point of view, it would be a theory. I think that this shows the limitations of science: Even if we had a neural science of consciousness, we would still have the nagging question of how any objective, third-personal phenomena could give rise to first-personal conscious phenomena. We could have a science of consciousness and still not understand it as the conscious person does. Such a science of consciousness would not show that conscious experience was eliminable or reducible to anything third-personal.

I am not suggesting that consciousness is nonphysical. Consciousness is physical in the way that all intentional properties are—by being constituted by aggregates of still lower-level properties. But knowing what constitutes instances of a property may not help us understand the constituted property. You don't understand the property of being a US dollar bill by knowing that US dollar bills are constituted by pieces of a special sort of paper.

In sum, I think that there may well be something we can call a 'science of consciousness,' but it will really be a science of neural mechanisms that constitute consciousness.

What are the most important open problems in contemporary philosophy of mind? What are the most promising prospects?

One of the most important problems in contemporary philosophy of mind is to keep the personal and subpersonal levels distinct. Personal and subpersonal levels are not just different levels of description, but—if my Constitution View is right—they are different levels of reality. Philosophers and scientists need not turn away from subpersonal explanations, but they should not suppose that subpersonal-level explanations supplant, reduce or eliminate phenomena at the personal level. What are needed now are theories that observe this crucial distinction.

The field of Medical Bionics provides an arena for observing the personal/subpersonal distinction. As a Practical Realist, I would advise pushing aside science-fiction thought experiments about zombies to consider real work on, say, neural prostheses. After the rather amazing success of cochlear implants, we have proof that machines can be integrated into organic brains in order to produce cognitive processing. Brain-machine interface work is very exciting and invites philosophical investigation into its ontological and ethical consequences.

2
David Chalmers

Professor of Philosophy, Director for the Centre for Consciousness
Australian National University, Australia

Why were you initially drawn to philosophy of mind?

Growing up, I was a mathematics and science geek. I read everything I could in these areas. Every now and then, something would point in a philosophical direction. Perhaps my most important influence was reading Hofstadter's *Gödel, Escher, Bach* as a teenager. I read it initially for the mathematical parts, but it planted a seed for thinking about the mind. Later, Hofstadter and Dennett's *The Mind's I* got me thinking more about the mind–body problem in particular.

At the University of Adelaide, I mainly studied mathematics and computer science. But in my first year, I needed an extra course, so I took one in philosophy. I didn't do very well in the course—in fact, it was the black mark on my undergraduate academic record. I remember thinking that philosophers were very difficult to read. Even Nagel's "What is it Like to be a Bat?," which now seems beautifully clear to me, seemed pretty obscure and full of jargon at that time. But the module in the philosophy of mind, in particular, left an impression on me.

I recall being told that Adelaide was where philosophers first developed the thesis that mental states were brain states. I was skeptical of the historical claim, but it turned out to be more or less right: this was the place where Ullin Place and Jack Smart developed the mind-brain identity theory in the 1950s. I was also skeptical of the philosophical claim: I wanted to believe that mental states were brain states, but I could not see how this could be so, and I was convinced that a much more radical and substantial theory of consciousness would be required to truly make the case.

I didn't formally study more philosophy in Adelaide, but I didn't stop thinking about it. I would talk about the problem of consciousness endlessly with my friends. It seemed even then that this was the most important unsolved problem in science. Every few months I would have a new theory, with my favorite being my patented "theory of abstractions", whose centerpieces were the claims that consciousness is an abstraction, and that every abstraction goes along with some degree of consciousness. I even presented a brief seminar on this theory to the mathematics department, as it was also part of the theory that numbers were abstractions. This led to the inevitable question: is pi conscious? My answer at the time was something to the effect that pi is conscious but asleep.

I went to Oxford in 1987 to continue my study of mathematics, but on the way I spent a few months hitchhiking around Europe. A lot of that time was spent by the side of the road writing in a notebook, working through all sorts of philosophical ideas. I thought that when I got to Oxford I would return properly to mathematics, but this didn't happen. I became more and more obsessed with the problem of consciousness, having a few ideas that seemed to me at the time to be breakthroughs. One idea was an argument that zombies, and more generally intelligent creatures without consciousness, were impossible (!), based on the idea that they would inevitably talk about consciousness. Another idea was a development of the abstraction theory into a theory of pattern and information. In retrospect, these ideas seem to me to be interesting although not as important as they seemed to be at the time. Still, the whole process has given me a lot of sympathy for people I often hear from with their own breakthrough ideas about consciousness.

Before long it seemed to me that I owed it to myself to develop these ideas properly, and that I should switch from mathematics to philosophy or perhaps cognitive science. Most of my friends and family thought that this was a crazy idea, as I had a track record in mathematics and no evidence that I would be any good in philosophy. Looking at the situation objectively I had to agree, but from the subjective viewpoint it felt like what I had to do. So I met with various Oxford philosophers of mind (Colin McGinn, Kathy Wilkes), and eventually with Michael Dummett, who was then in charge of graduate admissions, and very keen on getting mathematicians into philosophy. I wrote up papers on the two ideas above, and ended up being admitted to the Oxford graduate program in philosophy.

At the same time, I had doubts. My advisor in mathematics,

Michael Atiyah, who was an inspiring figure, returned from some time away and convinced me to give mathematics one more try. I also had the impression that Oxford philosophy was very conservative, and made very little contact with science. In retrospect this impression may have been exaggerated by the fact that a number of the philosophers in my college were Wittgensteinians. So I went back to mathematics for a little while. Not much changed, though. It seemed increasingly to me that contemporary mathematics had moved beyond the era of truly fundamental work, while the study of the mind was an area where the fundamental advances were still to come.

In the middle of 1988, I received a long letter from Doug Hofstadter, to whom I had sent my articles after writing them. He had liked the articles, and suggested that I move to Indiana to join the research group that he was just setting up there. I had no idea where Indiana was, but I went to visit and found both that it was a pleasant place and that the research group was terrific. So I pulled up sticks and moved.

Doug's research group was a tremendously stimulating environment. It was a house full of graduate students and postdocs in all sorts of areas, talking about every topic imaginable in cognitive science, AI, philosophy, and more. I thought initially that I could pursue my ideas from an AI direction, and I spent a lot of time programming connectionist models and the like. But it eventually became clear that to work on consciousness properly, philosophy was the best way for me to go. So I joined the Ph.D. program in philosophy, and belatedly took courses in the area. There wasn't much philosophy of mind at Indiana (though there was plenty of cognitive science), but I read voraciously in the area, to fill in the background that I lacked. I ended up compiling a huge bibliography in the philosophy of mind for this purpose, which has continued to this day on my website.

I still have large gaps in my philosophical education, especially in the history of philosophy, but overall I am glad to have taken the path that I did. In particular, I am glad that I had a chance to think about various ideas philosophically before I had read much about what the great philosophers had thought. One makes a lot of mistakes and reinvents a lot of wheels, but the thinking process itself is invaluable.

2. David Chalmers

What do you consider your most important contribution to the field?

The topic I have worked on the most is certainly consciousness. When I entered graduate school at Indiana, at the start of 1989, consciousness was not at all a fashionable topic. I remember being struck by the fact that there were hardly any books on the subject, either in philosophy or in cognitive science. Of course that has changed now! But initially, working on consciousness was a fairly lonely process. Still, I knew this was what I wanted to do: from my perspective, the problem of consciousness was the reason why a scientist might move to philosophy, while work on smaller topics in the foundations of cognitive science struck me as interesting diversions.

Coming into philosophy from the outside, it seemed to me that many philosophers were either not taking the problem seriously, seizing on cheap methods to deflate the problem that manifestly weren't up to the job, or were taking it too seriously and placing it outside the boundary of science. I've always thought that we need to acknowledge the problem and then face it head on. So I tried to do this, in a few articles and in my Ph.D. thesis *Toward a Theory of Consciousness*, which eventually turned into my book *The Conscious Mind*.

The Conscious Mind was much closer to being a traditional work of philosophy than I had envisioned at the start. Along the way, I had become convinced that a rigorous philosophical approach, bringing in tools from the philosophy of language and from metaphysics, was essential at least to getting clear on the foundational issues. Doing this that convinced me, contrary to my initial inclination, that a materialist approach to consciousness cannot succeed. So I became a sort of dualist. But I think of this dualism as growing naturally out of the scientific attitude: one needs to acknowledge (not dismiss) the data, and then come up with theories that are adequate to the challenges that the data pose.

I never really conceived of the book primarily as an argument against materialism. I had initially thought that this foundational material might take just the first chapter or so of the thesis, but it ended up taking up the bulk of the first half, and becoming the part of the book that is the most widely read. Still, some of the more speculative positive ideas survived in the second half of the book: for examples, a chapter on an information-based approach to consciousness is recognizably a descendant of my undergraduate ideas about abstraction. The ideas are put forward pretty tentatively, and I suspect that at the end of the day there may be more promising ways forward. But I hope that this sort of thing has at least encouraged people to think constructively about nonreductive theories of consciousness.

I had always thought that issues about consciousness and the mind-body problem were as important for scientists as for philosophers, and it was important to me to be able to present the central ideas in a way that would interest scientists. In 1994, I got a chance to do this, with the first "Toward a Science of Consciousness" at Tucson. I gave a half-hour talk on the problems of consciousness, starting with a distinction between the "hard" and "easy" problems and then presenting the central elements of a view on which consciousness is fundamental. Something about this caught people's attention, in a manner unlike any talk I've given before or since. This led to all sorts of terrific discussions, and ongoing productive interactions with scientists such as Christof Koch at Caltech and Roger Penrose at Oxford. It also led to my being invited to write an article on these ideas for *Scientific American*, and to a symposium on the ideas in the then-new *Journal of Consciousness Studies*.

It's obvious that much of the impact of these ideas was due to being in the right place at the right time. Scientists and philosophers were just returning to consciousness around this time, and distinguishing easy and hard problems of consciousness simply articulated something that many or most people recognized already. Certainly there's nothing wildly original about recognizing the problem. If anything, there's just something about the "hard problem" formulation that makes the problem hard to avoid. I like some of the arguments in my papers on this topic, as a way of making the case against reductive views of consciousness without technicality. But I can't really see the distinction between the hard problem and the easy problems, which has had the most influence among scientists, as a major contribution to philosophy.

One byproduct of all this is that a lot more people read my book on consciousness than I ever expected, both inside and outside philosophy. It's not an easy book for nonphilosophers, so I'm always pleased when I hear from nonphilosophers who have read it. I was also pleased that philosophers found a lot to chew on in the book, not just in the broad ideas about consciousness but in the connections to metaphysics and the philosophy of language. Many philosophers were returning to the topics of consciousness and the mind–body problem in the 1990s, so this was an exciting time.

I've also ended up working on quite a few other things, inside and outside the philosophy of mind. In the philosophy of mind I've thought a lot about intentionality, trying to develop a broadly Fregean and internalist account of the contents of thought, by developing some of the ideas from two-dimensional semantics that I used in *The Conscious Mind*. At the same time, in other work I've done with Andy Clark, I've looked at the idea that the cognitive processes can extend into the environment. So I seem to have ended up being both an internalist and an externalist, though I don't think that there's really a contradiction here.

I've always had a strong interest in AI and computation, too. More recently I've returned to computational ideas by thinking about the Matrix, which turned out to shed light on a surprisingly large number of other philosophical ideas, at least for me. To think straight about the Matrix, one has to think straight about the philosophy of mind, the philosophy of language, metaphysics, epistemology, the philosophy of physics, the philosophy of computation, and even ethics and the philosophy of religion. The paper I wrote on the Matrix is pretty close to being my favorite among all the papers I've written, and this is a topic that I'm hoping to return to.

Somewhere along the way, I became a philosophical holist. It seems that almost any area of philosophy is relevant to any other. When I first started in philosophy, I was really interested only in the mind–body problem, and questions about, say, sense and reference seemed to me to be nit-picky semantic questions. But to think properly about the mind–body problem, I had to think about metaphysics, and to think about that properly I had to think about the philosophy of language, and to think about that properly I had to think about epistemology, and so on. So I've ended up doing a fair amount of work in these areas, to the extent that I have a couple of books on these topics (one on meaning and content, one on foundations) that I hope to finish before too long. One pleasant side-effect of this holism is that it has made almost everything in philosophy seem interesting to me.

It's inevitable that work on more specialized philosophical topics has less direct impact than interdisciplinary work on broad themes. But I think that this sort of work is nevertheless crucial, not least to lay foundations for the sort of broader work above and to put it onto a more rigorous footing. I've also come to find it fascinating in its own right. The ideal, I think, is to pursue both big ideas and specialized details in parallel, always doing one with an eye on the other. I like to misquote Kant on this topic:

> big ideas without details are empty; details without big ideas are blind.

What is the proper role of philosophy in relation to psychology, artificial intelligence, and the neurosciences?

I have a complicated attitude to the relationship between philosophy and the cognitive sciences. For a start, I think that there is no firm distinction here. In any area of science, one can ask foundational questions. At a certain point, once the questions are foundational enough, one is doing philosophy. But there is no bright line, and the questions can be asked equally by scientists and by philosophers.

There are all sorts of different roles for philosophers to play in these areas. Most straightforwardly, philosophers can help clarify what scientists are up to, and help to distinguish and understand various important but ambiguous or ill-understood ideas in the sciences (here I think of work on the different notions of representation or of consciousness). Somewhat more ambitiously, philosophers can engage in the process of figuring out just what follows from various empirical results (here I think of work on blindsight or on change blindness, for example). Of course it is usually scientists who generate the data, but the path from data to theory is a process that often involves quasi-philosophical reasoning, and in which philosophers can play a central role. More ambitiously still, philosophy can offer guidance to the sciences, by pointing to promising avenues to explore (here I think of Fodor on modularity), or by making the case that some strategies are more likely to succeed than others (say, in devising a theory of consciousness). Finally, philosophers can sometimes make direct contributions to the sciences, whether by generating data (as experimental philosophers do), by proposing or proving some theoretical principle (as some Bayesian philosophers do), or by overturning others.

People sometimes say that philosophers shouldn't be prescriptive toward scientists. I don't really see why this is so. Scientists themselves are certainly often prescriptive toward other scientists, and their prescriptions are often based on foundational considerations. There's no reason in principle why philosophers can't do the same. Of course it's a good idea for philosophers to really know the science when they do this, though. And the prescriptions will usually be conditional: If you want to explain X, then doing Y won't be enough, and you'll have to do Z. Of course, as with most prescriptions, there is no guarantee that anyone will listen. And many prescriptions will turn out to be wrong. So I am generally in favor of letting a thousand flowers bloom, in science as well as philosophy. But this doesn't mean that some flower patches aren't more promising than others.

Just as interesting is the question of what roles the cognitive sciences have to play in philosophy. Again, I don't think there is any bright line here, and answers to foundational questions can be given equally by scientists and philosophers. Still, it's interesting to see the areas where the cognitive sciences have and haven't had a big impact on philosophy.

Most obviously, there have come to be huge areas—the philosophy of neuroscience, the philosophy of psychology, the philosophy of AI— that simply couldn't exist without the relevant sciences. Closer to traditional philosophy of mind, there are all sorts of foundational issues about how the mind works that have been transformed by work in science. Is the mind modular? Do we think using symbols? Are there unconscious processes? Are cognitive capacities innate? Still, these are questions that one should have expected to be empirical questions all along, albeit questions that require a lot of philosophical analysis.

When it comes to some of the really big central questions in the philosophy of mind, however—the mind/body problem, the nature of intentionality or of perceptual experience, the problems of mental causation and free will—it's not clear that these have been transformed by the cognitive sciences to the same extent. The sciences have certainly had an impact around the edges, not least by helping us to understand many specific processes and disorders involving consciousness, intentionality, perception, agency, and so on. But when it comes to some of the big traditional debates—those between materialism and property dualism about consciousness, between internalism and externalism about intentionality, between various metaphysical theories of perception, between compatibilism and incompatibilism about free will—the impact has been less than one might expect.

Of course some will chalk this up to the resistance of philosophers, and some will take it as evidence that these weren't the important questions in the first place. But I think something more is going on here. Whenever empirical results are brought to bear on the philosophical questions, the application requires some sort of philosophical premise to serve as a bridge. And in case of the big philosophical questions above, in order for this premise to be strong enough that the data bear directly on the question, the premise is typically so strong that it is almost as contentious as the philosophical views at issue. So disagreements about these philosophical views simply ramify into disagreements over the bridging premise.

This isn't always the case. Sometimes, when empirical results are applied to philosophical questions, the bridging premise is somewhat less antecedently contentious than the views in question. In these cases, one gets a sort of amplification from a less contentious premise to a more powerful conclusion. But in the case of questions such as those above, this sort of amplification is relatively rare.

I take the moral to be that the debates in question may well have a deeply philosophical core, one that is unlikely to be resolved by the straightforward application of empirical results. Instead, the core of the debates may well rest on conceptual, metaphysical, and normative issues that fall largely within the a priori domain. So philosophers should not feel embarrassed at spending a lot of time working in a largely non-empirical mode, as most philosophers do. Often this is the best way to get to the heart of the issue.

Different philosophers have different attitudes here. It is not uncommon for scientifically oriented philosophers to hold that there is something deeply old-fashioned or conservative about a priori philosophy, and that the real action lies in the sciences. Perhaps one's background makes a difference here. If one started in traditional philosophy, science can seem refreshing and liberating. But from my own perspective, starting in science, I moved into philosophy precisely because it seemed to address the big questions than science didn't settle. From this perspective it is no surprise that a priori methods should play a major role. I may well also be influenced by having a background in mathematics, which has made enormous progress using largely a priori methods.

Of course this is not to say that philosophers should ignore science. At the very least, philosophers should make sure that their ideas are at least compatible with scientific results. Thinking about science is also a terrific way to help one's thinking about philosophy, not least in expanding one's imagination. Scientific results can be expected to have a major impact on some philosophical questions, and at least a minor impact on almost all philosophical questions. But scientific results are just one tool among many in the philosopher's arsenal.

Is a science of consciousness possible?

Yes, I think that a science of consciousness is possible. In fact, I think that quite a few bits of it are actual, in contemporary work on consciousness in neuroscience, psychology, and other areas. I've spent a lot of time trying to help get the infrastructure for a interdisciplinary science of consciousness off the ground, through the "Toward a Science of Consciousness" conferences and through the Association for the Scientific Study of Consciousness, as well as through centres devoted to consciousness at Arizona and ANU. It seems to me that the recent explosion in the science of consciousness is one of the most interesting and important intellectual movements of our time.

There are qualifications, of course. I don't think that a successful science of consciousness can be a wholly reductive science of consciousness, cast in terms of neuroscience or computation alone. Rather, I think it will be a nonreductive science, one that does not try to reduce consciousness to a physical process, but rather studies consciousness in its own right and tries to find connections to brain, behavior, and other cognitive processes. If you look at the contemporary neuroscience and psychology of consciousness, this is just what you find. Any attempts at reduction of consciousness are extremely half-hearted. Instead neuroscience is largely engaged in finding neural correlates of consciousness, without making claims about reduction. Psychology studies the connections between conscious processes, unconscious processes, and behavior. This way, a lot of progress has been made.

I think that the science of consciousness also differs from many other sciences in that it gives an essential role to subjective or first-person data. In a way, each of our own conscious experiences provides the primary data that is distinctive to the science of consciousness. We cannot directly observe the experiences of others, so our access to consciousness is largely mediated by introspection (in ourselves) and verbal reports (in others). Assuming that we can take the deliverances of introspection and verbal report at face value – which is by no means always the case—these can be used to build up a store of first-person data about consciousness itself. One can then correlate this data with third-person data about brain and behavior, and attempt to integrate all these data via principles that connect them. I think that the principles of a satisfactory science of consciousness will always make ineliminable reference to subjective experience, though.

Of course it is very early days at the moment. We're greatly limited by what we know about the brain. Brain imaging tells one only so much, and the invasive techniques that can tell one more (such as single-cell recording) are largely limited to non-human animals and the occasional surgical patient. We're also limited by our methods for investigating states of consciousness. The science typically uses rough-and-ready introspective reports, but these are extremely coarse-grained. Ideally we would like to be able to use sophisticated and reliable introspective techniques, combined with some sort of rich formal language for expressing and analyzing states of consciousness. We don't have anything like that yet, and it's an open question whether these things are possible. But again, it's early in the day. After making a start on these topics in the nineteenth century, the sciences have only recently been returning to them. The proof will be in the pudding.

Ultimately, the hope is for a set of fundamental principles connecting physical processes and consciousness. If I am right about the metaphysics of consciousness, then these principles will have a status akin to that of fundamental laws in physics. I've speculated a bit about what these principles might be, but any theories that we come up with now will almost certainly be wrong. The science of consciousness probably has a revolution or three to go through before it gets to anything like its destination, and when it gets there, it may be quite unlike anything that we currently imagine.

Given this, though, I think we should be open to all sorts of ideas. I'm always pleased to see scientists and philosophers putting forward positive theories of consciousness. Even when they are wrong, one learns something from the attempt. When I first got into philosophy, I was disappointed by how little positive theorizing there was about consciousness. Philosophers seemed to have the sense that theorizing about consciousness should be left to scientists, while scientists seemed to have the sense that theorizing about consciousness should be led to philosophers. That situation has improved to some extent, but I'd like to see more of it. Of course this work often goes out on a limb, but sometimes one has to go out on limbs to get through the forest.

What are the most important open problems in contemporary philosophy of mind? What are the most promising prospects?

I take it that all of the most important problems in the philosophy of mind are still open. This applies most obviously to the mind–body problem and its various components, such as the problem of consciousness, the problem of intentionality, and the problem of mental causation. But the same goes for most of the other traditional problems in the area: the problem of other minds, the unity of consciousness, the nature of self-knowledge, the nature of concepts, and so on.

It seems to be in the nature of these problems that they are clarified rather than solved. Or perhaps they are solved to the satisfaction of an individual, or solved to the satisfaction of small groups or small communities. But they are never solved to the satisfaction of the philosophical community as a whole, for any extended period of time. Perhaps it is reasonable to doubt whether they ever will be. Instead, we might just end up with an increasingly good understanding of the fundamental disagreements on which debates over these issues turn, and with a conditional understanding of what one's theory should look like given one's view on these fundamental disagreements.

Still, one can make progress on these problems, and on a host of smaller problems. Often, philosophical progress comes from focusing in a new area where people had not much previously focused. For example, over the last decade or so, there has been an enormous improvement of our understanding of the relationship between consciousness and intentionality, after years in which the topics were largely treated separately in analytic philosophy. There are increasingly sophisticated analyses of the intentional structure of consciousness, and people are beginning to look at the converse question of the role that consciousness might play in intentionality. There are still rich pickings in this area, and I expect to see a lot more progress in the next decade or so.

On the mind–body problem, it's not surprising that I think that some of the richest pickings will come from developing nonreductive approaches to consciousness in real depth. One approach that is drawing increasing attention is that of Russellian monism: grounding consciousness in the unknown intrinsic properties of matter. The idea is too strange for some philosophers, but we've learned that the world is a strange place. I think that if someone can really take this idea and develop it properly, it has the potential to end up as a truly powerful approach to the problem.

There is also an enormous amount to be learned about specific aspects of consciousness. There have been many advances in the philosophical study of perception and perceptual consciousness in recent years. I think that we may be on the threshold of a period of advances in the study of conscious thought. Other aspects of consciousness that promise to yield a great deal in the coming years include temporal consciousness and the relation between consciousness and attention.

One can certainly expect that there will also be a huge amount of philosophical activity driven by the latest results coming from the cognitive sciences. Neuroscience will attract an increasing amount of attention. Although there is a reasonable amount of philosophy of neuroscience at the moment, it is surprising that there isn't more. I have begun some collaborative work with neuroscientists myself, on the question of detecting consciousness in patients diagnosed with vegetative state and related post-coma conditions. This is a place where neuroscience comes together with the philosophical problem of other minds in interesting ways. I think that philosophers have a lot to contribute to areas like this, and I hope that more philosophers will move in these directions.

Of course philosophy, like other academic disciplines, is subject to vicissitudes of fashion. This hurt the study of consciousness for many years, and more recently has helped it. In parallel, the study of intentionality saw a huge surge around the 1980s, followed by a swing away from the area as early promises seemed not to pan out. I have the sense that philosophers are ready to return to the study of intentionality, though, perhaps enriched by what we have learned about consciousness in the meantime, as well as by what we have learned in the philosophy of language.

Speaking for myself, I will continue to work on foundational ideas in metaphysics, epistemology, and philosophy of language, trying to pull together the details of a big picture that I hope can be used to shed light on many philosophical questions. At the end of the day, though, I am a philosopher of mind, and the problem of consciousness remains my first love. Before I die, I'd like to have one or two more cracks at coming up with a positive theory of consciousness. My older self says that this is probably quixotic, but my younger self says that one should at least try.

3
Daniel Dennett

University Professor, Austin B. Fletcher Professor of Philosophy
Tufts University USA

Why were you initially drawn to philosophy of mind?

When I encountered Descartes' *Meditations* as a freshman, I was fascinated and challenged. I thought his view just had to be wrong, but it was going to take some hard work to say why. Fifty years later, I haven't adjusted that opinion. I wasn't a budding scientist or even a science-phile then, but still it seemed obvious to me that the mind was the brain, and that there had to be a way of explaining intentionality non-miraculously. Qualia—I didn't encounter the term for a year or two—were a challenge, but I thought I could already see that no treatment of them as "intrinsic" properties had a prayer. So dualism was never attractive to me. I could feel the Zombic Hunch, and could thus see what people were talking about, but it struck me as a good candidate for the intuition to jettison, if we could. In the half century since then I've noticed a remarkable reluctance by many philosophers to even *consider* denying it. That strikes me as embarrassing: here we are at some kind of conceptual impasse, and something's gotta give! You'd think that people would at least *try out* the idea of abandoning their conviction that the zombie hypothesis makes sense. But for many of them, it is apparently inconceivable that zombies might not be conceivable after all. And among some of them I swear I detect a faint whiff of self-righteousness that might be expressed as moral disapproval of the very idea of challenging this idea. It may not be a *sin* to question qualia, but it is definitely not *nice*. This attitude has always amused me, but I suspect that my inability to conceal my amusement makes more enemies than friends.

What do you consider your most important contribution to the field?

I think the idea of the intentional stance—its relation to the design stance and the physical stance and the account of the role it plays across human inquiry—is probably my most important contribution, because it is the foundation for both the multiple drafts model of consciousness and the compatibilist account of free will I have developed. Both consciousness and free will are often—even typically—seen to be marvelous, mysterious, phenomena unlike anything else in the natural world ("real magic," in other words[1]). By understanding how the intentional stance is applicable to less awesome phenomena, we can see how (human) consciousness and free will are not stand-alone mysteries but decomposable into simpler phenomena, both synchronically and diachronically. That is, we can see how—in general, the details are still being worked out—to build a conscious mind out of unconscious (but intentionally interpretable) parts—homunculi—and how an agent can have free will though composed of parts that do not have free will; *and* we can understand how consciousness and free will could evolve out of simpler psychological and biological antecedents. I think the fact that the concept of the intentional stance has been put to such vigorous use (and some abuse) by the relevant sciences has also shown philosophers something about the role that we philosophers can play in the interdisciplinary quest to understand the mind.

What is the proper role of philosophy in relation to psychology, artificial intelligence, and the neurosciences?

Philosophical confusions are not restricted to philosophers and lay people. Scientists, whatever they may think of philosophy as a discipline, take on—and are guided by—philosophical assumptions,

---

[1] Lee Siegel draws our attention to the fundamental twist in his excellent book, *Net of Magic: Wonders and Deceptions in India* , (Chicago Univ. Press , 1991):

"I'm writing a book on magic," I explain, and I'm asked, "Real magic?" By *real magic* people mean miracles, thaumaturgical acts, and supernatural powers. "No," I answer: "Conjuring tricks, not real magic." *Real magic*, in other words, refers to the magic that is not real, while the magic that is real, that can actually be done, is *not real magic*. (p425)

It can't be *real* if its explicable as a phenomenon achieved by a bag of ordinary tricks—cheap tricks, you might say.

whether they do this reflectively or by unexamined hunch or habit of thought. I consider philosophy to play the role of uncovering and examining these guiding assumptions and clarifying the logical requirements and implications of the theories scientists propose. The scientific study of the mind is a particularly philosophy-heavy area of research, since the phenomena are so hard to describe neutrally (a task for which I designed *heterophenomenology*) and so hard to align with what we know about brains and the processes that occur within them. The gulf between the view from the inside and the view from science is unlike any other explanatory gulf in nature—even greater than the gulf between living things and inanimate matter, and it is no wonder that it remains so hard to bridge. It is probable that what makes this such difficult research is that some of the assumptions we take for granted are just false. Philosophy, with its lack of conceptual boundaries, its tradition of challenging everything, is well poised to uncover these stumbling blocks. In principle, philosophers could do this from their armchairs with only the most passing acquaintance with the stumbling forays of the scientists. In practice, however, engaging quite intimately and strenuously with the scientific questions and questioners provides a wealth of material for the imagination that one would be hard-pressed to conjure up on one's own. One of philosophers' greatest weaknesses is mistaking failures of imagination for insights into necessity. There is nothing like a heavy dose of empirical discovery to strengthen and discipline the imagination. And to those philosophers who recoil from the "conceptual naivete" of the scientists when they attempt to fathom their work, I say: First, ask yourself if their presumed naivete is getting in the way of their substantive research. If so, you have a fine contribution to make by sorting this out and enlightening the scientists; if not, you might like to reconsider the charge and see if what you have called naivete is just practical and defensible impatience with niceties that do not deserve so much attention.

There has been something of a reactionary swing in recent years among young philosophers of mind, back to the "classic" formulations of the problems and away from cognitive science, but I find this work to be invariably pinched and largely devoted to artifactual puzzles of no wider interest. By "leaving science to the scientists" these philosophers are making two mistakes: cutting themselves off from new ideas that could help them with their pure projects and walking away from one of the few domains of science that could actually use lots of help from well-informed philosophers. Their hermetically sealed, factually impoverished disputes also have an unfortunate side effect: they fuel the stereotype of the philosopher as somebody who plays word games and makes ignorance a virtue.

Is a science of consciousness possible?

Yes, of course. The defeatist idea that consciousness is a mystery beyond human ken has nothing going for it. The idea that is usually trotted out in support of this pessimism is one version or another of "cognitive closure": just as fish (we surmise) cannot be made to understand democracy and dogs cannot be made to understand mathematics, so there must be areas of inquiry forever beyond us finite, naked apes—and consciousness is the top candidate for being the humanly insoluble mystery. Why? Well, the brain cannot entirely represent itself so it cannot, in principle, understand itself—didn't Turing or Gödel prove something like that? These claims betray a misunderstanding of the nature of human inquiry and where it gets its power. First, putting our brains on the dimly imagined continuum with insect nervous systems at the bottom, and dogs and dolphins and chimps just next to us at the high, complex end, ignores the obvious fact that we're the only species that asks questions! Language gives our little brains a huge boost in cognitive power denied to all others. We have thinking tools—language itself, mathematics, microscopes and telescopes and statistics and a thousand other mind-sharpeners—that no other species has, and we get tremendous leverage from a division of labor. Whatever the Group Brain consisting of billions of human beings can do (abetted by the labors of billions before who have died but left us the fruits of their inquiries), can be done in summary form by just about any one human brain. (Our grandchildren can effortlessly understand scientific ideas that stumped the Nobel laureates of the last generation.) Curiously enough, language permits us to use formulae that we do not completely understand! (We can leave the deep understanding to the experts.) So the explanation of human consciousness will be composed at many levels by many disciplines and nobody will *have* to understand all of it in the detail in which it is confirmed. Thus even if the social psychologist and the linguist need to have a rudimentary appreciation of the role of the neurochemistry, they don't have to be capable of neurochemistry research, let alone the quantum physics that underlies it. And everybody will be able to understand the textbook version of the overarching theory, just as everybody can now understand the theory of life, evolution by natural selection, even if the details of methylation of DNA molecules or the dynamics of climatic pumping and habitat tracking remain fuzzy at best for most understanders. It is a special irony that Noam Chomsky is often cited as the authoritative source of the idea that our minds are cognitively closed, for Chomsky drew our attention to the marvelous feature of language that makes this a negligible surmise: because language is systematically productive—that is to say, its well-formed formulae are composed in ways that permit one to understand the wholes by understanding the parts—each of us can understand what might as well be an infinity of different explanations—some true, most false, but comprehensible when well-formed. The claim that consciousness is an insoluble mystery implies that the true explanation of consciousness could not be composed in, or translated into, language we can understand, that no chain of comprehensible explanations could ever lead to an explanation of consciousness. I have never seen anyone advance an argument for that conclusion.

What are the most important open problems in contemporary philosophy of mind? What are the most promising prospects?

We still need a good theory of semantic information. Both cognitive scientists and evolutionary biologists make heavy use of a concept (or concepts—it isn't clear if they are exactly the same) of information that is manifestly not the well-studied Shannon-Weaver concept, and nobody—to my knowledge—has propounded and defended a good theory of this concept. Does information about food preferences or nest building techniques by birds get passed through the germ line, in the genes, or does it get passed through social learning? We can say a lot about how to answer this question (do some cross-fostering studies, and see if the fledglings adopt the practices of their foster parents) but we don't have a good clean theory of the sort of information that can either ride along on the DNA or be picked up in the light as it enters the fledglings' eyes. Can the information that is picked up by Gricean implicatures also be transmitted in other ways? What is the relation between explicit and implicit information transfer by communicative acts? Should all differences that make a difference count as *semantic* information? (A dog growls at the stranger at the door. *Something* in the dog—something that might be a memory of a similar looking or smelling person who abused him, or might just be an emotional scar of sorts, or even an innate suspicion-mechanism directed at anything novel—was triggered by the encounter and provoked the growl. What information does it carry? How can we align the information of such states, whatever they are, with the sentences of natural or scientific language that articulate content explicitly?)

We are beginning to understand the tight interplay between our normative and indeed ethical notions and our ways of conceiving of the goings-on in our minds. This rapprochement of ethics and philosophy of mind (via neuroscience and evolutionary theory!) is a frontier on which much work still needs to be done.

From my vantage point I see the pace of discovery picking up. In the last decade or so, we've learned a great deal about the underlying mechanisms of the brain and how they might work together to create the "non-mechanistic" phenomena of mind. The fit between folk psychology and neuroscience is fitful and tantalizing—a mixture of sudden insights and frustrating complications. We are so close and yet so far. Our students can *begin* their careers with a detailed and flexible inventory of concepts, methods, and results that were unimagined by our professors when we were students. Along the way, the false starts and misbegotten agendas have often been inspired by visions that contained demonstrable philosophical errors and confusions, so we philosophers have not just been along for the ride.

4

Fred Dretske

Senior Research Scholar
Duke University, USA

Why were you initially drawn to philosophy of mind?

An early interest in epistemology—especially perception—shaped my later interest in (and approach to) problems in the philosophy of mind. One cannot think long about the relations that constitute an animal's perceptual awareness of the world without reaching definite—indeed, I would say irresistible—conclusions about the nature of the internal states required for such awareness.

It is, I think, this epistemological perspective that most clearly distinguishes my own work in the philosophy of mind from others. In Dretske (1969) I argued for a distinction between (what I called) epistemic and non-epistemic perception. Seeing a bug is like stepping on one, a non-epistemic relation to the bug: it does not require (though it is compatible with) knowledge of (or belief about) the object seen (stepped on). It does not even require understanding. You don't, that is, need the concept BUG to see a bug. This way of seeing is to be contrasted with epistemic perception: seeing *what* it is, seeing *that* it is a bug, seeing the bug *as* a bug, and *recognizing* it (as a bug). This distinction, embedded in our ordinary ways of describing our perceptual relations to the world, is vital for understanding the basic difference between perception and conception and, therefore, the difference between one's experiences of things on the one hand and one's thoughts and judgments about them on the other. A theory of mind that focused exclusively on propositional attitudes—mental states taking a that-clause as complement of the verb (seeing that, knowing that, thinking that, judging that, etc)—would be a theory of mind that was either wrong or seriously incomplete. If seeing is not believing in the theory of knowledge, neither is it in the philosophy of mind.

I have, as a result, always regarded naturalistic theories of the mind as confronting at least two fundamentally different problems: (1) those associated with the propositional attitudes (thought and belief) and related processes (reasoning and desire) that involved, in some essential way, deployment of concepts; and (2) those related to experiences and feelings, the qualia-laden states constituting our sensory and emotional life. No theory of the mind could be complete unless it had a story to tell about both. We need a theory that tells us what it is to think Judith is playing the piano, yes, but also one that tells us what it is to see and hear her play it. You can do one without doing the other.

Also basic to my view of the mind is the externalism I brought from my work in epistemology. Knowledge, or so I argued in Dretske (1969, 1971), is not a matter of justification, not a matter of getting your beliefs secured to a foundational rock by some evidential chain. It is, rather, a matter of such beliefs being connected to the facts in the right way, a relationship whose existence, because external or extrinsic to the system of beliefs, might be quite unknown (perhaps even unknowable) to the knowing mind. Sense perception is one way, the most direct and reliable way, of getting oneself so connected. The widespread use of measuring instruments in science and elsewhere is merely a way of extending these reliable connections to more inaccessible affairs. It later seemed to me that "information" was a useful notion to describe this external relation, and in Dretske (1981) I formulated an information-based theory of knowledge . The conclusive reasons (required for knowledge) of 1969 and 1971 became the information (a required cause of judgments qualifying as knowledge) in 1981. Since objective information, as I conceived it, was an intentional notion (a signal could carry the information that x was F without carrying the information that x was G even though F and G were extensionally equivalent concepts), information seemed like a useful tool in the philosophy of mind. The last few chapters of *Knowledge and the Flow of Information* were devoted, almost exclusively, to topics in the philosophy of mind. This, then, marked the transition of my primary interest and work from epistemology to philosophy of mind.

What do you consider your most important contribution to the field?

Most important contribution? Let me simply list a few of the fundamental ideas that characterize my own work in the philosophy of mind. Not everyone will agree about their importance—or perhaps whether any of them even constitutes a genuine contribution—but these, at least, are things *I* think are important to remember when doing philosophy of mind.

(a) Intentionality is not a problem in the philosophy of mind. It is already a part of the material world, not something that appears, magically, when mentality appears on the scene. The laws of nature (and a variety of relations that depend on such laws—e.g., indication, information) are relations between intensions (magnitudes, quantities, and properties), not extensions (sets of things that have these properties)—see Dretske 1977. So materialists (like me), people who want a naturalistic story about the mind, don't have to fret about reducing intentionality to something else. The problem is not intentionality, as such, but the kind (level, degree) of intentionality (Dretske 1981).

(b) Since many (maybe not all, but certainly many) mental states and processes are representational in nature (they have content), one doesn't have a fully acceptable naturalistic theory of mind unless one has an acceptable theory of representation (this is the higher level of intentionality mentioned above), a theory that explains how a physical state can express (say, mean) something false. I see no hope of providing such a theory that does not appeal to the past, to the way a system developed to process information. Only the history of a system can make it say (mean, express) something that is (as false content is) totally disconnected (causally and informationally) from the current state of the world. I tried to provide such a historically based form of externalism for concept-dependent states (thought) in Dretske (1981, 1988) and for concept-independent states (sense experience) in Dretske (1995). Just as physically indistinguishable marks on paper (in different languages, for instance) might have entirely different meanings (and in this sense be different words) because they have different histories, physically identical states (in different brains, for instance) that have different histories (either phylogenetic or ontogenetic) might be entirely different thoughts or experiences. They acquired, via these different histories, different information-carrying functions, and it is, or so I argued, these information-carrying functions that constitute the representational character of a physical state. The reason minds are so mysterious is that they not only do not supervene on the physical system possessing a mind (physically identical beings can be mentally different), they do not even supervene on the entire *present* state of the physical world. The makes it seem—almost—as if they weren't physical.

(c) Our ordinary picture of the mind not only assigns to thoughts an intentional content (= what is thought), but an explanatory role. The content must somehow be able to figure in an explanation of why agents do what they do. If Tim, wanting a beer, went to the fridge *because* he thought there was beer there, a theory of representation must give the content of this representation (that there is some beer there), whether true or false, a role in the explanation of Tim's behavior. If it doesn't, it fails to capture what, from an ordinary point of view, is absolutely essential to thought. If thinking that there is beer in the fridge doesn't explain why Tim goes there, Tim may as well not think there is beer in the fridge. What he thinks is irrelevant to what he does.

Explaining Behavior (1988) was devoted to understanding how this could be so, how thoughts could not only cause things (this is no problem at all if thoughts are material entities in the head), but whose content could explain things. On an externalist view of content (the only game in town as far as I can see) this requires that the external relations constituting the content of an internal state must explain why that state has the effects (on behavior) it does. I still see no way this can be done except by thinking of behavior not as bodily movements, but as a causal process culminating (typically) in bodily movements. Behavior isn't the bodily movement—the arm rising. It—raising your arm—is the causal process that results in these bodily movements. When A (some internal state) causes B (a bodily movement), the history of a system (defining A's content) might well explain why A causes B even though it is totally irrelevant in explaining B. It is the neurobiological properties of A (and the present configuration of the nervous system) that explain why the arm moves, but it is the content of A, an extrinsic (relational) property of A, that will explain why you moved your arm, why A caused B.

(d) A theory of consciousness is primarily a theory of perceptual experience, the kind of experience in which we become aware (conscious) of objects and their properties. We also speak of being aware (conscious) *that* things are so (facts), but fact-awareness is not the primary locus of the "what it is like" aspect (qualia) of conscious existence. Once one carefully distinguishes fact-awareness (thinking or judging that x is red) from object- and property-awareness (experiencing x as red), there is a problem (Chalmers dubbed it "the hard" problem): what explains the qualitative aspect of experience? What explains why it is redness (rather than blueness or squareness) that is associated with this physical state of the brain (that state of the brain one is in when one reports experiencing the color red)? A representational theory of experience (to be carefully distinguished from a representational theory of fact-awareness) is an attempt to answer this question.) I tried to deal with this question in Dretske (1995).

What is the proper role of philosophy in relation to psychology, artificial intelligence, and the neurosciences?

The proper role of philosophy? One can't do philosophy of mind in ignorance of what is happening in psychology, neuroscience, and artificial intelligence. About that almost everyone agrees. What isn't so easy is figuring out what a philosopher is supposed to do with this knowledge.

I have no particular views about this. I think philosophical problems arise from facts described in ordinary, non-technical, terms. Most problems in the philosophy of mind revolve around and take their life from such ordinary words as "see," "know," "aware," "conscious," "thought," "experience," and so on. Can you, for instance, see an object and not be conscious of it? There are a host of facts that were completely unknown forty years ago (I am thinking of the research on split brains, blindsight, change-blindness, unilateral neglect, and extinction) that have an obvious relevance to how one answers this question. I don't see how a philosopher can venture into this territory without a familiarity with these scientific facts. As far as I can see, though, the scientific facts, taken by themselves, do not provide an answer. And they never will. They do not provide an answer because they do not tell us what it *means* to see something or what it *means* to be conscious of something. Without that, without an understanding of what these words mean, the scientific facts are powerless to tell us whether one can see something without being conscious of it. All I learn from the scientists, for instance, is that certain subjects in certain circumstances do not report seeing x—report, in fact, not seeing x—when it can be shown they are receiving information about x through their eyes. This leaves one to puzzle over what the scientific facts show about either perception or consciousness. Can one see x, for instance, and not be able to report seeing x? What about small children and animals? Can one be conscious of x and think (and sincerely report) that one is not aware of x?

What about people who misidentify x? Can one receive usable information about x through the eyes and not see x? What about information about x one gets from newspapers?

If a question is expressed in ordinary language, as I think it usually is in the case of most philosophical questions, then no answer can be forthcoming from science until one is clear how the scientific facts—often expressed in some proprietary language—relate to the facts as ordinarily described. Analyzing this relationship strikes me as an important job for philosophers. Philosophers, of course, are not always the best (or most able) people to do it. Sometimes (as I read the literature) scientists are doing the job for themselves, and they are doing it very well, thank you. But somebody has to do it. Why not philosophers?

Is a science of consciousness possible?

A science of consciousness? I think there is as much hope for this as there is for a science of freedom or a science of knowledge (for my reasons, see above). This is not to say that science will not provide a wealth of information relevant to answering questions about consciousness (or freedom and knowledge, for that matter). It is just that science will, perforce, use ideas that are sharper, better defined, more operationally manageable, than the ordinary words (aware, conscious, see, free, intentional, know, recognize) used in the questions we are looking to science to answer. Science will provide the facts we need to know to answer questions about consciousness, but that won't make it a science of consciousness. Molecular genetics isn't a science of freedom even if it discovers facts that convince us (or some people) we lack freedom. A crucial premise—a premise over which compatibilists and incompatibilists will disagree—is whether one can act freely if one's beliefs and desires are genetically determined. That premise won't be supplied by science.

What are the most important open problems in contemporary philosophy of mind? What are the most promising prospects?

Most important problems? I have my own list. Everyone will. Near the top of my list is a question about the nature of conscious experience, the kind of experience one can alternately create and extinguish (in the case of vision) by opening and closing one' eyes.

I worried about this problem forty years ago, and I'm still worried about it. If concepts are not necessary for such experience (as they arguably are not in the case of a one-year old human infant or a rabbit), what is necessary? What is the point, the biological purpose, of conscious experience if it can occur in the absence of the kind of thoughts (motives, etc.) that help explain behavior? It seems to me that neuroscientific efforts to identify the neural correlates of conscious experience will shed light on this problem, but I doubt (for reasons given in the fourth question) whether it will be enough to solve it.

Another problem that does not seem to get much play these days is the causal efficacy of meaning or content. Most attention seems to be centered on providing a naturalistic theory of content. What gives some physical state of the brain the content: *this* (some perceptual object) *is water*? That is only half the problem. The other half is figuring out what relevance this (naturalized) content is to what the person does. If the person who thinks *this is water* picks up the glass and drinks it because (being thirsty) he thinks it contains water, how does the content of this brain state explain his behavior? If, as many philosophers think, content (meaning) is externally (relationally) constituted, and if (as also many philosophers think) a state's causal efficacy is determined exclusively by its intrinsic (non-relational) properties, it would appear that content is doomed to being causally irrelevant. Epiphenomenal. That, as far as I can see, is not a position anyone who is a realist about thought and experience can happily adopt.

Frankly, I don't see a lot of prospects here. I made an effort in Dretske (1988) but that (for reasons several critics pointed out in McLaughlin 1991) fell short of the mark. It did, I think, show something that is useful in this regard—how the extrinsic properties of a state (e.g., the information it carried) could be explanatorily relevant. It nonetheless failed to show what needs to be shown—how the intentional (representational) content of a state could be explanatory. This, for me, remains a troubling lacuna in an otherwise hopeful naturalistic project.

References

McLaughlin, B. 1991, ed. *Dretske and His Critics*. Cambridge, MA; Cambridge University Press.

Dretske, F. 1969. *Seeing and Knowing*. Chicago, IL; University of Chicago Press.

Dretske, F. 1971. Conclusive reasons. *Australasian Journal of Philosophy.*

Dretske, F, 1977. Laws of Nature. *Philosophy of Science*, 44.2.

Dretske, F. 1981. *Knowledge and the Flow of Information.* Cambridge, MA; MIT Press.

Dretske, F. 1988. *Explaining Behavior.* Cambridge, MA; MIT Press.

Dretske, F. 1995. *Naturalizing the Mind.* Cambridge, MA; MIT Press.

5
Owen Flanagan

James B. Duke Professor and Professor of Neurobiology
Duke University of Massachusetts, USA

Why were you initially drawn to philosophy of mind?

In college, my interests and talents landed me with the choice to go on for a PhD in philosophy or in experimental psychology, which in those days meant studying rats. I didn't do well with rats, plus I was interested in persons, not rats. So in 1970, I applied to graduate programs in Philosophy proposing to understand the nature of persons. My idea was to get to the bottom of *Dasein*, L'Etre, *Being* naturalistically. This was naïve, but I had what seemed a promising strategy for gaining traction on the problem of the nature of persons. Persons were especially interesting to me because I was one, plus persons have minds and persons have values. Minds and values are connected, and they present difficult epistemic and ontological problems. What and where are they? How can we know them? I was already a naturalist, or at any rate, an anti-supernaturalist, and thought that if there existed real knowledge about persons, mind, and value, it had to come from synthetic philosophical reflection on what psychology and the other human sciences teach or might discover. So I thought, and still think. A Quinean before I had read a word of Quine or met the man.

At that time, however, mind-science, depending on whether one was an optimist or a pessimist, was beset by theory diffusion problems or by paradigm chaos. Why were there multiple contenders for the right theory of persons and minds in psychology (behaviorism and cognitivism, with psychoanalysis still widely discussed) when mature sciences like physics, chemistry, and biology display paradigmatic unity? Two possibilities struck me as worth exploring: psychology was immature—methodologically and metaphysically deficient—or persons had no nature. My first book, *The*

Science of the Mind (MIT, 1984; 1991 2nd ed.), was an attempt to explore the theory diffusion (or paradigm chaos) problem by looking at the philosophical history of psychology over the previous century. (My dissertation, 1978, had been a critical study of B.F. Skinner's radical behaviorism, which located some of the shortcomings of radical behaviorism in the noble epistemology of the great positivists of the Vienna and Berlin schools, and not contrary to the still dominant view in the ontology of behaviorism). My tentative answer to my problem of why there was then (but isn't now) so much theory diffusion in mind science was that both my initial surmises were true: psychology was immature, unconfident of its methods and thus of its findings, extremely confused (sputtering dualistically inspired last gasps) about subjectivity and persons have less fixity in their nature, and thus more plasticity in their nature, than most other "things." We are possessed of a great deal of "nothingness," *le neant*, to adopt an existentialist turn of phrase.

What do you consider your most important contribution to the field?

The contribution I think most interesting, which is not, of course, the same as most important (I'll decline making that call) is my account of dream consciousness. That account of dreams seems an excellent example of what can be gained by judicious application of what I call the "the natural method." According to "the natural method" for studying the part of mental life that involves consciousness, one ought to blend insights from multiple sources, in this case, phenomenology, psychology, and neuroscience. By so doing one gains a surprising result, to wit: Waking-consciousness has an evolutionary function, but dream consciousness does not.

I first spoke on dream consciousness in April 1994 at Tucson I (Alvin Goldman, Dave Chalmers, and I opened the festivities on that first morning), and then later the same year in my Presidential Address to the Society for Philosophy and Psychology. I published a version of that talk as "Deconstructing Dreams: The Spandrels of Sleep," in the *Journal of Philosophy* (1995). I then presented a general theory in *Dreaming Souls: Sleep, Dreams, and the Evolution of the Conscious Mind* (Oxford, 2000) in which I claimed to solve these three philosophical dream problems (plus two other classics: Is there a reliable way to distinguish dream

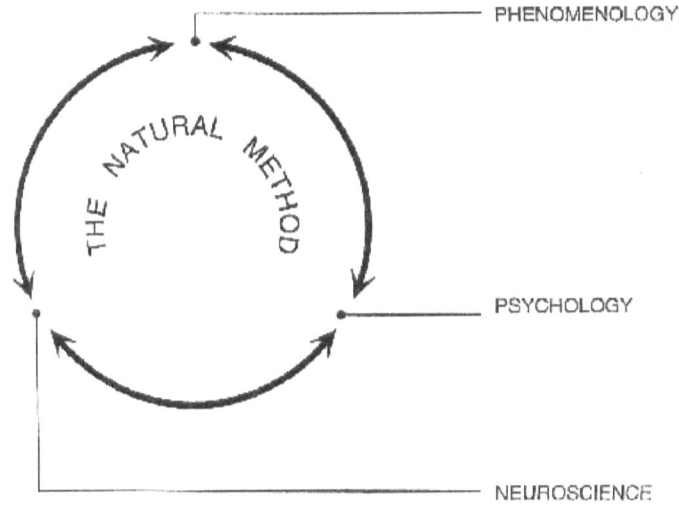

FIGURE 5.1.

consciousness for awake consciousness? Yes; Can I be immoral in dreams? No) at once:

1. Are dreams experiences that occur during sleep?

2. Is dreaming functional?

3. Can dreams fail to have an adaptationist evolutionary explanation but still make sense, still be identity expressive—and thus worth attention in the project of seeking self-knowledge?

The answers I gave, to these three questions, with supporting arguments, were Yes, No, Maybe.

The question that motivated my investigation of the phenomenology, psychology, and neuroscience of dreams in the first place was an obvious one about consciousness generally, and dream consciousness in particular: What is its function? My target was a common argument form that turns on the assumption that if there is a phenotypic trait and it is universal, then it has a biological function; it is an adaptation.

In *Consciousness Reconsidered* (1992), where I had proposed my own general theory of what consciousness is and how we ought to study it, via the natural method, I raised some worries about glib pronouncements to the effect that the function of consciousness is obvious. For example, if you weren't aware of things in your visual field (visually conscious) you couldn't see and would bump into things. Even Dan Dennett has fallen into the trap here, as for example when his panadaptationism gets the better of his skepticism about phenomenal consciousness and he writes that the evolutionary value of lust (as in feeling sexy, desirous) is obvious. But it isn't obvious. Many animals, most insects almost certainly, manage to mate and reproduce without the sexy feelings.

In *Consciousness Reconsidered*, then, I examined two related grounds for skepticism about glib adaptationism, which I labeled "consciousness inessentialism," and the "epiphenomenalist suspicion," respectively.

Conscious Inessentialism: For any intelligent activity i performed in any cognitive domain δ, for example, "doing addition" —even if we do i consciously (with conscious accompaniments), i can, in principle, be done without consciousness (without conscious accompaniments), for example, as "doing addition" is done by a calculator.

Epiphenomenalist Suspicion: Even in cases where consciousness always accompanies i in δ, for example, as it does when we humans "do addition," it [consciousness] plays no causal role in doing addition. Thomas H. Huxley, "Darwin's Bulldog" put the idea this way: "Soul stands to the body as the bell of a clock to the works, and consciousness answers to the sound which the bell gives out when it is struck... We are conscious automata."

I argued that computational functionalism made both *Conscious Inessentialism* and the *Epiphenomenalist Suspicion* seem very weighty, even convincing, and I argued that this was a good reason not to be a *computational functionalist* but rather to be a *Darwinian* or *teleological functionalist*. Teleological or Darwinian functionalism is interested in providing a theory of consciousness for actual mammalian minds, specifically human minds, not, in the first instance, a theory of any possible minds.

The right question to ask as a *Teleological* or *Darwinian functionalist* is: what function, if any, does sleep serve?—not what function does dreaming serve? The answer that falls out of close inspection of sleep neuroscience (especially Allan Hobson's work) is that sleep serves several different functions depending on whether it is NREM (restorative, filling endocrine tanks) or REM (memory consolidation and fixation), and that you get phenomenologically different varieties of dreaming (boring, perseverative in NREM; crazy and colorful in REM) for free, as a side-effect, a free-rider on what the brain is trying to accomplish by sleep. Dreaming is a side effect of sleep in the same way heartthrobs are a side effect of having a pump in a cavity. Heartbeats of course are useful in diagnosing heart problems. But this is a secondary function, not a biological function, not the reason Mother Nature invented hearts that make noise. Could dreams serve diagnostic functions, could they be used in the project of self-knowledge even if they occur as a side effect of a brain doing what it needs to accomplish via sleep? My confident answer was of the "sometimes, maybe" variety.

In any case, the reason I like this result, is that it undermines both the idea that consciousness is a homogeneous thing and that it is an adaptation *simpliciter*. We sleep for 33% of the time that we are alive, but the experiences we have during that third of our lives make no interesting difference to how we fare in the inclusive fitness sweepstakes. Furthermore, the theory is synthetic in a way appropriate to the role of the philosophical naturalist, with ramifications for sleep neuroscience (mentation that occurs during sleep is not in the service of sleep), depth psychology (deflating), philosophy of biology (adaptationism), philosophy of mind (function of consciousness), phenomenology, and philosophy of mind-science (homogeneity or heterogeneity of consciousness).

What is the proper role of philosophy in relation to psychology, artificial intelligence, and the neurosciences?

Here I follow Sellars and Quine. From Sellars we get the insistence that the job of the philosopher is to explain how things considered in the widest possible sense hang together in the widest possible sense. That's a paraphrase but it is close to the original. From Quine we get the insistence that philosophy, metaphysics and epistemology at any rate, are continuous with science.

With respect to mind, intelligent behavior, kinds of minds, then, the philosopher's job is simply more general, more synthetic than that of the scientist. The philosopher gets to ask questions such as, what is the function (if any) of consciousness? To address such a question the philosopher needs to read the relevant literature in all the relevant disciplines, which is fun. The government of course doesn't support such work, which is for the best for them and us.

Is a science of consciousness possible?

This is the trick question. My trick answer is this: There can be a philosophical theory of consciousness, but whether there can be a unified scientific theory of consciousness depends on what kind of thing consciousness is. Before I explain what this means, let me say this: It is exasperating to be at dinner parties and have economists and art historians and literature professors tell me "no one has a clue as to how to explain consciousness." This is akin to saying to a physicist or inorganic chemist that no one understands the nature of glass. The speaker doesn't understand the nature of glass I am sure, but, despite being a very difficult problem (is glass a solid or a slow-moving liquid?) our theories of the nature of glass are far advanced. The question of whether a true account of the nature of glass (if understood) would dispel the mysteries of glass for non-experts is irrelevant to whether we possess a satisfactory theory of glass.

Here one must distinguish as I did in *Consciousness Reconsidered* (1992) between an explanation of a phenomenon that is *satisfying* and one that is *satisfactory*. Water is H_2O. This is satisfactory as far as an account of what water is goes. Someone who enjoys the awe-of-it-all, might say "Far out, it is amazing, mysterious, I just don't get how that clear, colorless, tasteless stuff could have molecular structure." This reaction is, of course, completely irrelevant to the scientific and metaphysical question.

Many philosophers are what I call "mysterians." Some like Colin McGinn give arguments to justify their mysterianism, although I like to think I showed what is wrong with McGinn's arguments, but most (and alas it has now spread to the educated common folk) are into reporting just how amazing they think consciousness is, how intractable the problem is from both a philosophical and scientific point of view, as well as the fact that (even if they had read anything on the topic) they would not be satisfied with it as a scientific account. Whatever.

In any case, I do think that there can be a philosophical account of consciousness, but it might say, based on all the evidence, phenomenological, psychological, and neuroscientific, considered in a Quinean and Sellarsian way, that consciousness is not a natural or unified psychobiological kind around which a scientific theory should be built. My current view is this is the case. Spinoza (the first Quinean, so I claim) said (or would have said) that consciousness is a *property* or *aspect* of some kinds of mental processes. Sometimes properties or aspects get a science for themselves (electricity and magnetism), but normally they don't (there is no general theory of wetness or wet stuff; no theory of things that are red). Fifteen years ago I thought, based on some work of

Wolf Singer, Francis Crick and Christof Koch, that consciousness might be marked by 40 Hz oscillatory patterns (no one claimed that consciousness *is* 40Hz). Neuroscientists no longer favor this idea, so neither do I.

So what about a scientific theory of consciousness? It looks pretty clear that studying the mind-brain is a good approach because it picks out a domain with a unified overall biological rationale—minds equip creatures who possess them with (yet another) organ that helps those creatures survive, reproduce, possibly have fun, and so on. Furthermore, the parts of the mind-brain interact with each other and with other parts of the body and the natural and social world(s) in such a way that we will have a unified theory of the mind-brain. Since consciousness is just a property of the mind-brain, we will need an account of when and how and why (if there is a why) that property exists, emerges, and so on. I'd bet, however, against there being a scientific theory devoted just to consciousness. And I'd bet against it for Spinozistic reasons.

What are the most important open problems in contemporary philosophy of mind? What are the most promising prospects?

Philosophy of mind has been incredibly active over the last forty years. Committing philosophy in such a visible manner was necessary because in 1970 mind-science was in epistemological and metaphysical disarray. Now mind-science is more confident of itself and its direction. The scientific study of the mind, including the conscious mind—despite some naysayers, mysterians, and otherwise awestruck souls—has been made safe for scientific study. There is a broad naturalistic consensus that comes armed with a variety of fruitful ways of conceiving of the mind-brain relation and a mother lode of technologies and techniques to make the *terra incognita* of mind begin to yield its secrets. The gritty work is now in the hands of the mind-scientists as it should be. We, Quineans, are rightly in a wait-and-see pose for the next phase of synthetic work if and when it is needed.

One problem that could use good work immediately is on the logic of inferences to claims about the neural correlates of consciousness (NCC) and on the logic of inferences from claims about NCC's to stronger conclusions, e.g., about identities. I have already said that I think that there will be no scientific theory of consciousness separate from an overall theory of mind, and this because consciousness is only an aspect or property of mind, or of some mental states and processes, and not a faculty of mind, the way vision is. Nonetheless, it is important both for philosophy and for the mind-sciences to have an account of what features of brain states mark conscious ones off from ones that do not possess phenomenal properties. One reason this is important is to advance the project of de-mystification, eliminating the vestiges of dualism. Philosophy of mind has done a fine job of distinguishing among various possible kinds of relations between brain states and mental states—of brain states with phenomenal properties—relations of type identity, functional token-identity, kinds of supervenience, emergence, and so on. Nowadays there is excellent neuroscientific work—Christof Koch's on vision, for example—that has made real progress on the search for NCC. Philosophers of science generally, and philosophers of psychology specifically, could help a lot by explaining how the logic of various strength claims based on these correlations can and should work. To speak naively, what warranted the inference from the perfect correlation of water with H20 to the identity claim that water *is* H20? Are there different procedures for identity claims in inorganic chemistry and biology that mind-science needs to attend to? One obstacle to accepting even token-identity claims for conscious mental states comes, I claim, from thinking that satisfactory explanations must also be intuitively satisfying. My own view is that although most everyone accepts the fact that, e.g., the periodic table of elements expresses true facts about chemical type identities, most people don't get, nor should they get these identities in a way that is intuitively satisfying. What matters is that the experts find them satisfactory. In any case, examining the logic of inferences from correlations to type-identity, token-identity, varieties of supervenience, and emergence in other sciences that traffic is making such claims might help us see more clearly what good scientific practice requires for such claims to be warranted.

The role as a philosopher which interests me personally and that suits me now, at least in the near term, involves trying to advance a broad and humane naturalism and finding ways to explain how a scientific view of persons, their minds, and their lives is, or at least, can be, uplifting and neither disenchanting nor de-meaning. I started out interested in the nature of persons, and I am still at it. Mind, morals, and the meaning(s) of life. Now that's a good topic.

6
Samuel Guttenplan

Professor of Philosophy

Birkbeck College, University of London, UK

Why were you initially drawn to philosophy of mind?

When I did postgraduate work in Oxford in the late 1960s, early 1970s, the most important subject—the one that figured in most seminars and which generated the most 'buzz'—was philosophy of language. Indeed, so great was the interest in language that there was genuine institution-wide excitement when the university created a new position in linguistics, one intended to serve the then current philosophical agenda. Philosophy of mind did of course figure but it was more in the background, and was not thought of as the single subject it is today. The debate about the relation of the mind to the body—and the 'solution' broadly known as central state materialism—was perhaps the most discussed single issue that now counts as philosophy of mind, but that debate did not figure even as part of a whole subject in philosophy, much less a new one. If anything it was thought of more as a topic in metaphysics, and, aside from the then recent twist that Kripke's *Naming and Necessity* gave to discussions of identity theories, it was a debate rooted in the previous decade or two. The remainder of interest in philosophy of mind traded under the label *philosophical psychology*, a rather rag-bag (but important) collection of a prioristic, ordinary language and intuition-based studies of this or that notion, in what has broadly come to be called (I think unfortunately) 'folk psychology'. In any case, just as the debate about mind and body served a metaphysical agenda, many of the specific contributions in philosophical psychology served agendas in other more established sub-disciplines in philosophy. Of course this began to change in the UK in the 1970s (perhaps earlier in the US), and, though there are lots of reasons for the growth of philosophy of mind as a major sub-discipline, I think that it can at least partly be sheeted home to the interplay between philosophy of language and philosophy of mind. And, as I will explain, my early interest in philosophy of mind rested on this interplay.

One obvious reason for the pre-eminence of philosophy of language in Oxford in the early 70s was the publicaton of Michael Dummett's *Frege: Philosophy of Language* (1973). This book was keenly anticipated, and as soon as it did appear, it was devoured in seminars and discussion groups. Dummett's view that language was a key to metaphysics, that it in fact replaced epistemology in this regard, was reason enough for many to think of philosophy of language as the central discipline in philosophy. But there were others reasons which had less to do directly with the relation between language and metaphysics, and more to do with the links between language and mind. My own sense of the importance of the philosophy of language was always based on that connection. Even more strongly, I thought then and continue to think that one cannot do either of these subjects properly on their own, and I felt this even while I was engrossed along with others in thinking about problems in the philosophy of language, and writing my dissertation on *Truth in Interpretation*.

In Oxford, the groundwork for linking language and the developing subject of philosophy of mind had been prepared by the John Locke lectures of both Chomsky, and, perhaps even more significantly, Davidson (in 1969 and 1970, respectively). These lectures seem to have inspired the seminars that Gareth Evans and John McDowell offered, beginning in 1971-2. Following on from this, Quine's and Davidson's residence in Oxford in 1973-4, allowed me to organize the Wolfson College lecture series on "Mind and Language" in 1974. A certain skirmish that I had with some of the fellows of Wolfson illustrates my general point about the degree of interest these subjects generated. The non-philosophy fellows were worried that the topic chosen wouldn't generate the public interest that had come to be associated with Wolfson lectures. But in the event—and with very little publicity—the audience for the series averaged over 700 and more than filled the Examination Schools where they were held.

Throughout the period in which philosophy of language was ascendant, there was of course lots of interest in details about this or that natural language construction. But the central topic that figured in most of the discussions of language in Oxford was the notion of meaning itself. And, cutting a long philosophical story short, this view seemed to many of us that this notion could only be understood if it were taken, not merely as some special notion in philosophy of language, but as integral to the study of mind as well. Further, and even if it wasn't always said explicitly, meaning (sometimes 'sense', sometimes 'content') and mindedness were conceived of as inextricably interdependent.

One place where it was put forward explicitly in Oxford was in Davidson's Wolfson lecture, 'Thought and Talk'. Immediately after the lecture, Gareth Evans popped up to ask Davidson about the argument near the end of the paper purporting to establish the interdependence of thought and talk. Evans said that, perhaps because of his own carelessness, he had missed it. In fact, in one very short notorious paragraph, Davidson had said that a creature could only have a belief if it had the concept of belief, and that the latter required the creature to be an interpreter—a producer and consumer of meanings in a public language. And Evans was pointing out, in his usual style, that the first premise here, the one which does all the work, was wheeled in rather suddenly, and was not in any sense argued for. Still, I don't think that Evans really doubted that there was a significant interdependence between the uniquely human range of semantic abilities and a capacity for thought. It was just that he suspected that Davidson was too facile in arguing as he did for that connection. (Davidson tried again in print to fill that argumentative gap, but I don't think Evans would have found the argument in "Rational Animals" any more convincing.)

Against this background, it is easy to summarize my answer to the first question. I was initially drawn to the study of mind through the study of language. At the outset I shared the view then prevalent in Oxford that the very possibility of mindedness depended on meaning. Nowadays, that view is a minority one: most writers in the now ascendant philosophy of mind are perfectly happy with the dependence of language on thought, but are either dismissive of, or don't even bother with, the reverse kind of dependence. What could be more obvious, one often hears, than that there are creatures who perceive, desire, intend, act, choose, etc., but who are simply not, or not yet, language users. In one sense, I have sympathy for this view: in spite of Davidson's best efforts, I don't think that thought requires its possessor also to be a speaker of a public, natural language. However, I don't think that the interdependence thesis needs to be based on the model that Davidson offered, and I continue to think that meaning is a key to mindedness, and therefore a key to the subject matter of the philosophy of mind.

What do you consider your most important contribution to the field?

An initial disclaimer: almost certainly my most important contribution to the field has been my role in setting up the journal *Mind & Language* in 1986, and then having two long stints as Executive Editor, as well as constructing and editing the reference volume *A Companion to the Philosophy of Mind* (1994). Unlike others who will answer this question, there is no single thesis or set of theses or 'position' in the subject with which I am, or would like to be, publicly identified. Nonetheless, in my recent book on metaphor, I introduced a notion that I think can be important for the study of both language and mind. I shall say more about this shortly. First, though, something about *Mind & Language* and the *Companion*, not least because it will lay the groundwork for my answer to a later question.

For a number of years before the launch of the journal, several academics from philosophy, psychology and linguistics departments in London formed a reading group that met regularly. I recall these meetings as at first rather awkward: the ethos of each of these disciplines was, and to a large extent remains, quite different, and it wasn't always easy to find reading matter that would serve such an incubus interdisciplinary group. However, Fodor's *Modularity of Mind* proved to be an early and useful target text, and we found that as we came to understand underlying disciplinary differences, discussions became much more profitable. We even reached the point where psychologists 'allowed' philosophers to do some experimental work which was, in turn, informed by the contributions of the linguists in the group.

Mind & Language grew out of that reading group: its six original editors were the founding members of that group. In launching the journal we tried to keep hold of the lessons that we had learned— were still learning—about interdisciplinarity, but it hasn't been easy. Philosophers seem to have perceived *Mind & Language* as yet another place to fight their battles, and it has taken considerable effort to encourage submissions from psychology, linguistics and those working on computation, partly because the journal was not seen as, nor was appropriate to, the first publication of empirical work in those fields. Still, as the journal approaches its 25th anniversary, we like to think that we have had some success in promoting our original agenda. Through the yearly conferences we have organised—conferences on pragmatics, narrative, conditionals, objects, pretence and imagination, and names—we have actively encouraged the disciplines to work closely with one another. And we have encouraged contributions on topics that lend themselves to this kind of co-operation. One such obvious example is the debate about simulation theory. After we published Robert Gordon's original piece, which itself took off from some of Quine's remarks about the propositional attitudes, I encouraged Al Goldman and others to submit their work on simulation theory. Then, under the further guidance of Martin Davies and Tony Stone, the result was a discussion which ran and ran, and has had significant impact well beyond the disciplinary boundaries of philosophy.

From the feedback that I have had over the past fourteen years, not to mention the many reviews, I am pretty sure that *A Companion to the Philosophy of Mind* has had an impact on the subject. What I should like to point out here is just how difficult it was to make the choices needed to construct that reference work. The single most obvious difficulty was deciding how much work to include from neuroscience, psychology, linguistics and computing. Readers of the volume will see that I was economical here: while I commissioned some general pieces in these areas, I stuck pretty closely to the idea that this was a reference work in the *philosophy* of mind. At the time, I felt bad about this: having worked so hard to build up an interdisiciplinary journal, the table of contents of the *Companion* did not do much to advance that agenda. But the plain fact was that when the volume was constructed, genuinely cross-disciplinary work had not moved as far as one might have hoped or expected, especially given talk in the 1980s about a new subject of cognitive science (known sometimes too as cognitive 'studies'). Things have moved on since then, and this is making my task in updating the *Companion* a challenging one. However, it still surprises me that things haven't moved on as fast as was once expected they would. All those years ago, it seemed we were on the verge of seeing a new subject, one that would supersede philosophy of mind, certain aspects of psychology and linguistics, neuroscience, and work on artificial intelligence. But now, and to some extent then, one wonders whether what is in the offing is something genuinely new or is instead the rather more mundane replacement of several of these endeavours by a single more dominant one. (More on this in answers to later questions.)

As my answer to the first question suggests, my own work on

mind begins with what I regard as the inseparable bond between mind and language. In 2005 I published *Objects of Metaphor*, a book which contains the germ of an idea that, if not yet a recognised contribution to philosophy of mind, might become one. That idea comes in chapter 2 of the book, concerns predication, and it begins with what might seem an odd question: can objects (taking this liberally to include material objects, events, states of affairs and the like) serve in place of words in exercises of human semantic abilities? If the semantic ability in question is reference, the answer is surely 'yes'. We often—and naturally—use material objects, as well as sounds, events and even states of affairs as referential devices; for example, a salt cellar and pepper mill can stand in for—refer to—motorcars when telling a story at a dinner table. But of course reference is rightly thought of only as one of a pair of fundamental semantic abilities. The simplest kind of truth-directed speech act—what Quine called the 'basic combination'—depends on both reference and predication, and most philosophers pay at least lip-service to the idea that these two abilities are different and equal partners in the enterprise of saying something true.

These simple facts led me to wonder whether if like reference, predication was something that could be accomplished not simply with words, but with objects. For many reasons, some as obvious as the fact that 'predication' has the connotation of something done with words, answering this question is not straightforward. But I came to think that these difficulties can be overcome, and that we can and do recognize a way in which objects can function in something like the way that predicates do. Moreover, I came to see that this possibility can ground a rather novel approach to metaphor, one which doesn't go via a notion of similarity and closely related notions that have been a mainstay of accounts of metaphor for decades, even though the failings of these notions should be pretty obvious.

The idea that objects can themselves be predicates (or fulfill a predicative function) was always meant to extend beyond its use in connection with metaphor to a rather wider range of phenomena associated with language and mind. But the draft of my book was already too long, so I had to settle for the narrower subject matter, and pursue further developments in the volume I am now working on. With some trepidation, I have called it *The Roots of Categorization*, and it is contracted with Oxford University Press for publication in 2009-10. The background to my discussion in this book will be current work on children's acquisition of language, and I hope to show how my original ideas about predication can help us better understand the conceptual resources that are so clearly necessary for, and antecedent to, children's acquisition of natural language. It is also my firm intention to avoid the mistakes that philosophers often make when writing about empirical psychology (see my answer to the next question), and, though it is a tall order, I think that what I have to say will also shed light on the issue of mind-language interdependence.

What is the proper role of philosophy in relation to psychology, artificial intelligence, and the neurosciences?

My years as editor of *Mind & Language* have given me a keen sense of the *improper* role of philosophy in relation to these other disciplines, and perhaps saying something about this is the best way to get a sense of what the proper role might be.

The difficulties of achieving something like genuine interdisciplinarity that plagued the mind and language reading group all those years ago, can be seen in a magnified form in the kinds of things that pass my desk as editor of the journal. On the one hand, it used to be, and to some extent continues to be, quite difficult to get submissions that are interdisciplinary at least to this minimal extent: contributions that would be of interest to researchers in more than one field. Philosophers have been the worst offenders here, but they are not alone, and psychologists, linguists and AI researchers have at one time or another thought it perfectly reasonable to submit articles that could only ever be of interest to those in their own field, and all too often a narrow part of that field. On the other hand—and this is a greater problem—one often gets strangely uninformed submissions that purport to be interdisciplinary. Thus, there are papers from philosophers who don't seem to appreciate the demands of experimental work in psychology, but who nonetheless think it is perfectly reasonable to tell psychologists what must be the case with this or that way the mind works. The giveaway here is 'must': philosophers are wedded to arguing a priori, and this leads them to assert a kind of necessity underlying their speculations, even when the truth or falsity of these speculations needs to be established not by argument, but by experimental investigation. Similar things could be said about the level of interdisciplinary ignorance and methodological solipsism (using that term rather differently here) that one often finds in submissions from outside philosophy, but philosophers are the worst offenders. To be sure, there are some topics on which the disciplines seem to have come together, in particular, cases in which philosophers have taken on board whole swathes of empirical work. But my feeling is that in most of these cases it is more a matter of cross-disciplinary fact-gathering than a genuine unification of effort. So the question of the proper role of philosophy in respect to the other disciplines is still open.

As I noted in answering the second question, the relatively sudden appearance of 'cognitive science' a couple of decades ago promised some kind of fruitful unification of disciplines concerned with the many and varied phenomena of mind and language. But I don't think we are close yet. Though the analogy should be taken lightly, think, for example, of the way things were at the beginning of the nineteenth century in the subject we now think of as physics. Phenomena of light, heat, magnetism, electricity and mechanics were thought of as quite distinct subject matters, each with its own problems, apparatuses and methodologies. Unification came only after a long period marked by theoretical advances, not simply in each of these fields, but in the grasp of a wider picture of how the physical world worked. As a result, we have come to think of physics quite differently, and it takes considerable historical sensitivity to understand its original multi-disciplinary nature.

Though perhaps not in some of the ways it is presently done, philosophy might be the source for a wider picture of mindedness, and might in this way serve to launch a kind of unification which, though it cannot be quite like that which led to physics (as we know it), bears some resemblance to what happened in that subject. Among the disciplines that would be listed in a survey of cognitive science, philosophy is always mentioned, but invariably seems something of an outsider: its special concern with concepts and argument sit uneasily with disciplines whose main work is empirical. However, there are inklings of how philosophy might serve the unifying function described above: think here of how philosophical views of perception led researchers first to consider and then to find evidence of blindsight. I realize that this view of philosophy seems to inflate its importance, but the caveat that I mentioned earlier is crucial. If there comes to be a subject which supersedes the separate disciplines now focusing on various aspects of the mind, that subject won't be philosophy as it is now practiced. But then again it won't be any of the others either.

6. Samuel Guttenplan   55

Is a science of consciousness

It would be extremely foolish to say 'no' to this outright, especially after having just insisted that philosophers should not argue for things that are only ever going to be settled by empirical investigation. However, I suppose it wouldn't do any harm to make some obvious remarks about the way the question should be taken, even though a consequence will be a certain pessimism about answering the question affirmatively.

What most people mean when they wonder whether there can be a science of X is whether the methods of some particular science will help us understand X better. There are three questions that need to be addressed before we can make any further sense of this: What do we *now* know about X? What is the science in question? What would we count as *understanding* in this context? Where the X is consciousness, these obvious questions have anything but obvious answers.

What do we now know about consciousness? I really don't think that anyone should argue with the answer 'very little', but I think it is even worse than that. For I think we take ourselves to know more about consciousness than we do. It is now many years since I and a group of high-school friends discussed the strange fact that electrochemical goings-on in eyes and brains could produce experiences with what we thought of as such obvious 'filmic' values. We were not sophisticated enough to talk about explanatory gaps, though if questioned, we would probably have thought more in terms of a chasms. Moreover, had someone suggested any of the currently debated attempts to understand consciousness via various other putatively cognitive states and attitudes, either of ourselves or our nervous systems, I have little doubt but that we would have thought these proposals were in one way or another simply changing the subject; refusing, that is, to face the problem head-on (so to speak). In short, while we didn't think we knew much about consciousness, we did think we knew this much: there was a phenomenon of consciousness which was evident when one opened one's eyes in good light and took in the scene.

I now very much doubt that we do know even that much. It is not that I think we should give in to those who try to convince us that what seems the deeply mysterious phenomenon of consciousness is in some way just a complex arrangement of better understood cognitive states and attitudes, or that it is a pervasive illusion created by our possessing those states and attitudes. Far from it. But I don't think we should ever have thought that our understanding of attitudes was somehow easier than the so-called 'hard' problem of consciousness, or that we could use them to illuminate consciousness. In saying this, do not take me to be swelling the ranks of those who think we are simply not smart enough to understand consciousness. I do think we can make progress, but my hunch is that this will require us to abandon the idea that consciousness can be singled out—that it can by itself be the X in the first of the questions presupposed by the main one about the science of consciousness. Instead, we will have to think more about the intricate, and poorly understood, interdependencies among what we now describe as consciousness, perception, emotion, attitudes and, not least, human action.

One consequence of this is that any science of consciousness will turn out to be a science, not of some isolable phenomenon, but of human mindedness itself. And if, in answer to my second question, one opts for something like contemporary neuroscience, then the prospects for such a science of consciousness look dim. We have known for a very long time that without a functioning central nervous system, mindedness is absent. But that in itself doesn't help us understand mindedness itself. To be sure, there have been and continue to be many studies in neuropsychology showing how certain kinds of damage can lead to the disruptions of portions of our mental lives. And, more recently, there has been a torrent of brain-imaging results which, in a still rather crude way, show what is happening in the brain when a subject focuses on some task. However, even if one imagines these kinds of investigation being indefinitely refined, it is difficult to see how they could provide any *understanding* of what it is to have a mental life. Imagine someone trying to understand why people take trips by obsessively noting everything about road-infrastructure and the duration of every individual car journey and accident. If my hunch is right, we cannot understand consciousness without being prepared to take into account the full range of things which add up to human mindedness.

Admittedly, everything depends here on an answer to the third of my questions, the one about explanation and understanding. The issues here are too well-known for me to have anything new to say. In many cases, knowing what-happens-when—and why—is all that is required for scientific explanation, and thus understanding; in others, understanding seems to require going beyond, or at least off to the side of, scientific explanation. There are of course those who are prepared go that extra distance, and who see neuroscience as the best account we will ever have of what goes on in the human mind. I don't think this can be right.

What are the most important open problems in contemporary philosophy of mind? What are the most promising prospects?

As will be obvious from I have said above, what seems most pressing in the philosophy of mind is not any specific 'open' problem so much as the rather more difficult task of not being misled by too 'atomistic' a conception of the subject matter. In discussing the possibility of a science of consciousness, I mentioned the difficulties of treating—or even characterizing—consciousness in isolation from a wider range of other features of our mental lives. So, let me give another example here.

For a long time, the philosophy of action didn't figure as a central subject matter in the philosophy of mind, though there can be little doubt that it should have done. More recently, this has changed: to take just one example, the role of action in perception has been an area of great current interest, and this has been intensified by psychological work on, for example, mirror neurons. However, the change, while good in itself, has brought with it precisely the kind of problem that has I think made for trouble in respect of consciousness studies. For in ignoring, as is almost always the case, the careful philosophical literature on the nature of action itself, it is simply unclear what progress, if any, can be made in studying the role of action in perception. It is by no means easy to say what makes some event a human action; indeed it is not even clear that one is justified in assuming, as I just did, that we should think of actions as events in any ordinary sense. But there has been a lot written about these problems, and it should be taken on board when one looks at the role of action in perception. Simply assuming that the movement of various bodily parts, or anticipations of those movements, count as actions, is not only philosophically insensitive, it devalues whatever comes to be said about perception. It is no doubt true that many organisms, including human beings, integrate any sensory information received as a result of their movements in an environment with whatever is received by more passive sensory means. How a creature changes its location and orientation will certainly be a part of what that creature comes to discriminate, and these facts are certainly interesting. But there is more to the idea that perception and action are interwoven in human mental life than can be gleaned from these kinds of psychological results.

The example of action and perception certainly needs more spelling out than I have space for here, or than I am now in a position to give. For while I am convinced that the proper understanding of how each of these are implicated in the understanding of the other is a complex and subtle matter—one that requires sensitivity to both the philosophical and psychological literature—I have no particular advice about what the next substantial steps should be.

Further study of the interplay between consciousness and attitudes, perception and action—study that is not now being done in the serious way I think necessary—suggests then that the most important open problem in the philosophy of mind is that of learning how best to think about mindedness in the first place. It may well be that we can only discover that way when we come to have the unified science of the mind that I spoke of in answering the third question, or it may be that progress can be made in advance of that perhaps distant goal. But I think that we have often got too far ahead of ourselves in contemporary work on the mind, and would do well to draw back. Indeed, it might even be a good idea if philosophers of mind held back from offering their latest solutions to what they take to be the important problems. (Anachronism aside, Cicero could have been thinking of philosophy of mind when he said that there is no position too absurd for some philosopher not to have held it.)

7
Valerie Gray Hardcastle

Professor of Philosophy
Dean, McMicken College of Arts and Sciences
University of Cincinnati, USA

Why were you initially drawn to philosophy of mind?

In many respects, I can honestly say that I have always been drawn to the philosophy of mind, though when I was younger, I did not know that was what it was called. I was one of those rare students who went to college intending to major in philosophy, with the goal of studying mind.

As a young child, consciousness, sleep and dreaming, and death fascinated me. Raised without religion, I had a hard time imagining the finality of non-existence. (Actually, trying to imagine it terrified me.) I puzzled over why it did not bother me to consider that eons existed prior to my consciousness, though thinking about the eons existing after my consciousness would wink out did. I wondered why my meat was conscious but the "meat" of plants and tables did not seem to be. I worried that non-REM sleep was similar to death. These were the questions that fascinated me, but I had no idea that there was any formal program of study associated with them.

When I was sixteen, my father gave me a copy of Daniel Dennett and Douglas Hofstadter's *The Mind's Eye*. We also shared a copy of *Gödel, Escher, and Bach*. I realized then that one could get paid for investigating the mind. The rest, as they say, is history. Placing out of many of my general education courses, I filled my college schedule with philosophy classes and then classes in neuroscience, psychology, and cognitive science in graduate school.

What do you consider your most important contribution to the field?

When I entered the professional world of philosophy in the early 1990's, cognitive science departments were just forming around the country, and the idea that the various sciences that study the mind and brain could pool their intellectual resources to solve problems was really just beginning to take shape. The previous generation of philosophers of mind had set out the challenges of interdisciplinary work in the study of mind, and it was my generation's task to meet those challenges.

Broadly speaking, I am interested in the question of what science can tell us about being human, if anything. Hence, I work primarily in the areas of philosophy of psychology/cognitive science and philosophy of biology/neuroscience and in the intersection between the two. A constant worry in my research is how it is we should fit together different experimental paradigms across different levels of analysis and using different animal models. I recognize that I am often pegged as a philosopher of mind, but I am a fairly unusual philosopher of mind for I come to questions of mind as they arise in and around science.

Though I tend to operate under the assumption that empirical investigation can shed light on human experience, I am far from uncritical of science as it is currently practiced. Consequently, my publications are generally of two types. They use recent results from the cognitive sciences to inform current philosophical or theoretical debates, or they attempt to articulate appropriate frameworks for understanding scientific investigations, particularly in the cognitive sciences.

I work in the details, not so much in the broad strokes. Previous philosophers believed that brain science could contribute to our understanding of consciousness, human nature, the will, materialism, and so on. My job is to show exactly how this was the case in specific instances.

Under this larger motif, I have focused primarily on questions concerning the relationship between psychology and neuroscience. I became interested in this broad question as a graduate student in UCSD's interdisciplinary program in cognitive science and philosophy as I wondered how and whether psychological theories and data fit with what we know about the brain. I want to know how theories and data in the various cognitive sciences work together—if they do—and what this might tell us about the nature of explanation, reduction, scientific unity, and scientific practice, as well as what this might say about those aspects of being human we prize the most—consciousness, our emotions, our sense of self, and, to a lesser extent, rationality and sanity.

Looking back at my body of work, I believe my greatest contribution concerns how to meld the philosophy of science with philosophy of mind, when hitherto the two sub-disciplines rarely interacted with one another. Most of the issues found in traditional philosophy of science are recapitulated in (an empirically-grounded) philosophy of mind. In particular, philosophers of mind worry about what counts as appropriate empirical justification for a theoretical claim, how to determine which level of organization is the correct one for a scientific explanation, what explanations should look like, whether all explanations will or should reduce to some primitives, and how what is learned about the mind/brain should affect larger social, economic, and political decisions. At the same time, philosophers of neuroscience concern themselves some traditional aspects of philosophy of mind, including worrying how it is a brain can represent, if it does, and how and whether this representation ties to other notions of representation in cognitive science and beyond. My work crosses all these boundaries. Actually, my work blurs all those boundaries.

Along with a group of very talented colleagues, I see myself as a new sort of philosopher of mind, one who not only knows the relevant science, but also understands in a fundamental way the associated issues in the philosophy of science. In this way, we do not traffic in "data-borrowing"—using empirical results to prop up our favorite theories of mind—but we also engage with the science itself. We critique experiments, question interpretations, devise new ways of understanding collections of results. In short: we do the science as well as the philosophy.

What is the proper role of philosophy in relation to psychology, artificial intelligence, and the neurosciences?

I remember as an undergraduate student, Professor John Searle talking to me about how philosophy is essentially a gadfly buzzing around the livestock of science, irritating it and poking at it until all its flaws were raw and exposed. Though I do not think my views of philosophy are quite this violent, in many respects, I believe Searle was right. Philosophy at its best engages other disciplines and questions their fundamental commitments and assumptions. Philosophy of mind is no different. Good philosophers are at home in other disciplines, for philosophy is not so much a discipline in its own right as a set of tools one can use to query other ideas, claims, and assumptions.

But this perspective means that philosophers need to know a lot about other disciplines and how they actually work. If I had to summarize in three words or less the point I have been trying to make throughout my professional career, it is: "Details do matter." This is why it is important to be wary about claims most philosophers make about anything that is grand, sweeping, or applicable across lots of exemplars. This will also illustrate the other twelve words that describe the moral of my career: "The story is a lot more complicated than you think it is." It is going to be more complicated than philosophers think, and it is going to be more complicated than neuroscientists and psychologists think. It is all of our collective jobs to articulate the complicated story. It is philosophy's job in particular to understand the sciences it is trying to analyze and conceptualize.

Consider: we know that at the molecular level, mammalian brains are virtually identical—all neurons are composed of the same sorts of chemicals, which interact with one another in the same sorts of ways. This is not surprising, since basic physics and chemistry is the same whether one is talking about patterns of activation in a human brain or the electrical current zinging through a phone line. Further, just like at the molecular level, mammalian brains are remarkably similar to one another at a gross level. Indeed, the central nervous system in invertebrates isn't all that different from the mammalian central nervous system either. We find innumerable homologous areas, cell types, neurotransmitters, and so forth. This is good news, for it means we can study rats and fruit flies and gerbils and learn something about we work.

However, once we scratch the surface of different animal brains, we do find important differences. These differences will make a difference in how we theorize about how we think. For example, all mammals have roughly the same five end organs in their ears to support their auditory and vestibular systems. They work to keep their lateral semicircular canals in their ears parallel to the horizontal plane relative to the Earth, for keeping it in that position allows them to get the best possible information about head position in space. (The lateral canal is maximally excitatory to a yaw (left to right) head motion; keeping the canal in line with the horizontal plane allows the organ to detect this motion with the greatest accuracy.) But here, similarities end. Rodents ambulate with their necks extended, which keep their heads in an extreme dorsal position. Humans, in contrast, incline their heads about twenty degrees when walking naturally. Nevertheless, in spite of the extreme differences in how these mammals hold their heads, in both cases the lateral semicircular canal in the ear remains parallel to the Earth's horizontal. In general, we can correlate the differences in the shape of the semicircular canals in the ear with skull shape and the position that an animal's head is normally in. (It is an unanswered but intriguing question whether we find the canal structures we do because different heads evolved to be oriented in different directions or whether animals naturally hold their heads in different positions because their semicircular canals evolved differently.)

There are additional striking differences between herbivores and predators in brain structure, for creatures who munch on grasses and trees require much less precise environmental information than those who hunt moving targets in order to survive. Rodents, for example, have no foveae. To maintain visual fixation on a point, they move their necks, using what is known as the vestibular-colic response. The vestibular system in their ears tells them how their head is oriented and they use that information to reorient their heads in order to keep whatever object currently fascinates them in their line of sight.

In contrast, primates have foveae and we move our eyeballs to keep our target within the foveal area, using the vestibular-ocular response. This is a much more precise orienting mechanism, which allows us to move our eyes to compensate for changes in head position such that we can keep objects foveated for as long as we wish. For some indication of how important computing horizontal eye motion is to our brains, consider that the abducens (or VIth) nerve in humans, which controls horizontal eye abduction, feeds into one of the biggest motor nuclei in the brain stem. This ocular nucleus, which controls only one very tiny muscle, is only slightly smaller than the nucleus that controls all of our twenty or so facial muscles.

In more striking contrast still, bats do not maintain ocular position in the same fashion as the rest of the mammals. Because they fly and so have greater freedom to move in three-dimensional space, maintaining body position relative to horizontal is not an easy option. As a result, they use other sense organs, primarily hearing (the other half of the VIIIth nerve), to determine how their eyes should be oriented. Consequently, they need not rely on vestibular-ocular responses as we do, even though their bodies are equipped with such reflex machinery.

All of these anatomical and physiological differences are important when neuroscientists want to investigate something like how the brain learns to compensate for damage to the vestibular pathways. What may seem as small and insignificant differences from a broad mammalian perspective becomes hugely important as scientists seek to understand the particular mechanisms behind brain activity. Can they use animals with no foveae and a vestibular-colic response to learn about how foveated mammals recover their vestibular-ocular response? More generally, how well do particular animal models translate across the animal kingdom? Should we be allowed to generalize from experiments on a single species (or set of species) to how Nature functions?

Let us look further at this specific example. In all vertebrates, a unilateral labyrinthectomy (UL), or a lesion of the labyrinthine structure in one ear, gives rise to two types of ocular motor disorders. There are static deficits, such as a bias toward looking toward the lesioned side when the head isn't moving, and dynamic deficits, such as abnormal vestibular-ocular reflexes (VOR), which occur in response to head movements. In only two or three days following the UL procedure, the brain starts to compensate for its loss and the static deficits disappear. Since labyrinthine structures do not regenerate, and peripheral neurons continue to fire abnormally, whatever the brain is doing to recover has to be a central effect. Single neuron recordings from a variety of animals indicate that the vestibular nuclei (VN) on the same side of the brain as the lesion start to show normal resting rate activity as the brain learns to compensate for its injury. What the exact mechanism the brain uses for vestibular compensation is, though, is still unknown. Studies have shown that the brain does not substitute other sensory inputs or increase inputs from central regions that process sensory inputs, nor does it generate new synapses. A few data support the hypotheses that denervation supersensitivity or rapid hormonal changes could lead to vestibular compensation, but the effects of both appear to be small.

It is fairly easy to find significant differences in how organisms recover and compensate for vestibular damage across the animal kingdom. Frogs, for example, appear to rely on input from the intact labyrinth to regulate the resting activity of the vestibular nuclei. Mammals, however, do not. The recovery of their vestibular nuclei occurs independent of transcommissural inputs. In addition, static symptoms follow different time courses in different animals. In rats, spontaneous nystagmus disappears within hours after UL, while in the rabbit and guinea pig, it persists for several weeks. In humans, it may continue in one form or another for several years.

If we want to design therapies to enhance human vestibular recovery, then the differences one finds across the different animal models used to study UL compensation can make a big difference. Is there enough similarity in what frogs do to what we do that we can use them to learn about ourselves? How about a rat or a rabbit? Is the best model of our brain something close to that brain itself? These are actually philosophical questions. And they are more important questions than the thought-experiment driven multiple-realizability arguments of yore.

While there are many important commonalities among all members of the animal kingdom, there are also many important functional differences. In appreciating this fact, one should also appreciate that the details really do matter and that the final story, philosophical or otherwise, regarding how brains and thus minds work is going to be more complicated than we have ever dreamed. We all are similar, but we are also all very different. Whether we should emphasize the ying or the yang depends upon what we are trying to explain and why. Philosophers' job is to help decide which way neuroscientists, cognitive scientists, and psychologists should be going theoretically under which circumstances.

Is a science of consciousness possible?

Of course it is. The science of anything from the natural world is possible. The interesting question is whether a science of consciousness will tell us what we really want to know about the phenomena. My guess is that a lot of folk will remain unhappy with the results.

They will be unhappy because the real problem of consciousness is probably completely intractable. We will never understand consciousness in the deeply satisfying way some people expect from our sciences. The primary focus of debate in consciousness research, whether consciousness is a nonmaterial property of the universe, is off-target. The real debate should be over whether consciousness will occupy a unique place in our sciences or whether standard science will one day grow to encompass consciousness and make it understandable. In the end, I think consciousness will occupy a unique place.

Of course, much of our sense of understanding is bred by familiarity. Use begets familiarity. Because what we will learn in our science of consciousness will allow us to manipulate our world, a kind of understanding of consciousness will grow. Its more mysterious aspects will be identified, and we will understand better why certain aspects of consciousness will be beyond understanding. These things too are types of understanding, which will add to our sense that science explains consciousness and that we understand it.

But the real problem of consciousness involves reconciling two conflicting points of view: the subjective and the objective. Since science traffics only in objective points of view, it cannot solve or explain away the conflict. But it can do a lot of other things that it is supposed to do, like model, predict, retrodict, and generalize over conscious experience.

What are the most important open problems in contemporary philosophy of mind? What are the most promising prospects?

Honestly, I do not know. Instead, I will talk about the new directions the field is heading and why I think they are vitally important. These new directions are directly tied to the new directions we find in neuroscience and cognitive science.

Social neuroscience is an interdisciplinary field that explores the biological mechanisms underlying social processes and uses biological concepts and methods to develop and refine theories of social processes and behavior in the social and behavioral sciences. Social neuroscience emphasizes the complementary nature of the different levels of organization spanning the social and biological domains (e.g., molecular, cellular, system, organism, relational, group, social) and how multi-level analyses can foster understanding of the mechanisms underlying the human mind and behavior.

This new trajectory in neuroscience and cognitive science raises many important issues for both society and the social sciences, including: new ideas about what it is to be human; changing concepts of punishment and responsibility, the relationships among mind, self, and society; new forms of social control and behavior modification; the growing use of psychopharmaceuticals, changing notions of affect and desire; new accounts of alcoholism, drug dependency and addiction; altering the boundaries between normal and abnormal; and the blurring of distinctions between treatment and enhancement. As a consequence, there is a pressing need for critical reflection on neuroscience's claims, practices and technologies, and their social, political, and conceptual implications. This new area of research is known as *neuroethics*. In his book *The Ethical Brain,* Michael Gazzaniga defines neuroethics as: "the examination of how we want to deal with the social issues of disease, normality, mortality, lifestyle, and the philosophy of living *informed by our understanding of underlying brain mechanisms*" (emphasis in the original).

Though neuroethics arose out of concerns in social neuroscience and cognitive neuroscience, it has a conceptual home in the more established field known as *Medical Humanities*. Broadly speaking, medical humanities is an interdisciplinary field that applies insights from humanities (literature, philosophy, history, and religion), social science (anthropology, cultural studies, psychology, and sociology), and the arts (literature, theater, film, and visual arts) to medical education, practice, research, and theory. Bioethics, for example, is a sub-discipline of medical humanities. The humanities provide insight into the human condition, suffering, personhood, our responsibilities to one another, legal dilemmas, ethical decision-making; the social sciences help us to understand how the biosciences and medicine operate within cultural and social contexts and how culture and society interact with the individual experiences of self, illness, and well-being, and with clinical practice, health care systems, and biomedical research.

I think the jury is still out regarding whether neuroethics is a genuine new field in itself or whether it is the same old stuff dressed up in new clothing (lipstick on a pig?). Either way, it is clear that what we know about how humans' minds and brains work is at odds with some very basic assumptions in our society regarding how we should live our lives, how we assign responsibility and punishment, how we instruct our young, how we think, and how we should live together in harmony. At a minimum, philosophy of mind should be at the forefront of figuring out the implications of neuroscientific and psychological data for our legal and ethical frameworks. To date, we have not done a good job in managing these connections.

8
John Heil

Professor of Philosophy
Washington University in St. Louis, USA

Why were you initially drawn to philosophy of mind?

In the 1960's, when I came into philosophy, the mind-brain Identity Theory advanced by Herbert Feigl and J. J. C. Smart was creating the kind of stir that made it a natural choice for a Ph.D. thesis topic. My first publication, "Sensations, Experiences, and Brain Processes" (*Philosophy*, 1970) made up a part of the first chapter of my thesis, and appeared months before the thesis was completed. I argued that Smart's attempt to finesse the qualitative dimension of the mental by treating reports of sensations as 'topic neutral' was unsuccessful. From there, one thing led to another.

My graduate career had been lackluster, so I set out to learn philosophy on my own terms, first by teaching classes on subjects I thought I ought to know something about, then by snagging fellowship money that allowed me to attend classes and seminars in philosophically upbeat surroundings. I spent 1974-75 at Cornell with support from NEH, pursuing interests in Wittgenstein (the *Tractatus*), in linguistics, and in psychology. At the time I had the strong sense that mainstream cognitive psychology (as spelled out, for instance, in Ulric Neisser's *Cognitive Psychology*, Prentice-Hall, 1967) had tacitly embraced a Tractarian picture of the world and our thoughts about it. I pushed this thesis in various papers (culminating in "Does Cognitive Psychology Rest on a Mistake?", *Mind*, 1981) and in a course in the philosophy of mind I taught as a visitor at Brown in 1976.

I returned to Cornell in 1978-79, supported by an ACLS Study Fellowship. Study Fellowships were meant to underwrite work in areas other than that of the recipient's Ph.D. I passed the year in the Cornell Psychology Department, where Neisser and J. J.

Gibson were major forces. After years of resistance, Neisser had begun moving into the Gibson camp. (Gibson died in the fall of 1979, and Neisser departed soon thereafter for a chair at Emory.) The year at Cornell led to a book on perception (*Perception and Cognition*, University of California Press 1983) that reflected my understanding of Gibson, an understanding uncongenial to many self-styled Gibsonians.

In 1981, I was awarded a two-year fellowship from NIMH that took me to Berkeley. I was housed in the Psychology Department, but I spent much of my time brooding about issues in the philosophy of mind, most prominently the implications of the doctrine that the mental 'supervenes' on the physical. Donald Davidson, who moved to Berkeley the same year, came to exercise a profound influence over my thinking. My reading of Davidson, however, differed from the prevailing reading, a point to which I shall return presently.

In December of 1985, I presented a paper ("Are We Brains in a Vat? Top Philosopher says 'No'") at the Eastern Division APA meetings in Washington. C. B. Martin commented. The following fall, Charlie and I were thrown together as visitors at the University of Rochester. Our relationship during that term was often stormy, but I soon learned that, whenever we disagreed, no matter how confident I was of my own thesis, no matter how far-fetched Charlie's position struck me, I would ultimately concede. (Jack Smart later told me that this was a common experience for Charlie's interlocutors.)

Charlie eventually got me to recognize the importance of 'ontological seriousness' in addressing questions in the philosophy of mind, although it took a decade for the lesson to sink in. It wasn't until the early 1990's that it began to dawn on me that the interesting philosophical questions about the mind were really fundamental metaphysical questions. This was brought home to me in the course of editing, with my colleague, Alfred Mele, *Mental Causation* (Oxford, 1993) while completing my first, somewhat halting, attempt to treat questions in the philosophy of mind with ontological seriousness (*The Nature of True Minds*, Cambridge, 1992).

What became most clear to me during this period was just how little I knew about fundamental metaphysics. Like many philosophers of mind, I had set out to solve problems such as the problem of mental causation by picking and choosing metaphysical theses that suited my agenda. The results were, predictably, ontologically shallow and unsatisfying. Philosophy of mind is many things, but it is most fundamentally applied metaphysics. If you get the ontology right, central problems in the philosophy of mind take care of themselves.

I do not say that the *only* questions philosophers face in considering minds and their place in nature are metaphysical questions. We confront important epistemological and conceptual questions, as well, and we face the challenge of cobbling together a uniform conception of mind from all that the several sciences tell us about states of mind, mental operations, and the brain. Metaphysical problems occupy center stage, however. Our metaphysical conception of minds and their contents constrain the space of epistemological possibilities, for instance. Dualism allows for apparently easy access to the contents of our own minds, but makes access to other minds problematic. Materialism turns the tables, calling into question first-person authority.

The idea is not that we require a worked-out metaphysics to make progress in the philosophy of mind, but that we do well to understand the metaphysical options and their respective costs and benefits. Philosophers of mind too often treat substantive metaphysical views as though they fell from the sky. Such views—Humeanism comes to mind—are accepted as the defaults: presumed true until proven false. But in philosophy there are no default views, no heavyweight champs that retain their crowns unless decisively knocked out. Philosophy of mind has gone off the rails when it has unthinkingly embraced substantive metaphysical theses that turn out to make trouble in ways that escape detection. Problems we set out to solve, are, with depressing frequency, problems we create for ourselves. Metaphysics is too often pursued unselfconsciously.

What do you consider your most important contribution to the field?

My work on mental causation has implications for the way philosophers have come to think about the mind-body problem. We have, I claim, been too ready to assume that every significant predicate, every predicate that figures in the statement of a law, for instance, must designate a unique property. Suppose we grant, what seems obvious anyway, that most of the predicates we deploy in science and in everyday life apply to objects in virtue of those objects' possession of any of a possibly open-ended family of *similar* properties. Take the predicate 'is red'. This predicate applies to objects that are scarlet, crimson, and various other 'shades' of red. Think of these shades as ways of being red. The mistake would be to imagine that a billiard ball, *in addition* to being crimson, was red as well (on the grounds, perhaps, that not all red things are crimson). It is true that the ball is crimson and true that it is red, but these truths have a single truthmaker, the ball's being a determinate shade of red: two truths, one truthmaker.

Failure to recognize this homely fact about the application of predicates to the world underlies the argument for the multiple realizability of mental properties. Functionalists notice that the pain predicate, for instance, applies to diverse creatures in virtue of those creatures' possession of any of an open-ended family of properties, properties exhibiting similar 'causal profiles', properties endowing their possessors with similar dispositions. The key term here is 'similar'. Creatures in pain are *similarly* disposed.

Functionalists like to say that these dispositionally similar properties are 'realizers' of pain: there is the pain property itself, and there are its realizers. The problem is that, if we distinguish the pain property from its realizers, it becomes difficult to see how the pain property *itself* could play a role in producing behavior; pain's causal role would seem to be preempted by its realizing properties. I see nothing to be gained by positing 'higher-level' multiply realized properties in these cases. Just as a billiard ball can be red in virtue of being crimson—it's being crimson *is* its being red—so you can be in pain in virtue of being in a particular sort of physical state—your C-fibers are firing.

A view of this kind is close to what is sometimes called 'realizer functionalism', the kind of functionalism embraced by David Armstrong and David Lewis. I do not endorse functionalism, however. My belief is that states of mind are *both* dispositional and qualitative. What functionalism does is give us a description of the mind in dispositional terms, a description that is perfectly adequate for many purposes, but not the whole story.

Realizer functionalists are often accused of undercutting the science of psychology. If the nature of psychological states differs across species, even across individuals within species, how could we hope to formulate lawful psychological generalizations?

This line of criticism misses the point. The pain predicate applies to distinct kinds of creature in virtue of those creatures' possession of any of a family of dispositionally *similar* properties. Dispositional similarity is enough to ensure that generalizations about pains will hold true across individuals and species. What collects all the diverse physical properties together so that they fall under a single predicate? Well, as proponents of multiple realizability like to argue, the properties in question all play roughly the same role in the psychological economies of their possessors—where 'same' is understood as something like 'causally similar'. If we go this way, it is hard to see what is lost other than the problem of the 'causal relevance' of the mental.

One notable consequence of the view I am advocating is that the mental-physical distinction turns out not to be ontologically momentous. In this regard, my position echoes Davidson's. This might surprise some readers. I believe Davidson has been widely misunderstood, however, unfairly saddled with an insidious dualism he would never have dreamt of advocating.

Davidson distinguishes mental and physical *predicates* or *descriptions*, not mental and physical *properties*. (Davidson's rare uses of the word 'property' occur in contexts in which it is clear that he means by 'property' what we should mean by 'predicate' or 'truth about'.) Simply put, Davidson's contention is that whenever it is true that a mental predicate applies to an agent, it does so in virtue of that agent's being in a state that could be given a detailed physical description. (This is all there is to the 'supervenience' of the mental on the physical.) A single state is describable in two ways, the mental way and the physical way: two truths, one truthmaker. Philosophers have interpreted this as the claim that there is a single 'token' state possessing distinct mental and physical properties answering to mental and physical predicates, respectively. This is manifestly *not* Davidson's idea.

Davidson's 'anomalous monism' is not a thesis about the irreducibility of mental to physical *properties* (whatever that might mean). Rather it incorporates the claim that application conditions for mental predicates are orthogonal to application conditions for physical predicates. Mental descriptions are not translatable into or definable in physical terms. We have one world, variously describable: monism. The mental-physical difference is a difference in conception only. Davidson is right to align himself with Spinoza.

Thus interpreted, Davidson has little in common with philosophers who call themselves non-reductive physicalists. Ontologically, monism is fully 'reductive'. If reduction is taken to apply to descriptions or explanations, however, Davidson is indeed anti-reductionist. Non-reductive physicalists begin with the denial that mental descriptions are conceptually reducible to physical descriptions, and proceed to draw a substantive ontological conclusion: mental properties are distinct from, yet somehow dependent on, physical properties. This line of reasoning is not one that would ever have occurred to Davidson.

Nor is it useful to think of Davidson's brand of monism as a version of materialism or physicalism. Remember, the mental-physical distinction is not ontologically deep. When it comes to truth, physical descriptions are in no way privileged. If there is asymmetry, it amounts only to the fact that, whereas any feature of the world could be given a physical description, it is much harder to find mental descriptions for arbitrary worldly states. (In fact, in "Mental Events," Davidson provides a recipe for constructing a mental description for anything at all.) Both mental and physical descriptions can be true. Physical descriptions are not *more* true (as a physicalist would have it). This is compatible with the idea that whenever a mental description is true, its truthmaker could be given an exhaustive physical description.

All this is simply to say that I see the position I endorse as entirely consistent with Davidson's, rightly understood.

What is the proper role of philosophy in relation to psychology, artificial intelligence, and the neurosciences?

Like most philosophers of a naturalistic bent, I accept Quine's dictum that there are no sharp boundaries between science and philosophy. Most often this idea is interpreted as simply an injunction for philosophers to take the results of science more seriously. But Quine's maxim cuts both ways: philosophers aren't the only philosophers. Scientific discourse incorporates a lot of bad philosophy. It is naïve and ultimately self-defeating for philosophers to take on board scientific pronouncements uncritically. When we do so we risk losing our most important asset, the trait that makes us most valuable to our colleagues in the sciences, our critical edge.

I can illustrate by mentioning a mistake sometimes made by philosophers who insist that all inquiry begins with science. This is the mistake of moving from the fact that science is *silent* about some feature of the world to the conclusion that scientific findings *exclude* the feature in question. Thus, some philosophers have concluded from the observation that scientific laws concern only objects' powers or relations to the claim that science tells us that *all there is* to objects are their powers or relations they bear to other objects. The world is a massive structure in which the nodes—objects—are wholly constituted by their relations to other nodes.

Suppose I am right, however: properties of concrete objects are *powerful qualities*. Then science can be seen as providing an abstraction, a picture of the world couched in terms of powers or in terms of relations among actual and possible objects. Such a picture serves many important ends. It enables us to explain why things behave, or would behave, as they do, to predict objects' behavior and to manipulate features of our environment.

Even in such cases, however, we find appeal to objects' qualities unavoidable. Functionalists and connectionists like to pretend that all that matters are causal connections among states, the qualities of which are irrelevant. But, in the absence of a theory, it would be natural to think that states are very often suited to play the causal roles they play precisely *because* they have the qualitative natures they do. Pain states are apt for the 'pain role' because they are qualitatively as they are. C. B. Martin's longstanding emphasis on qualities of the material of mental imagery is meant to support a similar point.

Functionalists would dismiss such thoughts on the grounds that they are beside the point: a quality could have an influence on a system only if teamed with the right power. Were we to swap out the quality and retain the power, the system would be unaffected. Think here of fanciful cases in which neurons are replaced one by one with transistors in the brain of an unsuspecting subject.

This kind of substitution, however, presupposes that powers and qualities *could* vary independently. If we take properties to be powerful qualities, then the envisaged swap is not in the cards. The identity of a property is bound up with how it is and what it could do. These are not separable elements or 'higher-' and 'lower-order' properties. Properties differing qualitatively differ dispositionally. This view is hard to accept if you have been trained to think of powers and qualities as distinct kinds of property. But it is time we moved beyond this ill-conceived philosophical fable. (Consider just one liability of such a view: it makes our perceptual access to qualities utterly mysterious.)

Reflect on the sphericity of this billiard ball. Sphericity is a paradigmatic quality. But *in virtue of being spherical*, the ball has the power to roll in a particular way, has the power to make a particular kind of concave impression in soft clay, has the power to reflect light so as to look spherical.

Of course a ball is a complex object. You could construct a ball that outwardly resembled a billiard ball but wouldn't roll (because it was made of steel and in the presence of a powerful magnet) or would not make concave impressions in soft clay (because it was made of Styrofoam). But such examples show only that what a complex *object* would do depends on *all* the object's properties and their interrelations and on its circumstances.

I have gone on in this vein because I think it important that we remind ourselves that our interpretations of scientific findings can be affected by prior philosophical commitments. Ontology makes all the difference. Under the circumstances, it is advisable to be clear about our ontological presuppositions, to put our metaphysical cards on the table.

We have much to learn about the mind that we could only hope to learn through careful empirical investigation. Some of what we learn has implications for philosophical accounts of practical rationality, motivation, moral psychology, conceptions of the self. It is much less obvious that we are in a position to resolve through empirical investigation metaphysical puzzles about mental causation, for instance, or the relation of conscious experiences to goings on in the brain. On such matters we philosophers are on our own.

Is a science of consciousness possible?

A growing number of philosophers apparently regard consciousness as scientifically out of bounds. Science affords an objective 'third-person' account of the world, but consciousness is irreducibly 'first-person', subjective. By my lights this way of dividing the territory conflates epistemology and ontology.

We can allow that it is important to distinguish (1) *observing* someone's (or something's) being in a particular state and (2) *being* in that state. If the state is experiential, then the distinction is between undergoing an experience and undergoing an experience of an experience. One of the ways we philosophers make things difficult for ourselves is by imagining that experiences of experiences of something—a sunset, for instance, or the smell of a strong cheese—ought in some way to resemble the original experiences. When we look into the brain of someone undergoing the visual experience of a sunset, we see (as Colin McGinn puts it) only soggy grey matter. But what should we expect the experience of a sunset to look like? A sunset? Observing an experience need be nothing at all like having the experience.

My undefended assumption here is that consciousness is a feature of the natural world. This is bedrock, not something I would try to defend via philosophical argument. The only question is how consciousness fits in. Here again, we philosophers make things harder for ourselves than necessary by insisting at the outset on a deep division between the mental and the physical. The physical world, we think, is a colorless realm in which all there is to objects are powers to affect other objects. This is sometimes expressed in terms of structures or relations: objects, the relata, are constituted by relations they bear to other, similarly constituted objects. When we compare this drab, lifeless picture with the 'booming, buzzing confusion' of conscious experiences, we encounter an unbridgeable divide.

My belief is that properties—'natural properties'—of objects are at once qualitative and dispositional. In virtue of possessing a property an object is a certain way qualitatively *and* dispositionally. In virtue of being spherical, a ball would roll, would make a concave impression in soft clay, would reflect light so as to look spherical. Sphericity is a *powerful quality*. This was Locke's view and probably Spinoza's. It locates qualities where they belong: in the natural world. Consciousness is distinctive, not because it incorporates an ineliminable qualitative element, but because conscious qualities differ—qualitatively!—from non-conscious qualities.

The scientific problem is that of understanding the basis of conscious qualities in the brain. This is not a matter of seeing how something non-qualitative could give rise to something qualitative, but of seeing how something with the distinctive qualities of conscious experience could arise in the brain.

I have suggested that we make our job harder by imagining that qualities are exclusively mental and by expecting observations of experiences to resemble the experiences observed. We can make some progress by relinquishing these two prejudices. Note that this leaves entirely open what the qualities of conscious experiences are. Once again we philosophers have a knack for making hard questions harder by conflating qualities of experiences of objects with qualities of objects experienced. My experience of a fiery sunset is an experience of something red, but my experience is not red. Indeed, it is not easy to say what the qualities of conscious experiences are without mentioning qualities of what we experience.

This feature of experience, its 'transparency', has been used by some philosophers to identify qualities of conscious experience with qualities we represent experienced objects as having. There is something right about this, but it is not the whole story. There remains 'something it is like' to undergo a particular conscious experience, and this something is irreducibly qualitative. You can get a feel for this by imagining creatures with very different sorts of sensory system who have experiences of just what we experience. They experience in a different way, and this way is the locus of experiential qualities.

What are the most important open problems in contemporary philosophy of mind? What are the most promising prospects?

The fundamental task facing philosophers of mind is that of getting the ontology right. I believe that many of what are widely regarded as the most serious problems—the problem of mental causation, for instance—are self inflicted, stemming from a lingering analytic tradition that linguisticizes ontology at every turn. Just getting clear on the distinction between predicates and properties, understanding that distinct predicates can hold of objects by virtue of those objects' possession of a single property, and that a single predicate can hold of diverse objects by virtue of those objects' possession of distinct but similar properties can take us a long way toward a solution to the problem of mental causation.

If I am right, the problem of mental causation is not a big deal. A somewhat bigger deal is the problem of reconciling qualities of conscious experiences with features of conscious agents' bodies, most particularly their nervous systems. I have suggested already that we make this difficult problem altogether too difficult by conflating properties of conscious experiences with properties of experienced objects and by assuming that physical objects and states lack qualities. Once we acknowledge that every concrete particular possesses qualities, that properties of such objects are powerful qualities, the gap between conscious and non-conscious qualities is narrowed.

Progress in philosophy comes, not so much from the production of definitive solutions to difficult problems, but in the gradual recognition that we have been asking the wrong questions—or asking the right questions in the wrong way. I am optimistic. We seem to at last be poised to escape the treadmill of bad theories propped up and embellished with ever more intricate epicycles. The real question is: what will turn out to be the next big problem?

9

Douglas Hofstadter

College of Arts and Sciences Distinguished Professor of Cognitive Science

Director, Center for Research on Concepts and Cognition

Indiana University, Bloomington, USA

I will begin by addressing, very very briefly, questions 3-5, and then I will turn to questions 1 and 2 and will delve into them in some detail.

◆

What is the proper role of philosophy in relation to psychology, artificial intelligence, and the neurosciences?

Philosophy's proper role, as I see it, is to try to get at the essential nature of the more ethereal notions associated with the cited disciplines—for instance, the nature of purpose (teleology) and of causality, the nature of "the real" (which is intimately tied in with the nature of causality), the nature of life itself, the nature of collective phenomena in general (this also is intimately related to the question of what is "real"), the nature of desires and fears and hopes (etc.), and lastly, the nature of those elusive phenomena that are called "experience", "feelings", "meaning", "consciousness", "soul", "self", and "I".

Is a science of consciousness possible?

I believe it definitely is, and indeed that we are gradually approaching such a scientific understanding as we develop more and more sophisticated models of thinking and of causality, and more and more sophisticated understandings of the brain. Nonetheless, we still have a very long way to go, in my opinion.

What are the most important open problems in contemporary philosophy of mind? What are the most promising prospects?

The most important open problems that I see in the philosophy of mind are those that I referred to in my answer to the third question.

I think the most promising prospects for answering these questions will come from combining ideas born in numerous different disciplines, including philosophy itself, of course, but also cognitive psychology, perceptual psychology, social psychology, and cognitive science (including psychologically-inspired computational models of thought and its mechanisms, perhaps including some kinds of robotics, but not engineering-style artificial intelligence), neurology, linguistics, physics, and others. The crux of the matter will have to do with relating explanations on very different levels to each other (as I try to sketch a little bit in what follows).

Coming to a deep understanding of mind, consciousness, "I", and such elusive matters will, in my view, necessarily involve transcending a number of currently popular ideas, such as the "Chinese room" idea, the "inverted spectrum" idea, the idea of "qualia", the idea of "free will", the idea of "zombies", the idea that consciousness is a macroscopic quantum phenomenon (a bit like superconductivity or superfluidity), and the idea of the neurologist who supposedly knows every last tiny thing about what redness is, but who is vastly surprised when, after a surgical operation, the *experience* of redness is actually encountered for the first time. All these ideas will, I feel, have to tumble, sooner or later, in much the same fashion as phlogiston and caloric tumbled, centuries ago.

I guess that, having pointed out what I consider to be some unpromising avenues, I have implicitly pointed to their complement, which would be the promising avenues to explore.

◆

Now I turn to questions 1 and 2 and go into them in some depth.

Why were you initially drawn to philosophy of mind?

When, at age 12, I began to study French, I fell profoundly under its spell, amazed by all the differences between it and English, the language I'd grown up speaking and whose way of saying things

I had unthinkingly assumed was the way people *had* to express themselves. Prior to that, I had taken for granted that each foreign language was precisely isomorphic to English but simply used different words, so that there was always a perfect word-to-word mapping between sentences of language A and language B—an understandable but extremely naïve thought. When, to my wonderment, I realized that nearly anything seemingly "necessary" about language could in fact be otherwise, I plunged into French grammar, pronunciation, and vocabulary with unbounded fervor and endless, endless questions.

The next year, my father took a sabbatical in Geneva, and the daily games, bike rides, and jokes with my neighbor Roger, a Swiss boy of my age who was learning to be a *pâtissier* from his parents, helped enormously in converting the myriads of sharp, crystalline rules that came from my impassioned book-learning into automated reflexes that were far subtler and more fluid. The coexistence in my mind of wildly different ways of naming things and conceiving actions and relationships, plus the marvelous fact that I could somehow simply "will" one of those ways of cutting up the world to take over, intrigued me no end. How could all these mysterious things be happening inside my head? Who or what was really in control of it all? How was I absorbing hard-edged rules and, with no conscious effort, turning them into soft-contoured patterns? How could I just decide to "turn on" or "turn off" the French-language machine? Indeed, who or what was this "I" that could "at will" make all these internal things happen, ranging from events at a very high level (selecting the language) to an intermediate level (the ideas to be expressed) and on down to lower levels (words, phrases, and grammatical pathways, and also the rapid and precise chains of sounds, like a racer skiing down an intricate slalom course)? I wondered constantly about what was going on when, as the cliché would have it, I "thought in French" or "thought in English".

One of my strongest desires was to have no foreign accent. One reason was that I found the sounds of French to be extraordinarily beautiful, and thus, like a perfectionistic musician, I wanted to "perform" them flawlessly, but a second reason was that I rebelled ferociously against the idea that something other than *me* might contaminate the sounds that came out of my mouth. I couldn't abide the thought that anything "alien" might push me around. And what might that "alien agent" have been? None other than my brain. To put it starkly, this "I" was obsessed with the goal of *overriding its brain.* My "I" certainly didn't want to believe that its brain (or any physical thing inside that brain) could push it around, despite the clear evidence all around it in Geneva that *other* people's brains pushed *them* around, in the sense that anyone who hadn't learned language X by the time they were 10 or so was inexorably fated to emit sounds that instantly revealed them to be "alien". Their rigid brains betrayed them! I couldn't bear the thought that that ugly fate would befall *me*. I wasn't going to be a victim of my brain—not if *I* had anything to say about it.

My drive to attain a perfect accent in French thus launched a mortal struggle against whatever unknown physical force inside my head (where the "I" thing was also housed, oddly enough) might keep me from attaining my goal. Luckily, I had an innate gift for sounds and other aspects of language (this, too, was courtesy of my brain, but I don't think I ever felt myself to be a victim of my brain in *that* regard—to the contrary, I was *proud* of the good things that my brain gave me, gladly taking credit for them), and so, thanks to my brain's good luck of the draw and thanks also to huge amounts of extremely keen self-monitoring and intense practice, I was able to master the phonemes and intonation patterns of French well enough that my goal of accentlessness was pretty much attained by the end of our Geneva year. I had shown the world (or at least shown myself) that *I* transcended the mere *physics* inside my head. *I* was boss; *I* could push around lower-level forces with impunity.

Unfortunately there was a second monkey wrench threatening my intense desire to speak French in a native fashion. This was the deeply upsetting fact that often, right in the middle of a smooth French sentence, I would unexpectedly catch an English word or phrase popping up silently in my head, as if revealing to me that my external fluency in French—this supposed "thinking in French"—was all a lie and a sham, and that what was *really* happening was that my brain was unconsciously formulating every thought in its native language and then ultra-rapidly and still unconsciously converting it into a slick but fake Gallic surface form, using thousands of translation tricks that I had internalized by dint of all my hard work. This despicable thought seemed to imply the existence of yet another hidden enemy located inside my very own head.

As time passed, my French flowed ever more smoothly and fluently, and all sorts of lovely words and idioms and fancy structures would just come sailing out of my mouth without my knowing where in the world they had come from, yet there remained enough troubling "Anglo" moments that I couldn't totally shake the image of myself as a "fake bilingual". This hated idea nagged at me for many years and forced me to ponder at great length the mysterious hidden processes that underlie both my speaking and my thinking in any language, including English. Even today, I still ask myself "What does it mean, to 'think in French'?", although my answers are far more nuanced nowadays than back when I was a teen and everything seemed black and white, and when there were clearcut "victims of the brain" and "vanquishers of the brain".

◆

A second and very different impetus for me to ponder the mysteries of the human mind and human identity was that my youngest sister, Molly (nine years younger than me), had a profound mental handicap and never learned to speak at all, nor to understand more than a few rudimentary kinds of sentences ("Put on your napkin, Molly!"). On the outside, Molly looked like a normal girl, so something had to be wrong somewhere inside—and that could only mean in her brain. In fact, our parents considered brain surgery for Molly, though this was never done, since no one ever found anything macroscopic that was wrong.

The full realization of the tragedy of Molly became clear to our family when I was in my mid-teens, and of course it hit me very hard. It was the first time that I had been forced to think seriously about the fact that *what* we are, *how* we are, and thus *who* we are, must all come from physical activity—in other words, from physics—in a physical object inside our bodies. This fact seems totally obvious, in a way (and I had already confronted it "head on" in a somewhat different guise in my passionate struggles to override my own brain's biological limitations in speaking a foreign language), but somehow it also seems to elude most people totally, since we seem, instinctively, to be *anything but* "mere physical objects". (Indeed, that was the whole point of my battle against my own brain, where this abstract "I" was trying to get rid of any foreign accent and any remaining English substrate, which were flaws due to some "mindless" physical object—my brain—that had to be beaten by the abstract entity that was my mind and my *self*.)

The number of times I dreamed that Molly was normal and could speak with all of us is uncountable. Such dreams revealed that I had a tacit intuition that there was a different person hidden inside her body—the "real" Molly, the person who *ought* to have been part of our family. Decades later I was reminded of this intensely regret-filled feeling of "the identity that ought to have been" when the cover of one of my books initially came out with its title in the wrong typeface, and this "botched book" was distributed all around the country. I myself had lovingly designed that cover, and I was extremely upset, feeling that "the book that should have been" had been destroyed by someone's random carelessness. Luckily, that error was soon fixed and most copies of the book came out with the proper typeface, but Molly, on the other hand, was never fixed, and this image of "the real Molly" remains a strange kind of illusion—as if in some kind of Platonic heaven, there were a "normal" Molly, the person who she should have been and whom we all should have known, but who had been destroyed by some random act of carelessness. Such thoughts plagued me throughout my teen-age years, and even today, every so often in my dreams, a wonderful "speaking Molly" will appear and catch me off guard, leaving me in a state of great sadness when I wake up. And of course it was much worse for our parents.

When I was around 16 or 17, spurred by Molly's fate, I read a couple of lay-level books on the human brain, a topic that I found fascinating but also extraordinarily eerie and scary. (I was listening to Rachmaninoff's relatively little-known first piano concerto all the time as I read those books, and its chords "absorbed" all that eeriness, and to this day they evoke those same strange, frightening sensations that I felt as a teen-ager learning about the mysterious blood-filled blob that inhabited his own skull and turned him into a conscious being thinking about itself.) I learned that no one could put their finger (literally) on how thought worked in the brain, let alone where the "I" was, but I also learned that the results of surgeries and accidents and experiments had made it ever more clear that thinking and feeling were indeed physical activities in some kind of strange, gooey object made of billions and billions of spider-webby connections. All of this, combined with my introspections concerning my French, started to make me feel that my sensation of being an indivisible "I" that was totally "in control" of myself was most likely some kind of illusion, and indeed, when I was about 17 or 18, I wrote a "long" dialogue about it (four pages, which was indeed *very* long for me then!), using a modern-day Socrates and Plato to explore and express my belief that this "I" thing was essentially an illusion.

♦

Yet a third and again very different impetus to think about thinking was my encounter with computers in my mid-teen years. In 1960, when I was 15, my friend Charles Brenner taught me how to program Stanford's only computer (in the then very new and elegant recursion-based language Algol), and over the next few years I wrote many programs to do many different kinds of things. Whenever any of my programs ran, even though I knew exactly what the computer was doing, since I had written the program, I somehow wondered if it was "thinking" about the things it was working on. I could watch the console with its many hundreds of small orange flashing lights, and thus was privy to every bit of its "thinking", though of course I couldn't follow it, since it all happened so fast.

Sometimes it would be "thinking" about number patterns (I was a math major and I spent many years inventing and investigating intricate number-theoretical sequences), sometimes about its next move in a simple game, sometimes about how to construct a syntactically complicated sentence in English (or another language). Since I had already been convinced, by my musings about my ill-fated sister Molly (and by analogy, about all other people) and by reading books about the brain, that all thinking was physical activity in some physical substrate, the key question was *what kinds of activities* counted as thinking—and computation, especially when it involved the manipulation of language—seemed to be a candidate.

For that reason, my sentence-producing programs were the most provocative of all my computational explorations. Encouraged by Algol's built-in recursiveness, I came up with complex recursive descriptions of the grammars of the languages I had studied, and I used random-number generators to select pathways through these grammars and to select words to insert whenever needed. The words were not selected entirely at random, of course, but were subject to a number of semantic constraints, so that the sentences that came out often made considerable sense (many of them tickling my sense of humor because they were just a little bit "off" of what any human would have said). I couldn't help wondering how much this process resembled the actual production of sentences by a human, although I was very aware that humans choose their syntactic pathways and words not arbitrarily, merely following the dictates of random numbers, but according to *thoughts* that are behind everything and that guide every bit of the process.

And so a deep understanding of the way in which thoughts—those highly abstract, nebulous, impalpable, cloudlike things—could "push everything around" inside a brain (such as my own) became a beckoning goal to me.

I never truly believed that any of my programs were thinking—they were far too simple and too obviously mechanical (almost as mechanical as a cash register with its meshing gears)—but I wondered for years what it would take to make a computer *genuinely* think. I knew that any program, no matter how complicated, would still be mechanical in some sense of the term, but I also knew that the entire macroscopic world, in all its glorious complexity, came out of the basic laws of physics, and so in the end, everything had to be mechanical. It was just a question of complexity. It was a question, more specifically, of creating, through computation, these nebulous high-level patterns called "thought".

In other words, I had vague intuitions about the notion of "emergence" and believed in it, which means that I could imagine a very fine-grained substrate, entirely mechanical and deterministic, whose seething micro-activities gave rise to high-level patterns—thoughts—that resided on such a different level that they would seem detached from their substrate, would seem to "float above it" on their own, having behaviors that could be described without any reference to the substrate—indeed, without the describer having any knowledge at all of the substrate's existence. (Perhaps this idea of two vastly different levels, in some inchoate form, was what allowed me to think, in Geneva, that this nebulous thing called "I" could somehow get around the physical or biological limitations of "my brain".)

All the Algol programs that I wrote were hopelessly far from giving rise to emergent high-level patterns that resembled thinking, but I suspected that this vast gulf between my small programs and a gigantic program that would allow a computer to truly think must be, in essence, the same vast gulf that kept neurologists, who studied tiny neurons and other local phenomena, from being able to locate the gigantic swirling hurricanes of thought in the brain. It had to be because of the huge conceptual distance between phenomena that were taking place at extremely different levels.

— —

Last but not least, when I was about 15, I read with utter captivation the book *Gödel's Proof* by Ernest Nagel and James R.

Newman (and by a strange coincidence, the whole Nagel family soon became close friends of our family). From this charming and powerful book, I learned how the Austrian logician Kurt Gödel had revolutionized thinking about what mathematics was by revealing that strange vortices of self-reference lurked, deeply hidden but undeniably present, in a precise, mechanical reasoning system from which they had supposedly been perfectly and absolutely banished. This system was the set of axioms and rules of inference in Bertrand Russell and Alfred North Whitehead's heroic three-tome effort *Principia Mathematica,* which aspired to be a perfect formalization of all of mathematical thinking.

In *PM,* long prickly formulas encoded all possible statements, true and false, about sets and numbers—but luckily (or at least supposedly), the true statements could be mechanically sifted from the false ones by the magic of strict rule-following derivations from a finite set of axioms. Theorem after theorem was derived from earlier theorems by applying rigid rules of inference, with the ultimate starting points always being the axioms. This infinitely extensible stepping-stone-like process, always starting from the axioms and moving ever upwards and outwards, with one's hand being held at every step by one rule of inference or another, led one safely and dryly across the troubled waters of uncertainty, keeping one always on true territory alone, never contaminated by even a drop of falsity, moreover allowing one eventually to reach every last haven of truth. That is, all desired destinations were eventually accessible via the slow, cautious stepping stones of *PM.* Or so at least was the claim, and all mathematicians until Gödel took for granted that this was indeed the case. It seemed self-evident. How else could math be?

For some reason, however, Gödel was deeply skeptical that mathematical thought was so purely axiomatic and so utterly image-free, and his skepticism gave rise to long ponderings about the nature of formal axiomatic systems, and he began to see that such systems themselves were patterned structures whose properties could be studied—in fact, studied by mathematicians themselves. This led him to the idea that there was a deep connection between the abstract entities that *PM* formulas talked about (numbers) and the concrete visual patterns of symbols that decorated the pages of *PM.* There were two levels of such patterns of symbols. Firstly, there were the individual formulas themselves, and secondly, there were the grander patterns that constituted the pathways stepping delicately from one true formula to other true ones. Though these patterns were all typographical patterns, Gödel could see that he could replace typographical symbols by numbers, and then the patterns would all become number patterns.

By thus re-perceiving the precise, rule-based typographical patterns constituted by *PM* formulas as patterns involving numbers (in a sense, by applying math to itself in much the same way as it had been applied to many other domains, such as physics, chemistry, and so on), Gödel found that everything that one might want to say about the *formulas* of *PM* could be said by proxy, by talking instead about the formulas' code numbers, or Gödel numbers, alone. He also showed, most crucially, that the precise stepping-stone pathways constituting proofs in *PM*, daintily stepping from one true formula to another to another, were isomorphic to certain precise stepping-stone pathways among numbers alone. Since *these* pathways were purely *numerical* patterns inside the world of math itself, and since *PM* could talk about anything in math, there were *PM* formulas that could express these pathways and could talk about their properties.

The upshot of this was Gödel's stunning realization that certain formulas of *PM* could talk about the provability (or lack thereof) of other *PM* formulas and, strangest of all, that certain formulas might even make such assertions about themselves. Indeed, by exploiting the devilishly clever trick called "diagonalization" that had been dreamed up by the German mathematician Georg Cantor a few decades earlier, Gödel was able to build up a formula of *PM* that talked about itself (*i.e.*, about its own Gödel number), and in particular expressed the near-paradoxical thought that it itself was unprovable (*i.e.*, that no safe stepping-stone pathway led from the axioms' Gödel numbers to its own Gödel number). That is, Gödel found a statement of *PM* that said about itself, "I am not a theorem." Such a formula could not be a *PM* theorem because if so, it would assert a falsity. The result was that there were truths in math—he showed there were infinitely many of them—that were not provable inside *PM* (and the argument was fully general, applying to *any* system of axioms and rules of inference, not just to *PM*).

The revelation that self-reference lurked inside *Principia Mathematica* (and doomed it to incompleteness) rocked the mathematical world in 1931, and some thirty years later it rocked the adolescent me as well. All of a sudden, in the middle of terrain that seemed "flat" (*PM* statements talking only about *numbers*), something had flipped around like a snake eating its own tail, and had become "loopy" (certain special *PM* statements talked about *themselves*). Nagel and Newman's device of translating Gödel's self-referential formula into English by using the first-person pronoun "I" was perhaps a little facile (was a formula really a person? did it have the right to talk like one? to use the pronoun "I"?), but it had an incredibly powerful effect upon me, making me suddenly suspect that this kind of twisty loop inside a seemingly "flat world", brought into existence by a kind of code whereby "inert" numbers stood for higher-level patterns, might be what allowed an "I" to come into existence inside a brain, which was, after all, just a physical object that by all rights shouldn't have any more of a "self" or a first-person viewpoint to it than do, say, a waterfall or a hurricane. I began to suspect that Gödelian looping was at the origin of my own "I", and of course those of everyone else.

What do you consider your most important contribution to the field?

Probably my most important contribution to "the field"—that is, to the philosophy of mind (although I am certainly not a card-carrying philosopher of mind)—is my development, over the years, of the just-mentioned idea that the mechanism giving rise to the self-referential formulas Gödel discovered in *PM* is analogous to the mechanism that gives rise to an "I" in a human brain. In my writings, I have called such an abstract pattern a "strange loop", and I will devote the rest of my answer to explicating this idea and related ideas that, as a whole, form my vision of what a human "I" is.

As Gödel showed, a strange loop inevitably arose inside *PM*, even though, ironically, *PM* was explicitly constructed as a fortress to keep out self-reference, and a strange loop also inevitably arises in any brain with a sufficiently rich perceptual system and network of concepts (the brain of a normal human, in particular). Sophisticated brains, such as normal human brains, not only are *capable* of self-perception but *necessarily* indulge in it deeply and constantly, and out of this process results a very complex stable structure in the brain—the "I".

When I say "self-perception", I don't just mean looking at one's hand, hearing one's own voice, seeing one's face in a mirror, or other such basic perceptual experiences. I mean the gradual building-up, over years, of a profound sense of oneself as a unique causal agent in the world, having many abstract properties, such as one's physical and mental strengths (and weaknesses), one's friends and family members, one's interests (and dislikes), one's native language and native culture, one's musical resonances (and non-resonances), one's sense of humor, one's ambitions, dreams, fears, and ideals, one's huge chain of experiences, and a sense of all of this as amounting to a unified whole. This is the nature of any mature human "I", and we all automatically acquire such an internal structure by virtue of living in the physical world and among other human beings.

Why do we necessarily build up such a structure? Because we build up representational structures for *everything* that we are in close contact with—that's what the basic ability to perceive, supplemented by the more sophisticated ability to abstract, entails—and because we are obviously in intimate contact with our own bodies and minds and their unique modes of doing things for our entire lives. For this reason, building up an elaborate self-representation, far from being a quirky, rare, and pointless activity, is an automatic and highly useful reflex for any perceiving being that has the abstraction machinery that allows it to do so.

Although our self-representation is very complex, it is nonetheless extremely coarse-grained. This, too, is no surprise, since everything we perceive is drastically simplified relative to its full reality, because our sense organs are extremely coarse-grained. A glass of water sitting on a table provides a fine example of this: microscopically, it is filled to the brim with myriads of constant chaotic collisions, and yet to our eyes it is as still and stable as anything we know. Two glasses of water sitting side by side on a table are seen by us as virtually identical, despite their inconceivably many differences on a scale that is inaccessible to our perceptual organs.

We are built to ignore most of what we could in principle distinguish. We see only "an oak tree", when in fact its structure is hugely complex and totally unique on many structural levels. Likewise, instead of seeing Avogadro's number of infinitesimal things, or even just hundreds of smallish things, we see only "a dachshund" (or perhaps just "a dog"), "a pile of leaves", "a bridge", "a garbage dump", "an old woman", "a sly sneer", and on and on. We unconsciously filter out nearly everything that we could in theory focus in on, and this filtering—this left-and-right throwing-away of gobs and gobs of information—though it sounds negative and wasteful at first, is in fact tremendously positive and constructive. It gives us the power to make analogies, to abstract, to form new categories galore, to extrapolate, to dream up new ideas.

Our perception radically simplifies everything we come into contact with, and our perception of ourselves is no exception to this rule. We know almost nothing about our own body's functioning at lower levels, yet because we know how it works on higher levels, we feel on intimate terms with ourselves. Much the same can be said of our knowledge of our *selves*. Certainly very few of us know anything at all about "the human brain" in general, let alone about our *own* brain in particular. And yet we all know human brains intimately—both our own and those of other people—if we focus not on their gross anatomy or on the trillions of microscopic interconnections in them and the untold numbers of tiny operations they make day in and day out (like the invisible seething constantly going on in a seemingly serene glass of water), but instead on how, operating as wholes, they perceive things, remember things, make decisions, guide behaviors. In short, a human brain perceives itself not just a little bit, but extremely profoundly and richly, yet the resulting self-perception resides at such a high level, and involves such non-biological concepts, that no neurologist would call it a description of a brain.

If one considers television cameras, one can get a different sense for this kind of distinction involving levels of perception. Television cameras were originally designed as devices to transmit pictures of scenes and motions onto distant screens. This they do very well, as we all know, but that's only the tip of the iceberg. What televisions principally do today is purvey such things as *news* and *entertainment,* rather than transmit *physical scenes.* A soap opera is a conveyor of story lines, character traits, interpersonal conflicts, and types of morality, among many other high abstractions that I might cite. We don't watch soap operas for the colors and patterns picked up by the camera, but for the extremely abstract notions involving life and death, fidelity and betrayal, hope and despair, and so forth and so on, which those colors and patterns convey to our brains over long periods of time. Maybe a dog would find the visual patterns on the screen during a soap opera momentarily engaging, but that's not what *we* find engaging. Our world is infinitely more abstract than a dog's world, let alone a cockroach's world.

◆

It is here that I come back to link these ideas with Gödel's discoveries. Gödel saw that a system—*PM*—that had been created for talking solely about very concrete numbers and their properties was able to express ideas about things belonging to a universe that seemed far more abstract. To draw an explicit analogy, the numerical relationships expressed in *PM* formulas are like the colors and simple shapes that flash on a television screen, while the far more abstract statements that Gödel discovered secretly lurking in certain *PM* formulas are like the high abstractions that *we* see in soap operas, but that dogs and cockroaches are impervious to. It takes a far more sophisticated perceptual system to see Gödelian meanings in *PM* formulas than to see numerical meanings, which, after all, is what *PM* was built to express. But when one *has* that more sophisticated ability to see abstract meanings of *PM* formulas, then one can build on it and it's completely natural to construct many complex self-referential statements, of which "I am not a theorem" is only the first and simplest example.

Thus the "strange loop" in Gödel's work is a *perceptual* loop that allows a system that was built only to represent "simple" things (numbers) to twist back and perceive and represent *itself*, and itself is not a simple thing at all. Analogously, brains were originally built by evolution only to make very basic perceptual distinctions—"warmer" versus "colder", or "moving" versus "still"—things like that. But because of the "arms race" that evolution is—the constant and merciless competition between rival architectures—brains necessarily grew in sophistication over millions of years, and higher and higher capabilities of abstraction and memory evolved, until brains got to the point where their repertoire of categories was arbitrarily abstract and arbitrarily extensible. That fact characterizes the human brain. At some point, it surpassed a certain threshold of complexity and became a rich organ of perception (and therefore self-perception) at a highly abstract level. The analogous level of complexity in formal systems such as *PM* occurs when they are able to represent certain kinds of number-theoretical functions, and *PM* easily surpassed that level, so in retrospect it's not in the least surprising that *PM* could talk about itself—but even so, it caught the entire world totally off guard because no one had thought about things in that fashion before Gödel.

My ideas about human selves and consciousness are all based on this analogy between, on the one hand, the "simple" (Russellian) way and the "sophisticated" (Gödelian) way of looking at *PM* formulas, and, on the other hand, the "simple" way of looking at human brains (as networks of neurons that respond reflexively to external stimuli) and the "sophisticated" way (as rich storehouses and manipulators of highly interlocked ideas about life, death, hope, despair, fidelity, betrayal, cars, airports, dictatorships, democracies, racism, sexism, physics, and biology, among many other things). The fact that an "I" would grow up automatically inside such a sophisticated representational system as a human brain is, *a posteriori*, no more surprising than that self-reference would sneak automatically into the world of *PM* formulas.

♦

But ... such an "I" has a most peculiar quality attached to it—namely, that it seems to be a "prime mover" of sorts. Instead of being *pushed around* by physical law, it arrogantly *dictates* to physical law! That is, the "I" makes (or seems to make) decisions, and marshals large forces of muscles to carry those decisions out. This is exemplified by what I described when I spoke of the "I" who simply "willed" that his brain produce complex and flawless French sentences for him, and the brain dutifully obeyed (most of the time, anyway); likewise, the "I" commanded his muscles to produce sounds with a perfect French accent, and the muscles obeyed. As a teenager, the way I saw it was that my intense desire to have a perfect accent simply "pushed around" the churning soup of micro-stuff (the level of neurons and neurotransmitters, etc.) inside my brain. And I saw things this way because to me, the desires at the higher level were *far realer* than the invisible seethings at the lower level. The seething activities at that low level were simply "out of sight, out of mind"—or if, on rare occasions, I thought about them at all, then I envisioned them as being simply at the beck and call of "my" desires and hopes.

This kind of way of seeing the world is sometimes referred to as "downward causality", because the apparent cause lies at a high and abstract level in the hierarchy of descriptions of nature, and it seems to propagate its effect down to a low level—that of physics, where particles wind up getting shoved around by forces. Ideas push particles around, to put it succinctly. And then all of this downward causality is perceived by the brain itself, and it becomes an integral part of the story that the brain tells itself about the "I" that it houses. The brain tells itself that its "I" is a causal agent in the universe, and that its desires and dreams and dreads and so forth are what determine events in its body and in the rest of the world. All of this is locked in more and more as one grows up in the world, because we simply have no choice in the matter. Not only does it appear that way to us, but it is what everyone tells us, it is built into our language, and on and on.

The idea that "I wanted to do it, so I decided to do it, and so I did it" is far realer and far more important to us than the idea, say, that "the sun went down at 6 PM today". I chose this latter sentence very deliberately, since of course the sun did *not* go down at all—rather, the earth turned and the sun merely *appeared* to go down—but the idea of sunsets is built into our perceptions and our language, and it is something that would be very hard to get rid of. But getting rid of the idea of sunsets (replacing it, perhaps, with the idea of "earthspins") would be a trivial picnic compared to getting rid of the idea of the "I" as a causal agent. Getting rid of "I" as a prime mover would be even harder than getting the U.S. to convert to the metric system!

To survive in this world, we macroscopic creatures have no choice but to perceive things at a macroscopic level, where genuine physical causality, which exists way down at the level of particles, is replaced by mere probabilistic tendencies of very large things that are assigned verbal labels. And we are victims of this necessity. We *must* see our world in terms of categories whose reality is only approximate, because otherwise we would not survive.

The *strangeness* in our loop of self-perception, in short, is that by putting the higher level in the driver's seat, we distort causality, flipping it upside down. We intuitively posit a downward type of causality wherein abstract entities push around physical entities, as opposed to the sheer physical reality, which is that myriads of teeny-tiny law-governed seethings are all that there is to causality. The siren song of downward causality, which flows from higher levels to lower levels, though it is not *real* causality, is an inevitable and ubiquitous (though seldom-named) feature of the human view of the universe and of how we ourselves fit into it, and we all succumb to the charms of this siren song, like it or not. Doing so is an unavoidable fact of the human condition.

♦

Over the years, I've written about these elusive kinds of ideas in numerous books and articles, and in them I've invented and exploited many different metaphors. One of my favorites of these metaphors came from my pondering over a question posed by the celebrated neurologist Roger Sperry about the hierarchy of different forces at different levels of description inside a human brain. Sperry's question was: "Who shoves whom around inside the cranium?"

Inspired by this pithy question, I invented a hypothetical two-dimensional arena that I called the "careenium"—a giant frictionless billard table on which so-called "simms" (tiny spheres) careened around ceaselessly and bashed into each other, sometimes agglomerating into far larger structures called "simmballs" whose far slower-scale behavior could be perceived and described on its own level—the "simmballic" level, of course—and in my metaphor, simmballs did indeed *represent* things (they were intended to be thought of as being analogous to the physical realizations of concepts in a human brain). In the careenium, there were clearly different levels of description of the system, and on these different levels, and on their associated time scales (very fast motion or very slow motion), one could perceive different types of behavioral laws (*i.e.*, different levels of causality). This led naturally to my framing the analogous question to Sperry's question, and this question became the title and the topic of my dialogue "Who shoves whom around inside the careenium?"

Another metaphor that I have relied upon, and one that is closely related to the careenium metaphor, came out of a curious illusory phenomenon that I discovered many years ago when I was playing with a box of ordinary postal envelopes such as can be bought in any drugstore. For some reason, I reached into the box, grabbed all the envelopes at once (about a hundred in number), and squeezed my fingers together. To my great surprise, *I felt a marble* between my fingers. That is to say, I was convinced there was something *solid, spherical,* and *hard* lurking hidden among the envelopes—and it was floating right in the very middle of the box, to boot! Inspection quickly revealed, however, that there was no such solid, spherical, and hard object in the middle of the box or anywhere else in it, and that the marble I felt was a tactile illusion. It came from the fact that there were more layers of paper and of glue where the "V"'s of all the flaps were aligned—a very simple explanation for a very powerful illusion. What was *not* an illusion, though, was the set of basic perceptual properties of the *seeming* marble—of the "epiphenomenal marble", that is—namely, its location at the very center of the box, its felt diameter, its felt shape, its felt hardness, and so on. If one didn't know better, one might even ask oneself, "Could this marble be the green aggie I lost the other day when it rolled out of sight? If so, how on earth did it wind up inside this box of envelopes?"

96   9. Douglas Hofstadter

♦

   This hallucination of a "solid particle" where there is in fact just a collective phenomenon and no particle at all comes very close to a truly profound idea of modern physics—namely, that of *phonons*, which are "quasi-particles" of sound ("quasi-particle" is indeed the technical term) that propagate in the medium of a crystal (or a gas) and that bounce off of each other exactly as do "real" particles (*e.g.*, electrons, protons, neutrons, etc.) in the medium of ordinary space, and exchanging energy, momentum, and angular momentum. Today, roughly a hundred years after they were first envisioned (first glimpsed by Einstein in 1907, extended by Peter Debye in 1909, and then developed by many others), phonons are a crucial ingredient in all physical explanations of the nature of matter, as a glance into any text will reveal.
   Physicists long ago discovered that by far the most efficient and informative way of understanding the macroscopic properties of a solid—its heat capacity, thermal conductivity, electrical conductivity, elasticity, transparency, and so forth—is to think of the solid as pervaded by a "phonon gas"—that is, by myriads of phonons randomly banging into each other and exchanging energy, momentum, angular momentum, and so forth. Physicists know very well that they can also "reduce" any particular phonon into a very complex global pattern of excitation of all the atoms in the solid, thereby getting rid of the phonon and changing point of view so that all properties of the solid are seen as due to its atoms alone, and to their jiggling—but unfortunately, this shift in levels of description would make everything incomprehensible. This is because the phonon idea is a very efficient shorthand for an immense amount of coordinated lower-level jiggling happening inside a dense lattice of atoms, and it's hugely more economical to describe processes involving phonons than to talk about how billions of atoms are coordinatedly vibrating. Hence the only insight-providing explanations of the macroscopic properties described above depend on using the language of phonons. Phonons are indispensable to physics, *even though, if conceived of as genuine particles, they are fictions*. They are not *real* particles; they are *quasi*-particles. Why do I call keep on harping on this distinction between what is "real" and what is not? I will come back to that in a moment.
   Let's return to the hallucinated marble inside the envelope box. This marble clearly *is* a fiction—that is, there clearly is no marble anywhere in the box—and yet we can easily fall for the illusion

if we feel just reach in the box, squeeze, and feel it between our fingers. Now suppose there were no way for us to peer into the box and see that there's nothing there but envelopes (thus disabusing us of our illusion), and suppose moreover that the "marble" we were sure was co-inhabiting the box with the envelopes was incredibly useful to us in explaining the way our world (or at least some part of it) works; in that case, we would simply talk about it as if it existed—indeed, we'd believe that it *did* exist—and we might well never even think about the substrate of envelopes that gives rise to it. We might not even know about that substrate!

◆

Now we want to exploit this metaphor by carrying it back to the domain of brain and mind. The "marble" idea can be mapped onto high-level mental phenomena such as desires or hopes or dreads, or indeed, the "I" itself. We humans always talk about why we do things in terms of such abstract mental phenomena, blithely ignoring the microscopic (neural) substrate, because to us, those nebulous abstractions are the things that seem *truly* real. The brain, on the other hand, does *not* seem real to us ordinary human beings, even if we intellectually know of its existence and perhaps even know quite a bit about it. It doesn't occur to us that our very own personal dreads and hopes (etc.) could simply be "transformed away" by a move analogous to that of a physicist who suddenly recalls that phonons are really collective excitations of the trillions of atoms making up a crystal, and that despite their seeming reality, they are really *just a way of talking* about what is actually happening physically, in the deeper substrate. To believe that there are *real* particles in there is a hallucination, a crazy illusion. But *what an illusion!*

And that's the key point about our mental notions such as desires and dreads and, in the end, our "I": they are just illusions—but what powerful and useful illusions they are! Notions such as dreads and hopes (etc.) are very efficient ways of summarizing in a tremendously compact fashion the unimaginably complex (in fact, incomprehensibly complex) churning microscopic activities inside a physical object—the brain. Such abstract notions provide the best (most economical and comprehensible, even if only probabilistic) explanation of much of what we do, which endows them with a certain type of limited reality.

Why do I call them "illusions", then? Because it all comes down to where causality really resides. If one thinks that physical causality resides at the level of desires, dreads, and the "I", one is making a deep mistake. There are *no precise laws* at that level—just helpful heuristic patterns that can usually be relied on. That is not genuine causality. It is not where the laws of the universe really operate. It is just an efficient and usually accurate summary of tendencies.

The view we have of ourselves, based on collective phenomena that seem far realer to us than their invisible substrate, is similar to the nature of most of contemporary physics, which is pervaded from top to bottom by quasi-particles of all sorts. A description in terms of quasi-particles shifts levels upwards towards collective phenomena, and this allows deep insights to be made. However, the quasi-particles do not have the same status of reality as items such as atoms or electrons, since they can be "transformed away" and turned into global patterns of jiggling of atoms (or of other particles—or even of other quasi-particles, as is the case with the extremely esoteric entities called "second-sound phonons").

The language of quasi-particles encodes a vision whereby higher-level entities (the quasi-particles themselves) "push around" lower-level entities, and thus it is a model for the concept of downward causality, which, as I said earlier, is at the very crux of our self-concept, namely "I".

◆

Not surprisingly, downward causality has its counterpart in the world of Gödelian self-reference, though I won't go into it in any detail here. Suffice it to say that the high-level meaning of a Gödelian formula—"I am not a theorem"—is a guarantee that the formula is *not* a theorem, because (as I pointed out earlier) if it *were* a theorem, then it would be false. A false theorem is simply not part of *PM*. The downward-causality aspect of this situation becomes apparent when one recalls that every formula in *PM* makes a *numerical* statement (that is the original level of meaning that Russell and Whitehead intended), and so when we conclude that (because of its self-referential meaning) Gödel's formula is not provable but is true, we are *also* concluding that a certain *numerical* statement is not provable but is true. Yet in reaching this conclusion, we have never reasoned at all about any specific numbers involved, or about any arithmetical properties. This lower-level (number-theoretical) conclusion is forced on us not by reasoning about numbers but solely because of the *higher-level* meaning attached to the formula. This is a quintessential example of downward causality: the reason that something seems to happen at a low level flows from something happening at a high level. But one has to realize that there has to be an explanation purely at the lowest level as well, for otherwise one is verging on mysticism (mysterious holistic entities somehow magically "push around" the stuff where the laws actually reside, much along the lines of my youthful fantasy, as a teen-ager in Geneva, that my *self* could push my *brain* around).

When one attaches causality to higher-level items, acting as if the *genuine* causality did not reside on the lower level, one can get into trouble, because it may lead to conceptual confusions and ultimately to serious illusions. For example, our daily experience in the physical world makes us think that it makes sense to ask questions like, "Is *this* green aggie here the same marble as that green aggie that was over there a few moments ago?" Indeed, for physical marbles —marbles made of glass—such a question makes perfect sense. However, to ask such questions about *epiphenomenal* marbles (as in the box of envelopes) is to confuse patterns with physical objects. It's like asking about two identical poker hands at different tables using different decks, "Is this hand the same hand as that one?" The answer is "yes" on an abstract level (the level of poker) and "no" on a concrete level (the level of the physical cards), and which answer is "correct" depends only on how you wish to think about things.

With phonons, it's considerably trickier—indeed, physicists have had to learn to make their mathematics respect the absolute *indistinguishability* of phonons, so that, for instance, if two phonons collide and two phonons leave the scene of the crime, it turns out that it is not only meaningless but self-contradictory to ask, "Is the phonon that went off that-a-way the phonon that came in this-a-way, or is it the other way around?" Such questions, though tempting to ask, since phonons act in so many ways like microscopic pieces of matter (with energy, momentum, etc.), are simply unanswerable, and make no sense.

When many (even most) thoughtful people think about their own "I", however, they have a huge amount invested in its reality as a *real phenomenon*—as a "solid marble", almost a *glass* marble, floating all by itself inside a biological body, but without any substrate on which it is riding. Thoughtful people (*e.g.*, philosophers of mind) find themselves haunted by questions that would be natural to ask if the "I" were in fact a physical object. For instance: "If this pattern were destroyed *here* and recreated perfectly, atom by atom, in another medium, would it be *the same* person? Would it be *me*? And what if *two copies* of the pattern were created in different places—which of the two, if either one, would be *me*?"

Such people may use the word "pattern" in framing the question, but they usually don't believe, deep down, that *the pattern alone* is the nub of the matter; they think there is something *over and above the pattern* that makes it "be" one thing or another (namely, themself). It feels very uncomfortable to most people, including most philosophers of mind, to say that all that matters is *how a brain acts* and that's the full story, which implies that some kind of essential "me-ness" is merely a myth. Yet uncomfortable or not, that's where my story of the "I" winds up, in the end.

This doesn't mean that I avoid the words "I" and "me" (as can be seen from this essay). Like all other normal adult humans, I am *forced* by my nature as a language-dependent creature navigating in the world to use the word "I", and perhaps worse, to believe in the total reality of the concept nearly all the time. My "I" seems as real as real can be to the everyday me (I have an *egocentric* view of the world), just as the sun seems to me to set (I have a *geocentric* view of the world)—except the "I" seems intuitively far realer to the everyday me than does the setting of the sun. I have no choice in the matter, except when I am trying my hardest to understand these difficult philosophical matters, and then I can step back and try very hard to distance myself from my entrenched illusions—and to a small extent I can succeed.

But an "I"-less perspective, such as in rare moments I can achieve, will never serve me well in daily life, let alone play in Peoria. Adopting such a perspective in daily life would be about as perverse as trying to orient oneself in a supermarket in Peoria by asking Peorians questions that referred solely to quarks, gluons, and such micro-things alone. It wouldn't help you to zoom in on the potato-chip aisle. For that, you need to talk on a far higher level only—that of potato chips and supermarket aisles, not that of particles. The "I"-less view, in short, is a theoretical view of how things are that even its most hard-bitten proponents cannot put into practice in their daily lives, which is one reason that most people will find it so terribly hard to accept.

◆

A direct and inevitable consequence of my "I"-less view of the

"I" is that an "I" is merely an elaborate pattern that happens to be embedded in a physical substrate, but that what matters is only the pattern and not the substrate. This implies that the pattern can be copied in other media, and the copies can be made at various grain sizes (*i.e.*, having various degrees of fidelity), which means that the same "I" can exist, to varying degrees, in different substrates, in different places. The only one that is "privileged" is the one with the most detail; other than that, there is no meaningful answer to the question asking which one is the *real* "I".

I am not one to follow out science-fiction scenarios, however, and I'm not interested in talking about teleportation and such topics as if they were likely possibilities. Nonetheless, there is a more down-to-earth consequence of my view of the self (or the soul, or the "I"—I repeat that all these are interchangeable terms for me)—namely, that each adult human self actually exists in at least a few different human brains, to varying degrees. This is the case because there is a fairly decent coarse-grained copy of each adult human soul in the brains of those people who are emotionally the most closely linked to that person.

Copying someone else's soul in one's own brain is much as if one were copying a very fine-grained mosaic in the medium of stones of a much larger size. The result may seem very accurate when seen from afar, but because of its coarser grain it will inevitably be cruder and less complete when seen up close. However, there is no precise threshold between "fine-grained" and "coarse-grained" copies, whether in the domain of artworks or in the domain of human selves; all one can say is that I exist in the brains of my relatives and friends to varying degrees—and likewise, they in mine. This brain contains coarse-grained copies of each person that I know and care for deeply, and those coarse-grained copies are in fact that person's actual self, simply "diluted" in some sense. The more detailed a copy is, the more the person lives in your brain. In an extreme case (say, an Alzheimer's patient very dear to you but whose mind is just about all gone), the person may in fact be living more in *your* brain than they live any longer in their own.

Thus an inevitable consequence of my vision of selves as strange loops is that each self is blurrily spread out among a number of brains. We feel this spread-outness of our own self in our everyday interactions with those we are closest to, but it's simply not usually verbalized in these terms.

♦

Over a thirty-year span, through my various books—first in *Gödel, Escher, Bach* (published in 1979, and in which I first spoke of "strange loops" and made a connection between "I" and Gödelian self-reference), then in *The Mind's I* (coedited with Daniel Dennett and published in 1981, and which includes many easily accessible but provocative pieces of fiction or pseudo-fiction on self and soul), then in *Metamagical Themas* (published in 1985, and in which the "careenium" dialogue and several other relevant selections appeared), then in *Le Ton beau de Marot* (published in 1997, and in which I characterize translation as the the transplantation of pattern, leading directly to my vision of the spread-outness of each human soul), and finally in *I Am a Strange Loop* (published in 2007)—I have explored these ideas from many different perspectives. *I Am a Strange Loop* is my most recent and most focused attempt to pull all of these ideas together.

In *Fluid Concepts and Creative Analogies* (published in 1995), my graduate students and I described several computational models of the mechanisms of thought, and our goal was to show how concepts (and ultimately, creativity) emerge from myriads of very small processes acting in parallel, often competing with and combatting with one another (a little like an ant colony, as in the dialogue "Prelude... Ant Fugue" in *Gödel, Escher, Bach*). I believe that although the research described in *Fluid Concepts and Creative Analogies* is less concerned with directly attacking the elusive notions of self and soul, it is nonetheless only through a deep understanding of how cognition comes about that we will come to understand consciousness and "I", and that that book is therefore also a kind of tangential contribution to the philosophy of mind.

I will conclude by mentioning a very different and highly personal kind of contribution that I have tried to make to the philosophy of mind. This is the fact that when I write, I constantly rely on metaphors and analogies to get my ideas across, and I strive to avoid the many jargons and "isms" that, to my mind, plague the philosophy of mind and render it nearly opaque, even to someone like me who for decades has been passionately interested in what "I" means. I do my best to express myself in what I call "horsies-and-doggies" language—and that includes, fairly often, autobiographical anecdotes, since I believe that such anecdotes, through their directness and vividness, can often do a better job than any other kind of writing at conveying subtle and elusive ideas to one's readers.

I realize that this style does not appeal to everyone, and I hardly expect to revolutionize the rhetorical practices of the discipline of philosophy of mind by writing in my "horsies-and-doggies" style, but I am convinced that the issues that lie at the crux of this discipline deeply concern every reflective person, not just card-carrying members of the guild, and therefore the discussion of such ideas should be at least somewhat accessible to every thinking person. Unfortunately, this is incredibly far from the case today.

Just as it is very sad for youth to be given only to the young, so it would be very sad if philosophy of mind were reserved only for philosophers of mind. In my writings about the nature of the mind and the concept "I", I have tried to reach a wide audience, because I think that these issues matter to many, many people. They are, after all, about the nature of the proverbial "human condition". I hope therefore that at least some philosophers might on occasion be inspired to express themselves in an equally nontechnical fashion.

10

Terence Horgan

Professor of Philosophy
University of Arizona, USA

Why were you initially drawn to philosophy of mind?

I found a naturalistic worldview very plausible, and in particular I was gripped by Oppenheim and Putnam's classic article "Unity of Science as a Working Hypothesis." One especially pressing challenge for a broadly naturalistic worldview is to locate mentaliity in the physical world.

What do you consider your most important contribution to the field?

My stress on the challenge of providing materialistically kosher explanations of physical-to-mental supervenience relations—what I call "superdupervenience." And, more recently, my stress (sometimes in joint work with Uriah Kriegel and/or George Graham and/or John Tienson) on phenomenal intentionality.

What is the proper role of philosophy in relation to psychology, artificial intelligence, and the neurosciences?

Philosophy is continuous with these disciplines, and in my view is broadly empirical in certain ways even though some aspects of it can be effectively pursued from the armchair.

Is a science of consciousness possible?

Yes, insofar as it involves matters like mapping out neural/mental correlations. Whether such correlations are explainable in a materialistically acceptable way is a matter I am unsettled about. I would like think so, but I know of no remotely satisfying way of providing such explanations.

What are the most important open problems in contemporary philosophy of mind? What are the most promising prospects?

One important open problem is the issue of the relation between the phenomenal and the intentional aspects of mentality; I think prospects are good for defending a view according to which the most fundamental kind of mental intentionality is phenomenally constituted, and narrow; Uriah Kriegel and I call this "the phenomenal intentionality research program." Another open problem involves the truth conditions for agentive phenomenology—what they are, and whether or not they are satisfied. And another is the exclusion problem concerning mental state-causation of behavior, which I think is best addressed by going contextualist about the concept of causation.

11

Frank Jackson

Visiting Professor of Philosophy
Princeton University, USA
La Trobe University, The Australian National University, Australia

---

Why were you initially drawn to philosophy of mind?

I was taught by one of the most powerful advocates of the mind-brain identity theory, David Armstrong, in the 1960s at Melbourne University. My first philosophy job, in 1967, was in the philosophy department of another of the theory's most powerful advocates, Jack Smart, in Adelaide. The Adelaide philosophy department also contained one of the most perceptive critics of the identity theory, Michael Bradley. That meant I had plenty of exposure to the mind-brain identity theory from the very beginning of my career in philosophy. Moreover, the identity theory was very much the hot topic in Australian philosophy in the 60s, 70s and 80s and the debate over the theory set a good deal of the philosophical agenda outside the philosophy of mind. Philosophers of science discussed identity theorists' use of scientific reductions to illustrate and support their theory, and the way identity theorists used causal exclusion principles to argue against interactionist dualism; logicians discussed the identity of the identity theory; metaphysicians discussed whether identity theorists should re-state their view in terms of constitution—should identity theorists affirm that mental states are constituted by brain states rather than that they are literally identical with them; analytic ontologists discussed how identity theorists' claims that mental properties are identical with physical properties intersected with the debate between nominalists and realists about properties; and so it went.

How could I not be drawn to the philosophy of mind?

What do you consider your most important contribution to the field?

I think my most important contribution lies in what happened after I defended the knowledge argument against physicalism.

Some dual attribute theories of mind are a kind of mind-brain identity theory. According to them, mental states are brain states (maybe in the identity sense of 'are', or maybe in the constitution sense) but the brain states aren't your common or garden brain states. They have special properties, properties that outrun the kinds of properties to be found in the physical sciences. It is these properties that make them the mental states that they are—or maybe this is the case for those mental states with 'conscious feel'; dual attribute theorists often allow that some mental states, beliefs for example, are brain states having only physical properties.

The Australian identity theorists were very clear that their view was not any kind of dual attribute view. Their view wasn't simply that mental state tokens are brain state tokens. They held in addition that the properties mental state tokens have are, one and all, physical, are, one and all, of a kind with the properties that figure in the physical sciences. To mark this, they often called their theory 'physicalism'. Despite my exposure to the advocacy of Armstrong and Smart, my initial reaction was to adopt a dual attribute theory, and I sought an argument to support my conviction that the properties of mental states and in particular those mental states with feel outrun those of a kind to be found in the physical sciences.

The knowledge argument seemed ideally suited for the job. It can be put quickly. There's nothing in its statement about the analysis of mental language in functional or topic neutral terms (an issue that dominated early discussions of whether or not mental properties are one and all physical properties). There's nothing in its statement about the metaphysics of properties or about conditions of property identity. And, most importantly of all, the knowledge argument is intuitively powerful. As I said when I first advanced the argument, convinced dualists hardly need an argument against physicalism. They find it completely obvious from their own case that mental states with feel are left out of the physicalists' story about the mind. But the convinced want to convince at least some of the not yet convinced, and for that job we need an argument that rests on something intuitively compelling for as many as possible of the fence sitters. The knowledge argument seemed the answer to our prayers.

I now think that the argument fails to establish its conclusion and although I'd prefer to have championed the sound rather than the unsound, I think the knowledge argument has spawned many very fruitful debates. We have learnt a lot from the many objections made to the argument and from the replies to those objections. The argument has been an important stimulus to identifying of a range of central issues in the philosophy of mind and in philosophy at large. Here's a partial list. How are epistemic and metaphysical possibility related? What is the connection between information and possibilities? Are physicalists committed to the a priori deducibility of the mental from the physical? What's the relationship between properties and concepts? What, precisely, is the difference between knowledge how and knowledge that, and between knowledge by acquaintance and knowledge by description? Should we think of some mental concepts as directly referential? What happens to the knowledge argument if you take a representationalist position on sensory experience? Is there something about our relationship to our own mental phenomenal states that induces a kind of illusion about their nature? Of these questions I'd especially pick out the question, Are physicalists committed to the a priori deducibility of the mental from the physical? Although I changed my mind about the knowledge argument, I have consistently argued that the answer to this question is yes.

Of course many of the questions listed above were on the table before the knowledge argument became a central topic in the philosophy of mind, and those that weren't would likely have arisen in some other context, but I think the intuitive appeal of the knowledge argument and the urgency of its conclusion provided a powerful stimulus.

What is the proper role of philosophy in relation to psychology, artificial intelligence, and the neurosciences?

My position on this question disturbs some. It downplays the role of philosophy. It doesn't marginalize the role of philosophical reflection but it does give it a more modest role than some philosophers like. In my view, philosophical reflection can illuminate concepts like those of belief, intelligence and consciousness. It can, that is, illuminate what it takes to be a believer, to be conscious or intelligent. This intersects with questions about, for example, machine intelligence, in the following way. Armed with an account of what it takes to be intelligent, we can examine the way some given machine works and see whether or not that way counts as being intelligent.

What's involved in reflecting on a concept? That's a tricky question but here's a simple illustration to give the general idea. It can be tempting to analyze understanding a language in essentially behavioral terms. Understanding a word or sentence isn't like being in pain; there's no special 'feel' to understanding. One understands a language, you might speculate, to the extent that one gives systematically good answers to questions posed in the language in question, where giving good answers covers a whole range of responses, not just responses in words. A good response to 'There's a storm on the way' is to run for cover. But now think of someone who is good at answering the question, What is the natural logarithm of n? for a whole range of values of n, but whose ability rests *entirely* on their ability to find the right entry in a book of logarithms for each value of n. They don't understand logarithms. They understand how to use a table. This example—or rather what happens when we reflect on it—shows that getting systematically right answers isn't enough in itself for understanding. This tells us something straightaway about machine intelligence: a machine's delivering lots of good responses isn't in itself enough for the machine to count as intelligent.

The modest nature of the role I see for philosophy will now I trust be clear. Psychology, artificial intelligence, and the neurosciences will, we may suppose, discover all there is to discover about our capacities, how they are grounded in the way our brains and bodies work and are constituted, how our brains and bodies carry putative information about our surroundings in ways that guide us through the world, the evolutionary history of the various functioning parts of our bodies, and so on. These disciplines will make similar discoveries about non-human animals, computers of the future and so on. But these disciplines won't discover intelligence and understanding, or at least not intelligence and understanding *branded as such*. The question for philosophers is then whether or not what they discover, expressed in their terms, amounts to, counts as, say, intelligence or as understanding. Philosophers answer the question, Does being so and so count as being intelligence, being consciousness, having understanding or whatever? Neuroscientists, psychologists, the folk (our everyday observations are sometimes enough), computer engineers, biologists, or whoever, deliver the facts that fall under the heading 'being so and so'.

Here is a final example to flesh out how I think about the question (not that this way is original to me; I think it is pretty much the traditional way). Botanists discovered the causal relations between the number and spacing of tree rings, on the one hand, and the age and growth rates of trees, on the other. Did their discovery count as showing that tree rings carry information about age and rate of growth? You don't answer that question by doing another experiment. Another experiment may tell you more about, say, the mechanism that underpins the causal connection between number of rings and age but that in itself doesn't answer our question. You answer our question by reference to the concept of carrying information. *Mutatis mutandis* for the relation between psychology, work in AI and neuroscience, our everyday observations etc., and the existence of consciousness, and all that.

This way of thinking about the connection between philosophy and the empirical discoveries of psychology, the folk, AI or neuroscience allows that we should be open to the need to revise our concepts, that we should grant that some of our central concepts are vague and can reasonably be made precise in different ways, and that we should be prepared to introduce new concepts in the face of unexpected discoveries. No current computers have beliefs and desires but maybe sometime in the future the sensible thing to say will be that a certain computer has beliefs and desires on such and such a conception but not on so and so a conception, and it may well be an idle question which is the right conception—or perhaps the right thing to say will be that on our original conception of belief and desire, the computer lacks beliefs and desires, but on a conception we can reasonably regard as an improved relative of the old conception, the computer has beliefs and desires.

This example involves beliefs and desires and possible computers of the future, but it may be that a rather similar point should be made about the mental states with feel and human beings. Early defenses of physicalism gave a prominent role to analyses of pain that were designed to show how pain fits inside a physicalist view of our nature. It was argued that our concept of pain could be captured by something of the form

x is in pain if and only if x is K

where K is a specification that is transparently satisfiable by something whose nature is entirely physical. Often K was some sort of functional specification. Maybe nothing like this quite works. This will not matter too much if there's a successful analysis of the form

x is in pain* if and only if x is K

and where pain* is enough like pain. That is to say, we should allow as a possibility that conversion to a physicalist view of the mind will bring with it a recognition that we aren't in pain according to our current concept of pain but are in pain according to some concept that is close enough to our current concept. We have pain* and that's near enough.

It is plausible that something like this happens when one converts to four-dimensionalism about space and time. On the four-dimensionalist account, nothing changes over time in the sense of there being something wholly identical at two different times, while having different properties at the later time from those it ahs at the earlier time. What happens instead is that there are objects extended in space-time whose later temporal parts differ in their properties from their earlier temporal parts. Maybe we don't have change but we do have change*, and that's near enough.

Is a science of consciousness possible?

Of course. Consciousness is something we find in the natural world and everything we find in the natural world is a proper subject for science and a proper subject for theorizing. Possibly some, though not all, dualists would answer this question differently but not a physicalist cum naturalist about the mind like myself.

What are the most important open problems in contemporary philosophy of mind? What are the most promising prospects?

i) When we use space probes to investigate how things are on the far side of Jupiter or on the surface of Mars, we carry out a 'before and after' exercise on the probes and their instruments. We survey the possible explanations of the changes in the probes and their instruments in terms of hypotheses about how things are on the far side of Jupiter or on Mars's surface, and we take an hypothesis about Jupiter or Mars to be supported to the extent that it would provide, if true, a good explanation of the changes in the probes and their instruments. In carrying out this exercise, we take for granted the following principle: changes that don't discriminate are of no use to us. If we are wondering whether or not the rocks on the surface of Mars are predominantly igneous or non-igneous, a reading on an instrument that would be exactly the same in either case is of no use to us. We may have other reasons to favor one hypothesis over the other, but the reading itself is no help. Again, doctors who wish to test for whether or not a tumor is malignant need a test that discriminates between the two possibilities. A dye that turns from white to red if the tumor is malignant and does exactly the same if the tumor is benign is no use to the doctors.

There are a number of questions raised by these remarks. Could one say that the dye doesn't do the same thing in the imagined tumor example? Turning from white to red as a result of the action of a malignant tumor is different from turning from white to red as a result of the action of a benign tumor. One might ask whether what's crucial is that the dye turns from white to red in both cases, or whether this is known or believed or likely. And so on. All the same I think it is clear that there's some essentially correct thought behind the discrimination principle; what we have are issues about how to frame it and not about its essential correctness. For example, we may find it hard to explain exactly why it would be a mistake to argue that there's no problem with the dye test for malignancy, because turning from white to red for one reason differs from turning from white to red for a different reason; all the same, we and doctors know that this is the wrong way to go.

Now we can think of our bodies as kinds of space probes. We move through the world collecting information, or putative information, via the way the world affects our bodies. Most of the information is at the sub-personal level but we trust that some comes through to us at the personal level in terms of beliefs and perceptions. The discrimination principle tells us that to the extent that the beliefs and perceptions coming from the impact of the world on us are to be trusted, what we believe and perceive as a result of the impacts are a function of the distinctive effects of the environment. When different environments have the very same effect on us, these effects are not in themselves a reason for favoring one view over another as to which is the actual environment. This means it would be good to have a narrow notion of content for belief and perception; a notion of content, that is, on which what's believed and perceptually represented is a function of how one's body is, and the environment enters the picture inasmuch as it makes a distinctive difference to one's body, a difference that in turn feeds into personal level representational states like belief and perception.

There are, however, influential arguments to the conclusion that the content of belief and perception is wide across the board. It isn't as if beliefs and perceptions have both narrow and wide contents; they have wide contents exclusively.

I think the most important open problem in the philosophy of mind is showing where these influential arguments go wrong.

ii) How might one do this? This is a big question. Here I will simply identify two attractive thoughts which, in my view, underlie much of the thinking that leads to the 'all content is broad' position. Sometimes the role of these thoughts is explicit, sometimes it is implicit. I'll explain what they are and why I think they are mistaken, despite their attractions.

If we think in terms of representation, as I think we should, the issue of the content of personal level states is the issue of the relation between possible head states and possible environments. Contentful personal level states are states that represent. When I believe that snow is white, certain of my head states represent, in the way right for belief, that out of the possible environments I might be in, the one I am in fact in is one with white snow. The content of the belief is how the belief represents the environment to be, namely, as being one where snow is white. Likewise for perceptual states. But, except in trivial cases, relations hold in virtue of the nature of both relata. Object A's having more rough spots than object B is a joint effort between the way A is and the way B is. Surely, then, runs the thought, the belief content of a state of the head cannot possibly be settled by the nature of the head state alone. Ergo, the content must be wide; there is no kosher notion of belief content that supervenes on the nature of the head of the subject with the belief.

The mistake here can be illustrated using the example of the relation of having more rough spots. The following argument is valid:

A has more rough spots than B
A and C are exactly alike
Therefore, C has more rough spots than B.

Whether or not a given possible head state kind belief-represents a given environment depends on both the nature of the head state and the nature of the possible environment, but it doesn't follow from this that the belief-representation relation isn't a *function* from possible head state kinds to possible environments.

The second thought is one about the connection between content and truth of sentences used to express content. We use the sentence 'Some things are larger than other things' to express the content of the belief that some things are larger than other things. How does this connect with the idea that that belief represents that things are a certain way? Well, the sentence is itself a representational structure, and we can divide the possible worlds into those that are as the sentence represents things to be and those that are not. The first set will the worlds (possible environments) at which the sentence is true (it will include the actual world, as some things are larger than other things); the second set will be set of worlds at which the sentence is false (the worlds where everything is the very same size and the empty world).

However, the set of worlds where a sentence is true sometimes gets wrong how we represent things to be when we use that sentence. Suppose Fred says 'I am near something square' at noon, March 30, 2008. The worlds at which his sentence is true are those where Fred is near something square at noon, March 30, 2008. But that's not how he's representing things to be. He isn't saying who he is or what time it is, and the thought he's using the sentence to express isn't to do with who he is or when it is.

In my view, the way to get the representational content right for sentences like these is to look, not at the worlds where the sentence is true, but at the worlds, or more generally the centered worlds, whose actuality is consistent with the truth of the sentence: the worlds that might be the actual world consistently with the sentence being true, or the centered worlds that might be the actual world and center consistently with the truth of the sentence. In the case of our example, this will be the set of centered worlds with something square near their centers. How so? Because for each token of 'I am near something square', the actual centered world is the world of the token with the center being the actual producer of the token, and 'I am near something square' in X's mouth, or from X's hand, at T is true if and only if X is near something square at T.

How does this bear on the issue of wide versus narrow content? Suppose that Fred has a duplicate, Fred*, and that both utter 'I am near something square' at noon, March 30, 2008. The worlds at which their utterances are true will be different. Fred's sentence will be true at worlds where Fred is near something square at noon, March 30, 2008, whereas Fred*'s will be true at worlds where Fred* is near something square at noon, March 30, 2008. If the contents of their sentences and the thoughts they use to express them are the respective sets of worlds at which their sentences are true, it will follow that Fred and Fred*, despite being duplicates, have thoughts with different contents. However, if the contents of their sentences and the thoughts they use to express them are the respective sets of centered worlds whose actuality is consistent with the truth of their sentences, the contents of their thoughts and sentences are the same, namely, the set of centered worlds with something square near their centers.

We now have an attractive story to tell about how we get information from hearing sentences like 'I am near something square' issue from speakers' mouths or pens.

1. A hearer comes across someone producing 'I am near something square'.

2. The hearer infers that that person is a near-to-something-square center in the world they occupy at the time of speaking—from the posited content plus supposing the source of the sentence to be reliable and understanding the conventions of English governing indexicals.

3. The hearer knows they are in the same world as the speaker—that's *a priori*.

4. The hearer knows they stand in such and such a relation to the speaker—from observation.

5. The hearer acquires the belief that they stand in such and such a relation to someone near something square—putting all the above together.

We might highlight the importance of being able to carry out this kind of exercise by replacing 'something square' in the above by 'a land mine' or 'a radio-active source'.

12
Jaegwon Kim

William Herbert Perry Faunce Professor of Philosophy

Brown University, USA

Why were you initially drawn to philosophy of mind?

When I was in graduate school, in the late 1950s to early '60s, philosophy of mind was not yet fully established as a field of philosophy, separate from metaphysics and epistemology. I don't remember courses on the subject either in college or graduate school. There are two sorts of philosophers of mind—those who have come to the field from the science side and those who, like me, have come from traditional metaphysics. I did my dissertation on scientific explanation with Carl Hempel (a bad idea; Hempel was always kind and generous and I owe him much philosophically, but it's not a smart idea to do your dissertation on a topic on which your advisor is the world's foremost authority). My dissertation was not very good, but it did lead to my work on the nature of events. Writers on scientific explanation would routinely talk about explaining 'events'. As everyone knows, Hempel claimed that to explain an event one must derive a sentence describing that event from an appropriate set of premises. But what is an event? And what is it for a sentence to describe an event? Events are also causal relata. The proposition that every event has a cause figures prominently in Kant's 'Transcendental Analytic'. But why don't events show up in his table of categories? I couldn't find any philosophical literature on events, historical or contemporary, and this made me very curious.

Around this time, the mind-brain identity theory, of Feigl and Smart, burst forth on the philosophical scene. As you will recall, this is the claim that mental events are identical with brain events. What a neat idea, I thought. But, again, what are events? And when are events identical? I had no idea that Donald Davidson was thinking about events around this time. Anyway, this is what got me into the mind-body problem, and that led to other issues in the metaphysics of mind.

What do you consider your most important contribution to the field?

I suppose it's probably my work on the mind-body problem—on a cluster of issues like mental causation, the exclusion argument, reduction and reductive explanation, implications of multiple realization, and so on. Or perhaps my general work on supervenience. I am not sure.

What is the proper role of philosophy in relation to psychology, artificial intelligence, and the neurosciences?

I think that broad metaphysical issues of the sort I have dealt with, such as mental causation, supervenience, causal/explanatory exclusion, and the rest, should be of interest to researchers in the scientific fields you have mentioned. I don't think it has any direct bearing on scientific research, but I think it may help them to think and write more clearly when they touch on matters involving philosophy. If you think that this sort of philosophical clarity isn't something the scientists need or can use, or that, as serious naturalists, we should take science 'at its face value,' just look at the burgeoning literature by scientists on emergence and emergentism. The rampant confusions are sobering. I find it interesting that many of the students in my philosophy of mind course at Brown with majors in neuroscience, cognitive science, computer science, and such eventually come to take a serious interest the metaphysical issues about the mind. But what about the converse relation? What relevance do results in these fields have for philosophy of mind? I think that depends on the kind of philosophical problems one happens to be interested in. If you work on, say, the emotions or perception, you probably have to keep an eye on what's going on in the relevant sciences. In contrast, for someone like me, whose interest does not go much beyond the broad and fairly abstract metaphysical issues, I don't see that these sciences, at least the details of current developments, are of much relevance. I can't think of any possible new findings from neuroscientific research on consciousness that would, or should, change my mind, or anyone's mind, about the so-called explanatory gap problem, or about the causal efficacy of consciousness.

12. Jaegwon Kim   119

Is a science of consciousness possible?
Sure! That is, if we assume actuality entails possibility. There is a lot going on, as I take it, under the name 'consciousness research' in brain science. But is it a science of consciousness, or a science of the neural substrates of consciousness? Well, maybe we shouldn't be too picky. Will brain science produce an 'account' of consciousness? I don't think so—at least, not something that will remove the 'mystery' William James wrote about in 1890 in *The Principles of Psychology*. He said:

> According to the assumptions of this book, thoughts accompany the brain's workings, and those thoughts are cognitive of realities. The whole relation is one which we can only write down empirically, confessing that no glimmer of explanation of it is yet in sight. That brains should give rise to a knowing consciousness at all, this is the one mystery which returns, no matter of what sort the consciousness and of what sort the knowledge may be. Sensations, aware of mere qualities, involve the mystery as much as thoughts, aware of complex systems, involve it. William James, *The Principles of Psychology*, 1890 (reprinted edition, Harvard University Press, 1981), p. 647.

Psychophysical correlations are things 'we can write down empirically'—that is, we can make a list of them. The question, as Ned Block (I believe) once put it, is "Why do conscious states correlate with the neural states with which they are correlated?" If answering this question is part of giving a scientific account of consciousness, then, as James said over a hundred years ago, "no glimmer of explanation is yet in sight."

Giving a neuroscientific account of consciousness is one thing; there is also the converse question, namely the question what role, if any, consciousness can play as an explanatory construct in brain science? The term 'science of consciousness' suggests, tacitly, that this science is concerned, at least in part, with the theoretical role of consciousness (compare the science of heat, the science of gravitation, the science, or theory, of electromagnetism). It seems to me, though, that almost all brain scientists are what we might call 'methodological epiphenomenalists'. They don't think—at least this is what their theoretical practices seem to reveal—that conscious events and states, even if their existence is openly acknowledged, can have any theoretical role, that is, causal-explanatory role, vis-à-vis neural events and processes, or even in relation to other mental events.

What are the most important open problems in contemporary philosophy of mind? What are the most promising prospects?

Mental causation and consciousness; intentionality and mental content; and the normativity of the mental. As you know, these are among currently much debated issues in the field. I believe, though, that ultimately the most profound and challenging issues concern self and subjectivity. Of course, much has been written in this general area, but I don't think we even know what the central issues are, or how the problems are connected to one another. What we have is only a mass of data—often conflicting intuitions, problems, puzzles, and even mysteries—without any idea as to what sort of approach might yield a unified account, or what such an 'account' should look like. As far as I can see, this is a virgin territory. Perhaps we should go back to Descartes and Kant and start all over.

13
William Lycan

Professor of Philosophy
University of North Carolina, USA

Why were you initially drawn to philosophy of mind?

As a college senior in 1965, I took a course in it, taught jointly by Robert Tredwell at Amherst and John Brentlinger at UMass. We ended up reading Place and Smart, fairly new stuff at the time, and I thought the Identity Theory was both exciting and pretty clearly correct. Then in graduate school at Chicago I read Armstrong's *A Materialist Theory of the Mind*, which had just appeared, and the computational-functionalist works of Putnam. Meanwhile, Wittgenstein and others had called philosophers' attention to a variety of particular mental and perceptual phenomena, each fascinating in its own right.

What do you consider your most important contribution to the field?

The explicit introduction of natural teleology ("Form, Function, and Feel," *Journal of Philosophy*, 1981). Teleology had been implicit in the 'homuncular functionalist' works of Fodor and Dennett, following the psychologist Fred Attneave, but I brought it out and defended it as such. It's been influential, as witness the biologizing of functionalism and the whole current industry of teleosemantics. (But at least three people, Elliott Sober, Karen Neander and Ruth Millikan, had the idea independently of me even though they published later.)

The bio- and teleologizing of functionalism has brought a number of advantages. First, the older computational or 'machine' functionalist conceived *psychological explanation* in the Positivists' terms of subsumption of data under wider and wider universal generalizations. But Fodor, Dennett, Rob Cummins and others defended the competing 'function-analytical' picture of explanation, according to which behavioral data are to be seen as manifestations of subjects' psychological capacities, and those capacities are to be explained by understanding the subjects as systems of interacting 'homunculi,' each homunculus being identified by reference to the function it performs, and the various homuncular components cooperate with each other in such a way as to produce overall behavioral responses to stimuli.

Second, the machine functionalist's notion of functional 'realization,' the relation between an individual physical organism and the abstract program it was said to instantiate, had been too liberal (a simple matter of one-one correspondence). As Ned Block pointed out, if the population of China were organized so as to implement a program that is functionally equivalent to our brains when we feel pain, the nation would not experience pain thereby. Machine functionalism was also challenged by spectrum reversal cases; intuitively, the machine-functional roles of red and green visual sensations might be reversed while the sensations remain the same in experiential quality. Such counterexamples, and other difficulties relating to the 'feels' or experienced phenomenal characters of mental states, are blocked if we impose a teleological requirement on realization: a physical state of an organism will count as realizing such-and-such a functional description only if the organism has genuine organic integrity and the state plays its functional role properly *for* the organism, in the teleological sense of 'for.'

Third, machine functionalism's two-levelled picture of human psychobiology was unbiological in the extreme. Neither living things nor even computers themselves are split into a purely 'structural' level of biological/physiochemical description and any one 'abstract' computational level of machine/psychological description. Rather, they are all hierarchically organized at many levels, each level 'abstract' with respect to those beneath it but 'structural' or concrete as it realizes those levels above it.

Fourth, as previously noted, Dretske, Millikan and others have argued powerfully that teleology must enter into any adequate analysis of the intentionality or aboutness of mental items such as perceptual states, beliefs and desires.

I think my second most important contribution would be my early defense of the Representational theory of sensory qualia, the view that, e.g., the yellowness of the banana-shaped patch in my visual field as I look at a banana is the represented yellowness *of the banana*, not a property of my visual state, and the greenness of a green after-image is, not an actual nonphysical property, but a *physical* property of a *non*actual evanescent green blob illusorily represented by the subject's visual state.

(The Representationalist idea was not original with me; it was put forward by Elizabeth Anscombe in 1965 and by Jaakko Hintikka in 1969. But I believe I was the first to import it positively into mainstream philosophy of mind, in *Consciousness*, 1987—though it had been preëmptively criticized by Chris Peacocke in 1983.)

Of course, there has been steady resistance to the Representational theory, much of it following Peacocke, in the form of counterexamples: sensory states which differ qualitatively while allegedly differing not at all in their representational contents. In response to such a case, the Representationalist tries to show that there is after all a representational difference. Michael Tye has been especially good at that.

What is the proper role of philosophy in relation to psychology, artificial intelligence, and the neurosciences?

1. As usual, philosophy has both conceptual and methodological advice to offer, especially to psychology and AI. (This can be overdone. As my psychologist friend Paul Shulman once said, "We don't care what anything is *called*; we just wanna *measure* it.")

2. In my view, no philosophical view should contradict established scientific findings—period. (I subscribe to Locke's 'underlabourer' view of our discipline.) This requirement is easily satisfied, since it is rare for philosophy to be brought *logically* face to face with science, and one must doubt any claim beginning with "Science has shown that...," where what follows is couched in ordinary English. But:

3. In any area of philosophy of mind, the theorist should take the relevant scientific findings very seriously, even when those results do not legislate. For example, here are a number of claims that have been made about *pain* during the past fifty years—made a priori, or perhaps on the basis of introspection alone: that pain is 'self-intimating' (i.e., if one has a pain one is necessarily and perhaps eo ipso aware of it); that one's

belief that one is in pain is infallible and/or incorrigible; that pain is intrinsically unpleasant and necessarily motivates attempts to relieve it; that at least some pain is simple in that it does not have components. Not one of those claims has been confirmed by empirical research on pain (see, for example, the references in Valerie Gray Hardcastle's *The Myth of Pain*); each, though logically consistent with that research, is implausible in light of it.

Is a science of consciousness possible?

It's actual, and going great guns, if by 'consciousness' you mean roughly *awareness*, which is what nearly all working psychologists seem to mean by it. Here are some growth areas:

Attention and its relation to awareness and experience. William James famously held that we consciously experience all and only those stimuli that we attend to. But, interestingly, there is evidence that some attentional processing does not produce conscious awareness, so even if attention is necessary for consciousness it is not sufficient.

Information without awareness. There are many different sorts of case in which a subject is shown to have and use sensory information while unaware of possessing any such information. Perhaps the most dramatic of these is that of blindsight: patients with damage to striate cortex (V1) experience large blind spots. When stimuli are presented to their blind fields, they report seeing nothing; yet for some of those subjects, if they are asked to guess direction, motion, rudimentary shape or color, they do far better than chance, still with no awareness that their answers are anything but guesses. (And there is semantic priming.) There are several different theories of what is going on in blindsight, of which I think the most plausible is based on Milner and Goodale's finding that there are really two visual systems, one associated with the ventral cortical stream and one with the dorsal.

Inattentional blindness and change blindness. Surprisingly, we fail to notice even large and obtrusive events that happen right before our eyes, if we are not narrowly attending to the relevant sectors of our visual fields. Typically, when a subject does finally notice the change or is shown it in slow motion, s/he is astonished at having missed it until then. Several morals can be drawn. First, I think, that the focus of ordinary perceptual attention at a moment is much narrower than we would commonsensically suppose. Second, that even if attention is not strictly required for awareness, lack of it can produce dramatic lack of awareness.

'Filling in.' Everyone has a blind spot in each eye, because of there being no photoreceptors where the optic nerve leaves the retina. But no one notices this unless it is called to her/his attention in a fairly special, nearly experimental setup. Moreover, as James said, there are ubiquitous if tiny gaps in our experience—eye blinks, occlusions of objects by other objects, minute lapses of attention—yet we feel no gaps; our experience seems to us smooth and continuous. It is tempting to infer that the brain somehow 'fills in' the gaps. Research is beginning to reveal ways in which it does as well as ways in which it doesn't.

The temporal anomalies. There are well-known paradoxical cases in which we seem to become aware of a stimulus before it actually occurs. For example, in 'color phi', two adjacent lights of different colors are flashed in quick succession—say, first red and then green—and as in the familiar 'marquee' illusion, an observer seems to see a single light that moves from one position to the other. But subjects uniformly report that the light changed from red to green as it moved, i.e., 'the' light seemed to turn green before the green bulb came on! Some theorists have gone so far as to take these mysterious goings-on as evidence of mind/body dualism, but a nice naturalistic explanation has been offered by Dan Dennett and Marcel Kinsbourne.

Intentions, agency and control of behavior. It is natural to think that our deliberate actions proceed from our conscious decisions. But Ben Libet's experiments in the 1980s seem to have shown that some voluntary motor actions are initiated in the brain before the agent decides to perform them. It seems, then, that the role of consciousness in decision is sometimes illusory.

Unities and disunities. Normal consciousness displays a number of unities, synchronic and diachronic. We 'bind' separate detections of position, shape, color, texture and temperature into the perception of a single physical object such as a cup of coffee in our hand. We sense our own bodies as unitary physical objects. We experience change as such, i.e., first one thing and then another but in a single perception. These things and more need explaining, and are the focus of empirical work. And there are corresponding pathological disunities. For example, psychotics misidentify their own verbal thoughts as alien voices speaking to them; neurology patients may be alienated from their own limbs, perceiving them (horribly) as loose body parts of someone else's; Multiple Personality (now Dissociative Identity) Disorder speaks for itself. Perhaps the most extraordinary disunity of consciousness is that found in commisurotomized (split-brain) patients. Neuroscientists are trying with at least some success to parse these disturbing phenomena.

Moving to issues that have more directly concerned and puzzled philosophers: I believe science can also explain 'qualia' in the sense of sensory qualities. If the Representational theory of those is correct, then all that needs investigating is what external-world features our sensory systems detect, and how. That is a program already well underway in perceptual psychology.

Yet, according to me, there is one respect in which science cannot explain 'consciousness.' Joe Levine called our attention to the now famous 'explanatory gap': Even if God were to assure us that, say, the Identity Theory is true and that such-and-such a conscious experience *just is*, is strictly identical with, a firing of certain neural fibers, we would still lack an explanation of why those fiber firings feel to their subjects in the distinctive way they do. Indeed, to Levine it seems 'arbitrary' that they do.

Some philosophers deny that there is any such principled or ultimate gap. Against them, I insist that the gap is real and permanent. However (*Consciousness and Experience*, Ch. 3) I explain its existence in a way that is not only compatible with materialism, but positively predicted by the materialist theory of consciousness I favor. For now: Notice that assuming there is a permanent gap, it is not confined to consciousness in any sense or even to mind; there are many kinds of intrinsically perspectival (fine-grained) facts that cannot be explained. Suppose an opthalmologist explains why WGL is nearsighted. That does nothing to explain why *I* am nearsighted; nor could anyone or anything explain that (unless, of course, one *first* conceded the identity of me with WGL).

What are the most important open problems in contemporary philosophy of mind?

I'll mention three, each of which concerns intentionality or mental aboutness.

First, it's widely thought that of the two great difficulties faced by materialism, *intentionality* is tractable (as Jerry Fodor has put it, "Once Descartes figured out that intentionality is representation, a good graduate student can do the rest"), but issues of *consciousness, subjectivity, qualia* and the like are still deeply mysterious and materialists have barely a clue about them. I entirely disagree. Give me intentionality, and I have little trouble dealing with consciousness, subjectivity and qualia (*Consciousness and Experience*). It's getting intentionality in the first place that's the truly 'hard problem.'

Materialist psychosemantics has been mainly input-oriented: A brain state type is about X iff its tokens covary with, or are characteristically caused by, or have the function of indicating, or are asymmetrically dependent on, (etc.) X. There are, according to me, three great objections facing this project.

First, it treats only of concepts tied closely to the thinker's physical environment. But thoughts can be very abstract, and their contents far removed from the physical world. Philosophical thoughts are the obvious example ("A curious thing about the ontological problem is its simplicity"). And as always, there is nothing derivative or second-rate about such thoughts. As Brentano might have put it, thoughts can *just as easily* be about such abstract matters as they can be about water or tigers or your mother.

Second, input-oriented semantics addresses only thoughts and beliefs, and not more exotic propositional attitudes which do not have the function of being correct representations; see below.

Third, no current psychosemantics applies to any thought that is even partly metaphorical. N.b., nearly every thought you have is to some extent metaphorical.

Though Ruth Millikan's "consumer semantics" avoids the simpler objections to input-oriented views, it does not help much with any of the three problems just mentioned; after 30+ years of psychosemantics, they have barely been scratched.

(Of course, the materialist could abandon the psychosemantic project and fall back to a non-brain-based, whole-subject view of the propositional attitudes, such as Dennett's instrumentalism. I would not consider that calamitous, for the case of belief. However, it will not do for perceptual representation—which leads me to my next topic.)

My second important open problem is that of perceptual content. It seems obvious that vision, in particular, represents; your immediate environment looks a certain way to you, and it may or may not actually be that way. Yet in recent years that assumption has been challenged, by such theorists as Charles Travis and John Campbell. I do not find their arguments at all persuasive, but even if we agree that vision does represent, it is proving very difficult to say *what* (sorts of things), exactly, it represents.

A conservative approach would be to maintain that vision represents only sense-datum-type properties such as colors and shapes, corresponding to David Marr's "primal sketch." (Or perhaps it represents depth also, as in Marr's "2.5-D" sketch, and even volumetric shapes and distances, as in Marr's 3-D sketch.) But, surely, someone will say, vision also represents everyday objects such as shoes and ships and sealing-wax. After all, *object-recognition* is obviously one of vision's functions. Possibly for this reason, Jerry Fodor suggests that what vision represents are the properties mentioned so far *plus* those corresponding to Eleanor Rosch's "basic categories" such as 'dog,' 'shoe,' 'chair,' 'red,' or 'lady,' but no others.

Several objections will be made to that conservative view. First, we simply see and recognize individual things such as people (and their faces), not just properties or types of object. Second, we simply see and recognize things as socially characterized—dollar bills, post offices, square dances. Third, there is evidence that when we hear speech or read text, we directly perceive *meanings*, without having to derive those meanings from the phonemes or graphemes that are 'actually' perceived. Some liberals will go to the opposite extreme, and maintain that we can perceive (as such) electrons, social class, surges of monetary inflation, global warming, and the like.

How are we to adjudicate between conservatives, moderates, and liberals? Here, I believe, the issue deepens horribly, because no good methodology suggests itself. Introspection settles nothing. Our characteristic uses of the word 'looks' don't settle anything either; we use it in a very liberal way, with no implication that the appearance in question is purely visual and uninformed by sophisticated background knowledge. Nor can you appeal to psychosemantics, for every psychosemantics is itself tested against pre-existing judgments regarding what sorts of things visual states represent.

(In recent work, Susanna Siegel has offered a new style of argument for particular representational claims: the *method of phenomenal contrast*. It looks all right in theory, but is hard to apply. The developed instances of it I have seen are inconclusive; in particular, I don't know how Siegel might defend her characteristic premises against a Marr- or Fodor-style conservative.)

Unfortunately, the problem gets worse, because there are theoretical indications that visual content seems to have a more complicated, layered structure: According to the later Peacocke (*A Study of Concepts* et seq.), vision represents indexical "scenario" content—low-level properties nonconceptually, and high-level properties conceptually. I myself have argued (*Consciousness and Experience*, Ch. 7) that we represent high-level properties *by* representing scenario content and low-level properties. Alva Noë holds that we perceive high-level properties, though only as "present as absent," by actually-perceiving "perspectival" (elsewhere "appearance") properties. Susanna Schellenberg suggests plausibly that we perceive "situation-dependent" properties of external objects, and thereby the high-level properties of the same objects, the perception of the latter depending epistemically on that of the former. (Schellenberg's view is superior to mine, in that it does not require any element of illusion or seeing things that are not really there.)

Yet all of these 'layering' views merely assume, contra the conservative, that vision does represent some high-level properties.

It gets worse again, for we must consider aspect-perception and attentional phenomena. Aspect-perception has received shockingly little discussion in philosophy of mind (as opposed to aesthetics). It's invoked, especially as by Peacocke and others in putative counterexamples to the Representational theory of sensory qualities, but to my knowledge no one has positively investigated aspect-perception as a species of representation (again assuming it is one), or the relation between it and more basic, even layered, forms of visual representation. No one has solved Wittgenstein's original mystery: "'But this isn't *seeing!*'—'But this is seeing!'." Aspect-flipping, involuntary or deliberate, is a visual phenomenon, *or at least* it affects specifically visual phenomenology. But in some sense what is 'actually' seen doesn't change.

It's important to see that there are different subcases here. For example: perceiving ordinary objects under aspects (a bush is seen as a bear or vice versa); perceiving ordinary objects under *very high-level* aspects, such as 'harbinger of thunderstorm' or 'AIDS victim'; the pictorial seeing-as that Wittgenstein made famous, involving ambiguous figures such as the duck-rabbit; phenomena of selective attention or attentional grouping, as in Peacocke's dot arrays; and the use of ordinary objects as aspect representations of entirely different things, as when Jack Aubrey at the dinner table recreates a sea battle by using ordinary cutlery and plates and bottles to represent warships and their tactical movements.

My own hunch is that all aspect-perceiving is to be understood in terms of selective attention. But that is no more than a guess. The matter remains nearly unexplored by philosophers of mind.

My third open problem is that of propositional attitudes other than belief. (How many works have announced their topic as being 'the propositional attitudes' or even 'intentionality,' and proceeded to discuss only belief?) Consider hoping that p, rejoicing that p, being disappointed that p, loving that p, being embarrassed that p, being excited that p, regretting that p,.... Of course there is an understandable tendency to think that each of those more exotic attitudes is reducible to some complex of beliefs and desires, or at least that it inherits its propositional content from that of a related belief or desire. But even if that general idea should prove correct, there are still considerable difficulties in considering *desire* itself as a propositional attitude. The difficulties are all but unnoticed by mainstream philosophers of mind; their roots are in action theory and moral psychology.

Crudely, there are two main competing materialist paradigms for the explication of belief. One is interpretivist, stemming from Davidson and Dennett. As Dennett has it, a belief is, not an internal causal state of a subject, but only a holistic construct out of the belief *ascriptions* that would be made by a suitably placed observer, wielding certain norms of rationality and making the working assumption that people usually believe what they ought to believe (in the circumstances) given their sensory inputs, and they desire what they ought to desire given their needs. (Which is not to say that people do not *really* believe this or that.) The other paradigm is Fodor's: a belief is an internal cause of behavior, a brain state having both representational content, determined by a psychosemantics, and the functional role that's distinctive of belief as opposed to a different propositional attitude.

But desire fits neither of these paradigms, at least not comfortably. First, the term is almost universally considered ambiguous as between a 'thin' or merely 'formal' sense, in which any intentional action is trivially one that the agent 'desired' to perform, and a stricter sense, in which a 'desire' is a particular type of motivating state among others, and in which an agent may do something s/he has no 'desire' to do. G.F. Schueler argues that the disambiguation gives rise to a dilemma for Dennett: In the first sense of 'desire,' the notion cannot be used to predict behavior, in the way Dennett's epistemology demands; but in the second sense, it will often and understandably give the wrong predictions.

The ambiguity does not affect the Fodor paradigm, since Fodor's theory is clearly meant to apply to desires in the narrow, psychological sense rather than the broad formal sense. But now there are problems for the notion of desire *content*. On Fodor's view, the content of a propositional attitude is the semantic or propositional content of the internal representation in question. (One believes that p iff one hosts an appropriately behaved representation that means that p.) Of course the desire that p has such semantic content too, viz., that p; but (surprisingly) it is not that content that figures in real discussions of 'what' a person desires, what a person 'really' desires, when a desire is or is not *satisfied*, whether a desire can be 'false' in the sense intended by Aristotle, and the like. So far as philosophy of mind is concerned, these issues are wide open.

What are the most promising prospects?

For me, that's an awkward question. I have mentioned the three areas that I think are most daunting and in which little progress has been made; nothing promising there. The other issues that have dominated the literature, particularly those involving subjectivity, 'qualia,' phenomenal character and the like, are all ones I have addressed over the years, and *I* believe addressed fairly satisfactorily though of course not everyone agrees. My view is that every interesting feature of the mind can be explicated in terms of functional role and representation, and that is 'promising' enough.

Unfortunately, as I've indicated above, I also believe that our understanding of representation itself is in terrible shape, and I know of no good way forward. So, depending on how we choose to individuate 'prospects,' maybe there are no promising ones at all. I can only hope for a breakthrough.

14
Alva Noë

Professor of Philosophy
University of California, Berkeley, USA

Why were you initially drawn to philosophy of mind?
Everything in philosophy is connected with everything else. There are not really philosophical sub-disciplines. Philosophy begins in wonder and confusion and it frequently ends in wonder and confusion. What we are seeking, what we are working for, the aim of philosophy, is understanding. We seek a kind of self-transformation that consists in the achievement of understanding. This is what we learned from Socrates, and from all the great, landmark figures in the history of philosophy. This idea that in philosophy everything is connected to everything else is something that I think I first encountered in the work of philosophers of the early to middle 20th century. I am thinking of the Logical Positivists and the Vienna Circle. And of course of Wittgenstein. I am also thinking of streams of philosophical activity of the later 20th century that flow from this earlier movement; streams such as "analytic philosophy," "ordinary language philosophy," "linguistic philosophy," etc. The picture that emerges: the philosophical mind directs itself to this question or that, from questions about language to questions about mathematics, from questions about freedom to questions about mind. But it is always the same philosophical method, always the same style of questioning, that puts itself in play. I once heard a philosopher discuss personal identity; he'd come to a place in the discussion where things turned on the idea of the continuity of consciousness. At that point he threw up his hands and declared: I don't do philosophy of mind! I've always found that an incomprehensible thing for a philosopher to say. In philosophy, questions just don't segregate themselves that way.

Which is not to say, of course, that the terrain of the philosophical landscape is flat and undifferentiated. Hardly! Questions about mind and number and truth and freedom arise in the strikingly different intellectual quarters. Philosophy aims at understanding, so it is always guided by local puzzlement.

Puzzlement about the nature of mind and consciousness is at the very heart of philosophy and the stakes have always seemed very high. What greater puzzle is there than that of our own nature and our place in the world around it? And what better way to investigate that central issue than by thinking about the nature of our cognitive, the nature of our perceptual capacities?

I said that there are no philosophical sub-disciplines. But of course, in a very real sense, there are. Within philosophy as a whole there are what we can think of as subcultures. There are smaller communities of people working on this or that question, working with and in response to each other. It has been said that philosophy is a conversation going on through the ages. To enter into the conversation today, you need to pick up the threads that are being carried on, coming to us from history. So a philosophical engagement with the historical figures in our field is really a way of moving forward in the field. I like this way of thinking in philosophy very much; but I would add: there isn't one conversation which is philosophy, there are hundreds. And each of these smaller conversations reproduces in the small this dynamic property that we see in philosophy as a whole, namely, communication with and responsiveness to one's interlocutors, past and present. So, from the standpoint of this more anthropological conception of disciplines and sub-disciplines, there are sub-disciplines of philosophy.

What do you consider your most important contribution to the field?

My work today is animated by three ideas.

First, experience is an achievement, or performance, of the person or animal. Experience, or consciousness, is not something that happens in us. It is something we do. Our experiential lives, like our lives themselves, unfold in an environment, in a world. The title of my new book sums up the view pretty well: *Out of Our Heads: Why You are Not your Brain and Other Lessons from the Biology of Consciousness* (Farrar Straus and Giroux, February 2009). Our mental lives extend out of our heads. A person is not a brain, an assemblage of cells and associated molecules. And crucially: this fundamental fact about ourselves is what science, what biology, teaches us. The whole problem of the nature of mind and experience is, really, a problem about bringing our lives into focus for biology. The idea that the science of mind should be biological is something to which philosophers and cognitive scientists pay lip-service. But the really striking thing about much work in cognitive science—I'm thinking of computational theories of mind, the whole information-processing model of mind—is how biological it isn't.

In fact, the problem of mind and consciousness and the biological problem of life are really one and the same. Life is not something you find inside an organism. Life is not something that is carried on in isolation from dynamic exchange with the environment in which an organism finds itself. Life is an achieved balance that is carried out by the organism in a situation. There are internal correlates of life (e.g. neurobiological, molecular biological). But there are also environmental correlates of life. Animals create environments – nests, houses, hives. They create worlds. Environments in turn shape animals. To understand life we need to look beyond mere biochemistry to the ecology of being.

Mind is a phenomenon of life; it is a biological phenomenon, but one that needs to be understood at an ecological level rather than at the level of molecular biology. Our mental powers are actualized thanks to our embodiment and thanks to our situation. We are out of our heads. We are performing. We are at home in the world.

Turning now to a second idea that animates my research: I see my work over the last thirteen years (since finishing my PhD in 1995) as providing steps towards what I now think of as a general theory access. Traditional approaches have it that the world shows up for us *as represented*. Visual experiences, for example, are thought to represent what is going on around us. Our capacities for thought and imagination in turn are taken to be representational capacities. I reject this sort of approach. The world shows up for the conscious mind not as represented, but as available, or as accessible. The foundation of access is the possession by the human being (or animal) of skills, of capacities, for achieving contact with the world around us. Perception is an activity for exploring the world making use of background skills and knowledge. Seeing relies on one particular repertoire of skills, while touch, or hearing, and the other sensory modalities rely on different repertoires. The different sensory modalities are different styles of skillful exploration of the immediate environment. Thought, imagination, are also styles of achieving contact with the world around us, but relying on rather different skills. All reference is conscious reference; all perception is thoughtful; much thought is more or less perceptual. We don't build up internal models of the world—not in thought or perception. The world is there, for us, thanks to the fact that we have the skills to pick it up or to reach out and touch it or to grapple with it.

A general theory of access will treat thought, perception and imagination as modalities of skillful access. Technology—and here I mean not only tools, implements, buildings, but also linguistic technologies and indeed pictorial technologies—enhances our skills of reaching, and so also enhances or alters the world that shows up for us. The theory of access takes the central phenomenon of mind to be that of *presence*. The world is present for us. The world shows up. The fact of consciousness really is this: a world shows up for us. We are carried along in a stream of meaningful activity. Other people are present to me. Cars, buildings, political campaigns, baseball games, defeats, catastrophes, births, and deaths, these are all present to us. They show up for us. A meaningful world is present for us. The character of our feelings, of our feeling states, can only be looked at in this larger setting of our meaningful encounter with the world around us. One way to sum this up: the problem of consciousness is really an aspect of the problem of intentionality. We are directed towards and confronted by an environment. All our mental states are in this sense responsive or receptive. All our mental states have content that tends to outstrip their mere receptivity.

A third idea: philosophy is transformative. Philosophy aims at understanding, as I said before. No philosophical argument ends with a QED, as Gilbert Ryle once claimed. Philosophy is necessarily a teaching enterprise; it is necessarily a persuasive enterprise. For all that, I do not believe that philosophical problems are the special property of academic philosophers. Philosophy happens everywhere, in life, and in science. A philosopher must be deeply engaged with science, as with life. I also think that a good natural scientist is likely, at least sometimes, to need to come to grips with philosophy, even if it may run against his or her temperament to have to do so. As someone who works primarily in the philosophy of mind, I view neuroscientists, psychologists, roboticists, evolutionary biologists as colleagues. We are working together on a common enterprise, bringing different skills and insights to the task.

In my view, there is especially profound need for philosophy in the field of the study of consciousness. There's simply too much uncertainty and even confusion about what the phenomena are. What is consciousness? Experience? Attention? Memory? The study of these questions is thoroughly philosophical but can only be productively undertaken in an interdisciplinary setting.

I would also say that other disciplines than those of the natural sciences are important sources for collaboration with philosophy and science in pursuit of an understanding of experience. For example, art is a domain in which it is possible directly to investigate the character of consciousness. This is the topic of my current research. The whole problem of "getting a work of art" is, I think, a good metaphor for the project of phenomenology. The problem of seeing a work of art with comprehension—whether a painting, or a dance, or a piece of music—is a version of the problem of bringing the world itself into focus for perceptual consciousness. And so, reflecting on the work of art, probing it, investigating it, exploring it, is a perfect analogy for what we need to do if we want to bring the character of our own experience into focus for ourselves. This is something we must do if we want to make experience a subject for science.

I've said that philosophy aims at understanding, that no philosophical argument ever amounts to a straightforward proof. That this is something that many philosophers have lost sight of. The hardest choice a philosopher faces is that of deciding what the battles are that need to be fought. Refuting the claims of others is pointless, at least as an end in itself. I think every student of philosophy should ask him or herself: how am I advancing the cause of enlightenment? What especially bothers me is that sometimes philosophical writers adopt a stance of false rigor, and false clarity. As philosophers, we're in the business of communicating.

What is the proper role of philosophy in relation to psychology, artificial intelligence, and the neurosciences?

As I offered above, philosophical problems arise in science and for science. Philosophical problems are distinct from empirical, natural scientific problems. But it is a mistake to think they have a life or existence separate from natural science or indeed from problems in our social and political life.

In practice, we can make a distinction between a mature science and an immature science; the more mature a science becomes, the easier it is to segregate philosophical problems that might arise for the discipline from the kinds of problems that arise on a normal basis for working scientists. It sometimes happens that philosophical problems arise in the course of the day-to-day workings of scientists. In contemporary physics, for example, there are live, outstanding philosophical problems, and not only at the outer-reaches of the theory "(e.g. where physicists are trying to formulate a unified theory of everything). I'm thinking of the sort of problems thrown up by quantum mechanics concerning locality and indeterminacy. But by and large natural scientists in the mature scientific disciplines can get by without asking themselves distinctively philosophical questions. One influential metaphor: science is like a superstructure; scientists build the structure up; philosophers explore the foundations. If you are working on the upper stories, you can leave concern with the foundations to others.

In any case, the mature sciences—I'm thinking of physics and chemistry—were not always mature. And in the early days it was hardly possible even to draw a distinction between what belongs to the natural science as such and what belongs to its philosophical foundations. In the early days, I suppose one can say, there are only foundations to work on. It is no coincidence that physics was once called natural philosophy. Newton's great *Principia Mathematica* carried a subtitle to the effect that it was a work in natural philosophy. And certainly it is easy to find in Newton's writings discussions (for example about the nature of color) that are is every sense philosophical. And by the same token, if we look at the writings of philosophers around that same time, we see that they are filled with what could only be characterized as natural science.

The point I'm leading up to should be obvious. The study of cognition and consciousness, whether in psychology or in the neurosciences, is very much an immature science. If you open a contemporary textbook such as Kandel, Schwartz, and Jessell's *Essentials of Neural Science and Behavior*, you will encounter a good deal of writing that could only be described as philosophical. For example, Kandel and his colleagues argue that "the appearance of our perceptions as direct and precise images of the world is an illusion." When it comes to an immature science such as a science of consciousness, one can hardly even differentiate the work of the philosopher from that of the scientist. When it comes to understanding consciousness, science and philosophy are on a par. Philosophy and science need to work together if there is to be progress.

And the exciting thing is that they are now working together in the field of the study of the mind. There is a tremendous flurry of collaboration between philosophers and cognitive scientists. And this is a good thing. It is a productive relationship, although in many ways it is a fraught one. Philosophers have cultivated a style of thought which is strange and even confusing to outsiders. For example, philosophers like to reason dialectically. This goes back to the beginning in the work of Socrates. What I mean is, philosophers like to work their way to a good position by first trying out bad positions. Philosophers canvas alternatives and achieve positive results through processes of elimination. At least this is very often the case. Scientists, for their part, have an intellectual style that strikes most philosophers as unnatural. I have in mind thinking experimentally. For scientists, something is only a worthwhile idea once you come up with an experiment to investigate it further.

In fact, the tension between philosophy and science is much deeper than mere styles of thinking. Early analytic philosophy announced as its very program the separation of matters of fact from matters having to do with meaning, language, and logic. In the *Tractatus*, Wittgenstein propounded that philosophy is either above or below the sciences, it's not at the same level; it is not one of the sciences. Sciences make statements that are true or false; philosophers analyze the conditions on the possibility of making statements. Philosophers are interested in the bounds of sense, not in this or that domain of inquiry. These ideas—ideas we find not only in the early analytic philosophers, but also in late 19th century French Posivitism and also in the work of Neo-Kantians— are an important philosophical legacy. Philosophy in the analytic tradition likes to pretend to a certain pro-science attitude. Certainly, analytic philosophers endorse the enlightenment values of rationality and inquiry. But I think you find a much closer alliance between working scientists and philosophers working in the Phenomenological tradition, especially in France. For example it is only in the last few years that we see anything like the kind of knowledgeable engagement with neuroscience on the part of philosophers that was in evidence in Merleau-Ponty's *The Phenomenology of Perception* (first published in 1945). One can see the influence of Merleau-Ponty's work, moreover, in the work of neuroscientists in France today (and elsewhere in Europe).

Since the 1960s things have gotten much worse, in large part because of oppositions and splits within philosophy. I won't here go into the complex interaction between British and American philosophers, on one side, French and German philosophers on another, and natural science on a third side. Critically, this recent history has meant that the coming together of scientists and philosophers as they have in the last few years in the cognitive sciences has the air of something new, when really, it's a kind of the return to the way things would have been if not for the intervening schisms.

Is a science of consciousness possible?

If by a science of consciousness you have in mind a discipline producing the kind of knowledge we enjoy in physics, that is, employing the kinds of reductive, mathematical styles of thought we find in physics, then I think the answer to this question is no. But if you mean instead: will it one day be possible to understand consciousness, that is to say, to make sense of it as a natural phenomenon, one that belongs to our biological nature, then I think the answer is: of course there will be a science of consciousness! But a science of consciousness will not look any more like physics than evolutionary biology does.

There will not be a *neuro*science of consciousness, if this is taken to mean an explanation of consciousness exhaustively in neurological terms. Consciousness, as I have said already, is not something that happens inside us—not inside our brains, or anywhere else. The brain and nervous system are necessary for consciousness, but not sufficient. Here again it may be useful to make a comparison with the problem of life. In one sense, we understand the molecular, chemical nature of life. We understand how the combination of the right chemical building blocks constitutes the protein building blocks of life. But in another sense we do not understand life in molecular or chemical terms. And the proof of this is straightforward. Not only are we unable to produce life from the combination of inorganic chemicals in a test tube, but we are barely able to understand why this is so. We are right to believe that our biological life depends on what goes on in our bodies, and, in particular, that it depends on our biochemistry, on the way we are put together. But at the same time, our life is not itself merely a chemical process. Life takes place where the interior physical system is situated dynamically in relation to the outer environment.

We know how life begets life, but we don't know how mere chemicals come to life. I entirely reject the appeal to divine intervention or the supernatural in this stage of the discussion, just as I reject the appeal to an immaterial soul in the attempt to explain consciousness. There's a good reason why we can't explain consciousness in terms of what is going on in the brain alone, and also why we can't explain life in terms of inorganic chemistry: consciousness doesn't happen in the brain, and life is not a chemical reaction. To understand consciousness, and to understand life, we need to look at organisms in their environmental situation.

So, can there be a science of consciousness? Yes. Just as there can be a biology, a science of life. We're making progress towards these goals.

What are the most important open problems in contemporary philosophy of mind? What are the most promising prospects?

I have answered this already. The central problem for the philosophy of mind, as I understand it, is to develop a biological theory of our active lives. Let us call such a theory a biological theory of access. Such a theory will explain how the world shows up for the conscious mind.

15
Hilary Putnam

Cogan University Professor Emeritus in the Department of Philosophy

Harvard University, USA

Why were you initially drawn to philosophy of mind?

In the late 1950's, an argument for dualism known as the "grain argument"[1] was advanced in the philosophy of mind. (The objection—that it is 'unintelligible' to suppose that qualities whose 'grains' are as different as those of neural properties and phenomenal properties are, in reality, identical—is an early ancestor of both Jackson's 'knowledge argument' and Tom Nagel's 'what it's like to be a bat' argument.) Although my "Minds and Machines" was later seen as important—by myself as well as by others—primarily because it suggested the functionalist account of mental states, the reason I wrote it was to argue that *if the grain argument is right, it is available to a robot as well*, and hence the form of 'dualism' it is supposed to establish could not be a threat to materialism. Basically, I argued that the underlying 'dualism' is the 'dualism' of *knowing about a psychological property via a description* and *'knowing' about it by exemplifying it oneself*, and that this is an inevitable dualism, even for machines. (I still think this argument is sound, by the way.)

Having dipped my toe in the water of philosophy of mind by writing that paper, I was led to go on and reflect further on functionalism, on the synthetic identity of properties, and related topics. Another source of my interest in philosophy of mind was a revulsion against behaviorism, particularly Norman Malcolm's pseudo-Wittgensteinian version thereof, which attracted a lot of attention at the time.

---

[1] A good (later) account is Michael Green, "The Grain Objection," *Philosophy of Science*, 46 (1979), pp. 559-589.

What do you consider your most important contribution to the field?

Proposing functionalism. Although I am no longer a *computer-program* functionalist, the idea that *our mental states are best conceived of as ways of functioning and exercises of those ways* still seems right to me. Although not in the 'internalist' (and reductionist) sense that that went with the model of those states as "the brain's software".

The reasons I gave up that model are three: 1) it cannot be the case that there is a one-one mapping of such mental attributes as *believing something, hoping for something, desiring something*, etc., onto precise kinds of software, as functionalism hoped. If such states are 'realizable' in software at all, they are so in infinitely many different ways. We might call this *the computational plasticity* of mental states; 2) According to the 'externalist theory of reference' I developed in "Is Semantics Possible" and "The Meaning of 'Meaning'", reference and meaning are not simply in our heads; meaning and reference are 'transactional', that is, they depend on both the organism and the environment, and they cannot be simply be read off from our brains without looking at the kinds of interactions that take place between the brain, the rest of the organism, and the environment; if they are functional states in some sense (as I believe they are) they are functional states with 'long arms', that is they are *environment-involving* ways of functioning; 3) as a corollary of 1) and 2), the crucial notion of *sameness of content* between thoughts cannot be simply a matter of sameness of 'program'.

In any case, the question whether our minds/brains are best thought of as computers is important and exciting. Here, happily, is an area in which philosophers and scientists do talk to each other and recognize the profit in doing so. Also, although I now think that the computer-program functionalism I proposed was too simple, it still seems to me an excellent entering wedge into the philosophy of mind in our post-computer age.

What is the proper role of philosophy in relation to psychology, artificial intelligence, and the neurosciences?

To be a gadfly, of course.

Seriously, I learned from my teacher, Hans Reichenbach, that the most exciting task of philosophy of science is to combine clarification of the concepts of science with reflection on the implications of scientific theories, both proposed theories and theories that are not considered to be confirmed, on great metaphysical issues. That seems to me to be the role whether the science in question is physics or psychology or artificial intelligence or neuroscience.

Is a science of consciousness possible?

I can't answer this question with a simple 'yes' or 'no'. If the presupposition is that consciousness is a 'mystery', I don't agree. I am still a 'functionalist' in the wide sense that I think that having a functional organization of the kind humans typically have or sufficiently similar to what humans typically have (of course that is really a 'family resemblance' affair) is all there is to having human consciousness (and analogously for chimpanzee consciousness, pussy-cat consciousness, etc.). The familiar objections (e.g. the 'knowledge argument', the 'zombie' argument, Kripke's argument in *Naming and Necessity*) fail to convince me. But, of course, there is a great deal to be *learned* about what sort of (environment-involving) functional organization that is. For me, that is the real 'problem of consciousness'.

What are the most important open problems in contemporary philosophy of mind? What are the most promising prospects?

I can only say that the problem I find most *interesting* is the problem of perception. But everyone has his own pet problem. And there is an enormous amount of work to be done no matter what problem one finds interesting or what approach one favors.

Hilla Jacobson of Ben Gurion University and I are currently working on a monograph on perception. Here is a sketch of our approach, which we call 'transactionalism'.

First, by way of background, the current approaches that Jacobson and I take most seriously are *intentionalism* (Dretske, Tye, and many others), *disjunctivism* (McDowell, Martin, and a number of others), and *phenomenism* (Ned Block, in particular). Each of these approaches we see as having insights and oversights, and we believe our approach will preserve the insights and avoid the oversights. One great advance in the discussion, in our opinion, is that none of the philosophers just mentioned thinks of perceptual experiences as objects in an 'inner theater' that we 'observe' with the aid of an inner perceptual capacity called 'introspection'. As Reichenbach long ago argued (*Experience and Prediction*, 1938), our perceptual experiences are states that we have, not objects that we observe; and as he further argued[2] our awareness of our perceptual experiences does not issue in 'incorrigible' reports. These points are now widely accepted, although Reichenbach's anticipation of them seems to have been forgotten.

But there are further issues about which there continues to be serious disagreement. One concerns the question whether perceptual experiences and their 'relatives' (illusions, hallucinations, etc.) are just "flat psychological surface"[3], with no intrinsic connection to anything in the environment. This is Ned Block's picture (the picture of these experiences as "mental paint"). We, along with both the disjunctivists and the intentionalists, hold that such a description, in addition to being inadequate to the phenomenology of such experiences, gives too much away to skepticism of both the Cartesian and the Kantian varieties.[4] In addition, intentionalists and disjunctivists disagree about whether there is a 'highest common factor' present in veridical perceptions and hallucinations/illusions. Both intentionalist and disjunctivists defend 'naïve realism', however, which they identify (mistakenly, in our view) with the idea that the description of the perceived public property also exhausts the qualitative character ('phenomenal character') of the experience, while Block argues [correctly in our view] that it does not).

Let me explain our criticism of the approaches just mentioned in a little more detail:

(1) *Disjunctivism.*

Like Intentionalism, which I shall describe next, Disjunctivism, a position introduced by J.M. Hinton in a 1967 article in *Mind* titled "Visual Experiences", has the ambition of reviving and reinterpreting naïve realism, that is the view that the objects of veridical perception are the objects we see in our environment (in the

---

[2] Hans Reichenbach, "Are Phenomenal Reports Absolutely Certain", *The Philosophical Review* 61(2) (1952), pp. 147-159. See also "Reichenbach and the Myth of the Given", in my *Words and Life* (Harvard. 1994), pp. 115-130.

[3] William James, "The Tigers in India", collected in his *The Meaning of Truth*, describes conceptual representations in this way, although he had a "natural realist" view with respect to *perceptual* experiences.

[4] On the difference between Cartesian and Kantian skepticism, see James Conant, "Varieties of Skepticism", in Denis McManus (ed.), *Wittgenstein and Skepticism* (Routledge, 2004).

case of visual perception), and not our own sense data. Nowadays, this is hardly controversial. Even Ned Block, while defending 'qualia', explicitly attacks the 'inner arena' picture of our relation to those qualia. We need to dig deeper to expose the differences.

Not only do disjunctivists and intentionalists hold that veridical perception extends all the way to the environment itself, but they hold that the qualities we perceive are simply the qualities of the objects we see (I confine attention to visual perception, which is the most discussed case). That is why I said before that "Both intentionalist and disjunctivists defend naïve realism, however, which they identify (mistakenly, in our view) with the idea that the description of the perceived public qualities of the object we see (in the case of a veridical visual experience) exhaust the qualitative character ('phenomenal character') of the experience." This indeed distinguishes them from Ned Block, the "phenomenist", who argues that different perceivers not only may have but in fact do have quite different 'qualia' when they look at, say, a green picket fence, and that none of these 'qualia' can be identified with *the* color of the picket fence. But it does not distinguish intentionalists from disjunctivists. Also, since for reasons I shall describe, Hilla Jacobson and I agree with Block on the psychological facts, though not with his conception of visual experiences as "mental paint", and yet we consider ourselves too to be defending (and interpreting) 'naïve realism', it is clear that it isn't enough to say "I am a naïve realist in the philosophy of perception". One has to say *how* one proposes to be a 'naïve realist'.

What makes disjunctivism the most radical of the 'naïve realist' positions is the denial that veridical experiences and illusions (even the perfect hallucination supposed to be produced by Nozick's famous "experience machine") *have anything in common.* Of course, if one were plugged into the experience machine, one wouldn't be able to tell that I was not experiencing real colors, a real picket fence, or whatever. But, according to Hinton and his followers (John McDowell, Mike Martin) that is not because the hallucination and the veridical experience have a 'highest common factor'. According to Hinton's classic paper, even referring to both the veridical perception of an object and the corresponding hallucination as 'experiences' is misleading!

(2) *Intentionalism.* According to intentionalism, perceptual experiences have *representational content.* (Most intentionalists hold that this is not the same as 'conceptual content', but this is an epicycle I shall not enter.) They are thus, *not* flat 'mental paint';

they tell us how the environment is (or at least claim to do that, when they deceive us). Thus the perfect hallucination of the green picket fence and the veridical perception of the same *do* have a 'highest common factor' according to intentionalists. However, as already said, intentionalists and disjunctivists both hold that *the description of the perceived public qualities of the object we see (in the case of a veridical visual experience) exhaust the qualitative character ('phenomenal character') of the experience.*

Most, if not all, of the intentionalists we know of, beginning with Dretske, hold that the content of a mental representation is the 'information' it carries in something like Shannon's sense of 'information'. Call this familiar version of intentionalism 'reductive intentionalism'. In principle, there is room for another version of intentionalism, a 'liberal naturalist' version, which takes intentionality to be irreducible without 'transcendentalizing' it. Thus a liberal naturalist could agree that the intentionality of both words and perceptual experiences is something that can be scientifically as well as philosophically studied, something that depends on causal connections and on what Ruth Millikan calls "normal biological functioning", something that many different sciences can contribute to our understanding of as well as many sort of conceptual inquiries, while *denying* that one can reduce the intentional to the non-intentional. Indeed, with this much of a 'non-reductive intentionalist position' Hilla Jacobson and I would agree.

What makes reductive intentionalism tremendously implausible is the difficulty in seeing what it means to say that 'information', in, say, Dretske's sense (which is simply a matter of what a mental representation covaries with in the subject's environment) can be the same thing as 'phenomenal quality'.

This is not the difficulty that leads disjunctivists to reject intentionalism, however. According to disjunctivists, to concede that there is a highest common factor in the case of the hallucination and the correspond veridical experience is to surrender to the skeptic. They claim that only by denying that there is *any* highest common factor can we preserve the idea that veridical experiences *justify* and do not simply 'trigger' our beliefs about them. In our view, this is a mistake. No philosophy of perception can claim to be 'the only' way to answer the skeptic—not even if we agree that what we want is more than a 'reliabilist' account of justification.

(3) *Phenomenism.* Block, who is the principle representative of this position, rejects the 'inner arena' picture—that is, the 'qualia' he posits are not objects that we 'observe' (although he does not go

into sufficient detail about his alternative picture, in my view)—but otherwise his account resembles a classical sense-datum story. We are able to attend to qualia on his account, and they are inside our brains, and non-representational. In our view, the fact that a green object may look different to different subjects no more shows that the *capacity to have that look* is not a property of the object seen (say, the picket fence), than does the fact that the picket fence has a different look in bright sunlight and when a cloud passes over the sun. Looks, in my view, are *capacities that objects have* (and realizations of those capacities), not properties of a supposed 'mental paint'.

(4) *Transactionalism*. Last but not least, let me very briefly sketch the alternative Hilla Jacobson and I favor.

As already mentioned, one problem that we see with both disjunctivism and intentionalism has to do with in the claim that the description of the perceived public qualities of the object we see (in the case of a veridical visual experience) exhaust the phenomenal character of the experience. *There are many counterexamples to this claim.* Here are three (for simplicity of exposition I confine attention to visual experiences, but similar points apply to the other sensory modalities):

(i) The picket fence has a different look to someone who has astigmatism and to someone with 'normal' vision.

(ii) In the case of vision: when they look at a white surface, most observers will observe a slightly different look when they view the surface with the left eye closed and when they view it with the right eye closed. (One look is 'grayer'.) This is not explained by appealing to parallax: the explanation is that there are slight but significant differences between the macular areas of the two eyes. (Try it yourself.)

(iii) The data cited by Block, Hardin, and others, showing that a given shade of green looks 'pure green' to some observers and 'yellow green' to others, and that there are reasons to think that neither observer misperceives the shade in question.

One fact that this illustrates is that both disjunctivists and intentionalists are still in the grip of the 'spectator' view of perception that Dewey, Gibson, and others have criticized; they fail to see the extent to which what we perceive depends on a *transaction* between ourselves and the environment, and hence fail to see that the properties we perceive depend on our nature as well as the nature of the environment. (Which is why we call them 'transactional properties'). Once this is recognized, there is room for an account which preserves what is right in talk of the 'transparency' of perceptual experience—namely, the idea that in a successful perception we experience properties of the picket fence (or whatever), and not properties of our own minds or brains, while leaving room for recognition of subjective as well as objective factors in perception.

A second problem has to do with what both disjunctivists and intentionalists say about hallucinations and illusions. Since this is a huge topic, I will confine attention to just the case of what might be called 'philosophical hallucinations', that is, the sort of hallucination imagined by myself when I imagined "brains in a vat" and by Nozick when he imagined an "experience machine".

Disjunctivists simply deny that there is such a thing as a 'phenomenal quality' or even a common 'intentional content' common to the hallucination and the corresponding veridical experience, while intentionalists say that both exist (and are in fact identical), and the phenomenal quality is simply the 'information' that reaches the brain.

My own view is that (environment-involving) 'liberal functionalism' is the right way to think about this. A hallucination, *functionally* characterized, is a state in which it appears to the subject that the subject is perceiving, say, a green picket fence. Thus hallucinating a green picket fence is not *directly* a world-involving state (there doesn't have to be a picket fence, or indeed anything at all the subject is seeing), but its functional characterization refers to such a state ('perceiving a green picket fence'). Since I still believe that Commander Data and I could both have the same mental states (a corollary of my original version of functionalism that I still subscribe to), it is not the case that hallucinating is a *neurologically* characterized brain state; it is, rather, a *functionally* characterized state of the organism.[5] It is part of this 'functionalist' view that ('philosophical') hallucinations do have content (something radical disjunctivists deny); intentionalists are right in seeing the hallucination as involving the organism's being misinformed about the environment. The 'tricky' question is the status of the hallucinated objects and qualities.

Quite simply, what I think is that the hallucinated white picket

---

[5] David Lewis's version of functionalism makes it a necessary truth that the famous android "Commander Data" and I cannot have the same sensations, although the higher level property of "being sensations" is one some of our mental states have in common; but Lewis offers no *psychological* arguments at all to justify building this into his version of functionalism.

fence has the ontological status of a *fictional entity*. (What is that status? Pick your favorite story about such entities as Hamlet!)[6] I don't only mean to say that perception involves an intentional content which is similar to a proposition expressed by a sentence with an empty name; rather I want to point to the sense in which hallucinations are similar to intentional states that concern specifically *fiction*. When I get engaged with the fiction, Hamlet, who isn't real, *seems real* to me. He seems to be presented to my mind in a way in which the king of France surely isn't, if it's just the intentional object of my reading Russell's famous sentence. Likewise, in a perfect hallucination, the orangish picket fence, which isn't real seems real to me. Hamlet and the picket fence seem to me real; it isn't only that the proposition that they exist, or some specific predicative proposition about them, seem to me to be true.

How does this compare with intentionalism? Intentionalism treats all experiences, veridical and non-veridical alike, as, in effect, *representations*. According to intentionalists, the difference between a veridical experience and a non-veridical one is like the difference between a true newspaper article and a false one. In contrast, Hilla Jacobson and I think of veridical experiences as *externalistically* characterized states of the organism, states that essentially involve the object perceived. Hallucinations do not involve an object perceived, they do, indeed, only *represent* an object as perceived, but that is the case because they are, so to speak, defective states; they are malfunctions. Veridical perceptions *involve* the object, they don't merely 'represent' it. Thus even if intentionalists were to agree that the status of the hallucinated picket fence is similar to the status of a fictional entity, their account of the nature of veridical perceptual experiences would still be very different from mine.

How does transactionalism compare with disjunctivism? In agreeing that the qualities that are presented in a veridical perceptual experience of the picket fence are real (albeit 'transactional') properties of the *fence* while, at the same time, denying that the 'qualities' that are seemingly presented in a hallucination are properties of any real object, it goes a long way towards disjunctivism. I think, in fact, it preserves what is right in disjunctivism.

---

[6] Of course real entities can have fictional counterparts; Napoleon was a real person, and is also a character in *War and Peace*. Similarly it is possible to have a hallucination about a real person or thing.

I shall close by briefly considering two objections that are sure to occur to my readers:

First, it may seem that fictional characters are too 'abstract' to be experientially presented, too abstract to even *seem* 'real'. In part this objection underestimates the extent to which an imaginative person can experience a fictional scenario as 'real'; in my own case, there are portions of *The Wind in the Willow* that I read when I was about ten years old which I could swear that I *saw*. But in any case, the degree to which a fiction seems 'real' depends on the mode of presentation of that fiction, and hallucination is obviously a functionally different mode of presentation than, say, reading a novel.

Second, and sharpening the above objection, it might be argued that while indeed a fictional character can seem fully real if the fiction is acted on the stage, the 'reality' belongs to the actors and the scenery. So, this line of thought continues, there have to be 'actors' and 'scenery' in the case of a hallucination, and what could they be but our brain states?

Well, if you think it is a priori that a functionally identical but physically differently realized person (e.g., Commander Data) couldn't have the same experiences you do, you may find yourself forced back to the idea that what you experience is your own brain states (in all cases? or only in the case of hallucinations?). Not only does it make it difficult to see how our experiences can justify beliefs about the external world (one of the insights of McDowell's *Mind and World*), but it makes the sort of functionalism that I favor a priori false, which makes it extremely dubious, in my view. On the other hand, if what you claim is that what we experience (in the case of an hallucination) is a *functionally characterized state of our own brains*, then I would say that this view is compatible with my account IF (but again that's a big 'if') the right account of fictional entities is that they are functionally characterized states of the organism. But I will not decide here whether that's the right account of fictional entities.

16
David Rosenthal

Professor of Philosophy

Coordinator, Interdisciplinary Concentration in Cognitive Science

City University of New York Graduate Center, USA

Why were you initially drawn to philosophy of mind?

In the summer of 1956 a half-year correspondence began between Roderick Chisholm and Wilfrid Sellars, prompted by Sellars' having sent to Chisholm page proofs of his forthcoming "Empiricism and the Philosophy of Mind." In their letters, Chisholm and Sellars debated various issues about how to understand the intentionality of mental states. Their principle dispute was about whether, as Sellars argued in his article, one can understand and explain the intentionality of thoughts by appeal to the independently understood intentionality of speech.

Sellars' still seminal, monograph-length "Empiricism and the Philosophy of Mind" appeared that year in the first volume of *Minnesota Studies in the Philosophy of Science*.[1] A couple of years later the Chisholm-Sellars correspondence itself appeared in the second Minnesota Studies volume,[2] along with a reprinting

---

[1] Wilfrid Sellars, "Empiricism and the Philosophy of Mind," *Minnesota Studies in the Philosophy of Science, volume I: The Foundations of Science and the Concepts of Psychology and Psychoanalysis*, edited by Herbert Feigl and Michael Scriven, Minneapolis: University of Minnesota Press, 1956, 253-329. Reprinted with minor changes in Wilfrid Sellars, *Science, Perception and Reality*, London: Routledge & Regan Paul Ltd., 1963, 127-196, and republished as *Empiricism and the Philosophy of Mind*, with commentary by Robert Brandom and Richard Rorty, Cambridge, Massachusetts: Harvard University Press, 1997, and in Willem deVries and Timm Triplett, *Knowledge, Mind, and the Given*, Indianapolis and Cambridge, Massachusetts: Hackett Publishing Co., 2000, pp. 276-205.

[2] Roderick M. Chisholm, and Wilfrid Sellars, "Intentionality and the Mental," *Minnesota Studies in the Philosophy of Science, volume II: Concepts,*

of Chisholm's important "Sentences about Believing."³ The correspondence immediately provoked an excited, inconclusive, and often perplexed reaction among many in the philosophical community.

A few years later, I was a graduate student at Princeton, where Richard Rorty had come to be deeply influenced by Sellars' thinking on these and many other issues. I became intrigued by the questions posed in the correspondence, and undertook a dissertation under Rorty's direction to try to sort those out various issues about intentionality, and see where the truth lay. In addition to having Rorty's penetrating guidance, I was very fortunate that Sellars visited Princeton in the spring of 1965. I met with him virtually every Tuesday afternoon for what turned into an informal tutorial, which led the following semester to my own, subsequently published correspondence with Sellars about those questions.⁴

Sellars argues in "Empiricism and the Philosophy of Mind" that we can understand intentional mental states as folk-theoretical posits, originally invoked to explain the occurrence of speech acts as well as rational behavior unaccompanied by speech. Such states are posited as having properties analogous to the semantic and illocutionary properties of speech acts, and those posited properties are the intentional content and mental attitudes of intentional states. After a time, individuals come to have subjectively unmediated first-person access to many of these posited intentional states.

Chisholm had argued that we cannot understand the relevant properties of speech acts except by seeing the speech acts as caused by intentional states. I argued that Chisholm's argument seemed compelling only because the folk theory Sellars described had come to be deeply entrenched in our commonsense ways of thinking about speech and thought.

Following Sellars, I argued that since we can in fact understand others' speech acts and we plainly have no access to their thoughts

---

Theories, and the Mind-Body Problem, ed. Herbert Feigl, Michael Scriven, and Grover Maxwell, Minneapolis: University of Minnesota Press, 1958, pp. 507-539.

³Roderick M. Chisholm, "Sentences about Believing," *Proceedings of the Aristotelian Society*, LVI (1955-56): 124-148.

⁴"The Rosenthal-Sellars Correspondence on Intentionality," *Intentionality, Mind, and Language*, ed. Ausonio Marras, Urbana: University of Illinois Press, 1972, pp. 461-503. Also online at: http://www.ditext.com/sellars/rsc.html

independent of their behavior, access to thoughts cannot be necessary to understand others' speech acts. So it must be possible to understand the semantic properties of speech acts independent of understanding the intentional properties of thinking.

I had originally imagined that I might specialize in some area of the history of philosophy, ancient or early modern, or perhaps in social and legal philosophy. But I became so intrigued by these issues about intentionality, mind, and language to let them go. And it came to seem to me, as it does still, that these issues are among here most fundamental in philosophy, and that getting straight about them would have a big payoff in understanding many other issues.

What do you consider your most important contribution to the field?

The work I've done in philosophy that's most widely discussed has to do with the higher-order-thought theory of the consciousness of mental states that I articulated first in the early '80s and have expanded on and developed since.[5]

After graduate school, I wanted a change from the issues of my dissertation, and turned to questions about mind-body materialism, which were discussed very heatedly in the '60s and '70s. The main problem for mind-body materialism was widely thought to be consciousness, by which people had in mind the consciousness of qualitative mental states. How could a materialist view do justice to what it's like for one to be in a qualitative mental state?

It seemed that, to be convincing, an answer to this question would need to rely on more than just good arguments in defense of materialism. One would need in addition to provide a satisfactory explanation of consciousness, and in particular of qualitative consciousness. I did not think that the eliminativist program of Rorty, Paul Feyerabend, and Paul Churchland[6] was acceptable, and at the end of an article arguing as much I put forth in outline a theory of consciousness.[7] On that theory, mental states, includ-

---

[5] See, e.g., *Consciousness and Mind*, Oxford: Clarendon Press, 2005.

[6] E.g., Rorty, "Mind-Body Identity, Privacy, and Categories," *The Review of Metaphysics* XIX, 1 (September 1965): 24-54; Feyerabend, "Materialism the Mind-Body Problem," *The Review of Metaphysics* XVII, 1 (September 1963): 49-66; and Churchland, *Scientific Realism and the Plasticity of Mind*, Cambridge: Cambridge University Press, 1979.

[7] Keeping Matter in Mind," *Midwest Studies in Philosophy*, V (1980): 295-

ing qualitative states, are never intrinsically conscious; so mental states, again including qualitative states, often occur without being conscious. The conscious states differ from those that are not conscious because of the occurrence in the conscious cases of some factor extrinsic to the state itself.

It's clear that when a mental state is conscious, the individual who is in that state is in some way aware of the state. If one is in some mental state but wholly unaware of being in it, that state does not count as being conscious, on any intuitive, commonsense understanding of consciousness. So the extrinsic factor that differentiates conscious from nonconscious mental states must be some kind of awareness of those states that are conscious. So the important thing would be to see what kind of awareness is operative here.

David Armstrong had argued, following Locke and many others, that the awareness is perceptual in nature.[8] But it seemed to me that no such higher-order perceptual awareness actually occurs. For one thing, there are no higher-order mental qualities, and no awareness will count as being perceptual if it altogether lacks such qualities. The only alternative is that we are aware of our conscious states by having higher-order thoughts (HOTs) about those states. A HOT is simply a thought to the effect to one is in a particular mental state.

For the target state to be conscious, one's awareness of it must seem to arise spontaneously and without any mediation. This will be so if it seems subjectively that there is no inference or self-observation that leads to one's awareness of the target, that is, if one is aware of no such inference or self-observation. The HOT theory can easily provide for this. For one thing, the HOTs are seldom themselves conscious, since there will seldom be third-order thoughts about them. Because HOTs are seldom subjectively available, it won't seem subjectively as though the awareness of mental states that results from such HOTs is mediated. Positing HOTs can thus explain how we are aware of those of our mental states that are conscious.

322.

[8] D. M. Armstrong, *A Materialist Theory of the Mind*, New York: Humanities Press, 1968; second revised edition, London: Routledge & Kegan Paul, 1993; "Is Introspective Knowledge Incorrigible?", *The Philosophical Review* LXXII, 4 (October 1963): 417-432. See John Locke, *An Essay Concerning Human Understanding*, ed. Peter H. Nidditch, Oxford: Clarendon Press, 1975/1700, e.g., p. 105 (II, i, 4).

Positing such HOTs to explain how conscious states differ from mental states that are not conscious has turned out to have many theoretical benefits, allowing informative explanations of things that it's unlikely any other theory can handle. For example, HOTs allow informative explanations of why a state's being conscious coincides with its being noninferentially reportable, why thoughts are always conscious when they're expressed verbally though not when they're expressed by nonverbal behavior, and why our conscious mental lives appear subjectively to be unified.[9]

The HOT theory fits nicely with Sellars' account of the connection sketched earlier between the intentionality of thought and that of speech. Sellars argued that we could see mythical ancestors as having posited inner states with intentional properties to explain verbal and nonverbal behavior. The ancestors that deployed that theoretical structure would in time have come, he urged, to have first-person access to some of their intentional states. But as students of Sellars have noted, he glides rather quickly past the question of how it is that this first-person access might come about.[10]

The HOT hypothesis provides an informative answer. On Sellars' account, our mythical ancestors posit intentional states to explain their own speech acts as well as those of others. Sellars usually presents this positing as an early stage for human thinking about mind in general. But he also occasionally notes that we can understand such positing also as an early stage in the development of each individual.[11] With practice, each person will become adept and habituated to applying to oneself the folk theory that posits intentional states.

As with the application of any folk theory, in time this positing of intentional states will become relatively automatic. At that point. one's simply being disposed to say something will by itself dispose one to ascribe to oneself a internal state that has intentional properties that correspond to the speech act's semantic properties. This disposition to ascribe an intentional state to

---

[9] See *Consciousness and Mind*, chs. 2, 10-11, and 13, respectively.

[10] All Sellars says is: "And it now turns out–need it have?–that [one] can be trained to give reasonably reliable self-descriptions, using the language of the theory, without having to observe his overt behavior" ("Empiricism and the Philosophy of Mind," §59).

[11] Sellars, "The Structure of Knowledge, Lecture II: Minds," in *Action, Knowledge, and Reality: Critical Studies in Honor of Wilfrid Sellars*, ed. Hector-Neri Castañeda, Indianapolis: Bobbs-Merrill, 1975, pp. 316-331, II.

oneself will result in a thought to the effect that one is in that very state. Because one comes to have a HOT that one is in that state, the state itself comes to be conscious, and one thereby has first-order access to it. The HOT hypothesis helps sustain Sellars' theory of the nature and origin of our folk understanding of intentionality.

It's widely acknowledged that the most difficult aspect of consciousness is the consciousness of qualitative mental states, which has been the focus of much discussion in connection with mind-body materialism. And many have thought that, however well the HOT theory may handle the consciousness of intentional states, it cannot handle qualitative consciousness, that is, there being something it's like for one to be in qualitative states. Qualitative consciousness may indeed be intractable to explanation if one regards qualitative states as essentially conscious, so that such states cannot occur without being conscious. But qualitative states do often occur without being conscious, as in subliminal perceiving.

So being conscious cannot be essential to a state's being qualitative. And even when qualitative states are conscious, their being conscious, which they have in common, is distinct from the qualitative character, which differs from one state to the next. So in addition to a theory of what it is for mental states to be conscious, we also need an independent theory of what it is for mental states to have qualitative character.

Unlike Sellars' view of intentionality, which fits well with an informative theory of consciousness, his view about qualitative mental states makes it more difficult to explain consciousness. For one thing, Sellars held that qualitative states are necessarily conscious, which makes for a mystery about how such necessarily conscious states could fit within the natural order. In the face of that apparent mystery, therefore, Sellars seeks to sustain mind-body materialism by holding that the commonsense conscious qualities we think of our mental states as having can somehow be relocated in a new guise within an ultimate materialist framework.

But Sellars' actual account of qualitative mental properties can be detached from his insistence that mental qualities cannot occur without being conscious. And once we drop the view that mental qualities always occur consciously, Sellars' account of mental qualities yields, with some adjustment, an informative theory of mental qualities independent of consciousness.

As Sellars observed, our folk descriptions of the mental qualities of perceptual states appeal to the similarities and differences that hold among those qualities. And we can get a handle on the similarities and differences that hold among mental qualities that occur in perceiving by noting that they are parallel to the similarities and difference that hold among the physical properties we perceive. Just as we can understand the intentional content of thinking in terms of the semantic properties of speech, so we can understand the mental qualities of perceiving in terms of the perceptible properties of physical objects.

And that insight about mental qualities can, moreover, be readily detached from claims about the consciousness of qualitative states. Mental qualities are the properties of perceptual states in virtue of which we discriminate perceptible properties, whether such discriminating occurs occurs consciously or not. So we have in Sellars' insight about mental qualities the making of an informative theory of qualitative character, a theory that can fruitfully combine with an independent theory of consciousness.

On this theory of mental qualities, we individuate each mental quality by reference to its position in a quality space distinctive of the perceptual modality in question. And that quality space is homomorphic to the quality space that defines the physical properties discriminable by that modality. Since perception can discriminate perceptible properties even when the relevant perceptual states fail to be conscious, the resulting theory of mental qualities is independent of consciousness.[12]

This homomorphism theory of the mental qualities fits well with the HOT theory. On the HOT theory, a state is conscious if one has a thought to the effect that one is in the state in question. So when a qualitative state is conscious, the HOT in virtue of which it's conscious describes the mental quality of its target in terms of that quality's position in the relevant quality space. This enables the combined theories to deal effectively with a number of traditional issues, such as the alleged conceivability of inverted or absent qualities, and also to fit comfortably with many empirical findings, such as masked priming, confabulatory consciousness, and blindsight (see §IV).

---

[12] See *Consciousness and Mind*, chs. 5-7.

What is the proper role of philosophy in relation to psychology, artificial intelligence, and the neurosciences?

Every discipline seeks to establish boundaries that are reasonably well recognized, based on features that help fix those boundaries. But the accumulation of knowledge and development of theory in the last century or so has made such boundaries ever more difficult to draw. Mathematics now gets input from physics, and there are increasing disciplines that build bridges between adjacent sciences, such as physics, chemistry, and biology.

A traditional way to delimit philosophy has been to urge that philosophy, like logic and mathematics, deals with truths that hold independently of any empirical input. But as W. V. Quine, Sellars[13], and others have forcefully driven home, this tradition is indefensible. It is very likely impossible to isolate either a purely conceptual or a purely empirical aspect of any truths whatever.

Work in philosophy of mind does somehow seem different from research in experimental psychology, cognitive neuropsychology, and related areas of scientific investigation. But if we follow Quine and Sellars in rejecting the idea that some sentences are true come what may, we can't account for that apparent difference by saying that philosophy of mind deals with pure conceptual analysis or metaphysically necessary truths.[14] And philosophy of mind must in any case respect findings in experimental psychology and cognitive neuropsychology, and is at least to that extent continuous with those fields.

Many follow Quine's suggestion that philosophical work involves the search for truths that are located near the center of our web of belief.[15] Such truths seem to resist revision, but only because rejecting them would prompt us to reject such a large number of other beliefs as well. In contrast, disciplines such as experimental psychology and cognitive neuroscience work to establish truths

---

[13] Quine, "Two Dogmas of Empiricism," in *From a Logical Point of View*, Cambridge, Massachusetts: Harvard University Press, 1980, pp. 20-46; Sellars, "Is There a Synthetic A Priori," in *Science, Perception and Reality*, London: Routledge & Kegan Paul, 1963, pp. 298-320.

[14] For useful doubts about the metaphysical necessity, see Jerry A. Fodor's Eastern Division APA Presidential Address, "What is Universally Quantified and Necessary and A Posteriori and It Flies South in the Winter?", *Proceedings and Addresses of The American Philosophical Association*, 80, 2 (November 2006): 11- 24.

[15] Quine, W. V., and J. S. Ullian, *The Web of Belief*, New York: Random House, 1970.

located nearer the periphery of that web of belief. Because those truths have sparser connections with the rest of the web, their ties to empirical discovery are more salient.

This model does far better at capturing the difference between philosophical investigation and work in adjacent areas than a model that construes philosophy in terms of conceptual analysis. Little in Aristotle's *Metaphysics* or Descartes's *Meditations* or Kant's *Critique of Pure Reason* seems to be intended as conceptual analysis, proper. It's more credible to see these works as theorizing about various topics at a very high level, further removed from immediate empirical input than the sciences. Like philosophy, physics tells us about substance and physical reality and psychology about the nature of mind and knowledge. But theory building in the sciences is relatively tightly connected to empirical input. Philosophy, by contrast, is theorizing at a relatively abstruse, sometimes speculative level. The difference between distinctively philosophical work and work in the sciences is a matter of degree, not of kind.

This way of seeing the difference explains the many fruitful interactions between philosophical and more strictly empirical work on the mind. Philosophy cannot and should not try to dictate to the sciences, about the mind or anything else. But philosophy can suggest and evaluate theoretical contexts within which we can seek to understand the empirical findings of experimental psychology and cognitive neuroscience. Philosophy of mind can help guide the theorizing that occurs in the sciences proper.

Indeed, some psychologists and cognitive neuropsychologists have welcomed theorizing from the philosophy of mind in what seems to be just this spirit. Thus, neuropsychological theorizing by Lawrence Weiskrantz and Edmund T. Rolls[16] and psychological theorizing by Zoltán Dienes and Josef Perner[17] have taken on aspects of the higher-order-thought model. In the opposite direction, Austen Clark has invoked work in psychophysics to develop a powerful

---

[16] Lawrence Weiskrantz, *Consciousness Lost and Found: A Neuropsychological Exploration*, Oxford: Oxford University Press, 1997, pp. 71-76; Edmund T. Rolls, "A Higher Order Syntactic Thought (HOST) Theory of Consciousness," in *Higher-Order Theories of Consciousness*, ed. Rocco J. Gennaro, Amsterdam and Philadelphia: John Benjamins Publishers, 2004, pp. 137-172.

[17] "Executive Control without Conscious Awareness: The Cold Control Theory of Hypnosis," in *Hypnosis and Conscious States: The Cognitive Neuroscience Perspective*, ed. Graham Jamieson, Oxford: New York: Oxford University Press, 2007, pp. 293-314.

theoretical account of mental qualities that addresses and resolves many concerns traditionally found in philosophical writing.[18] And Daniel C. Dennett's powerfully evocative appeals to experimental findings in theorizing about consciousness[19] are a model of how fruitful the interaction can be between philosophy of mind and scientific research.

It is doubtful that philosophy of mind will disappear or merge into those scientific disciplines; relatively speculative, high-level theorizing will continue to be fruitful and interesting. But there is every reason to expect that such productive cross-fertilization will continue to grow.

Is a science of consciousness possible?

The scientific study of consciousness is not only possible; it's actual and under active development.[20] Doubts about the scientific treatment of consciousness stem mainly from seeing qualitative consciousness as accessible only from a first-person point of view. Qualitative consciousness is a matter of what it's like for one to be in a state with qualitative character. And it's tempting to hold that what it's like for an individual can only be known by that individual. If so, my conscious experience of red physical objects might, for all anybody can know, be what it's like for you to experience green objects, and conversely.

There are two compelling reasons to doubt that our knowledge about conscious qualitative character is limited to such first-person access. One reason stems from considerations that pertain to the so-called other-minds problem. In many circumstances, you will know whether you're in pain and I can at most guess. But sometimes there can be no serious doubt about whether you're in pain, even from a third-person point of view. If you suffer great bodily damage and you're writhing and crying out in an agonized way, nobody who sees you can have any serious doubt

---

[18] *A Theory of Sentience*, Oxford: Clarendon Press, 2000.

[19] *Consciousness Explained*, Boston: Little, Brown and Company, 1991; *Kinds of Minds: Toward an Understanding of Consciousness*, New York: Basic Books, 1996; *Sweet Dreams: Philosophical Obstacles to a Science of Consciousness*, Cambridge, Massachusetts: The MIT Press/A Bradford Book, 2005.

[20] For work from two decades ago, see Anthony J. Marcel and Edoardo Bisiach, eds., *Consciousness in Contemporary Science*, Oxford: Clarendon Press, 1988.

about whether you're in pain. Successful pretence may occur with middling pain, but not with excruciating, agonizing pain. I may not know exactly how your pain feels to you, but it's simply silly to suppose you might not be in pain.

So in certain cases at least we have third-person access to others' mental states. The trick in philosophy of mind is to make the occurrence of such third-person access fit theoretically with the acknowledged first-person access we have to many of our own mental states. But just as we should not seek to solve that problem by jettisoning or even minimizing our first-person access, so we mustn't jettison or minimize our third-person access.

We need, then, a theory of qualitative character on which we can explain both first- and third-person access. The combined homomorphism and HOT theories described above are one good way to go. Together they show how we have first-person access, by way of HOTs about our own qualitative states, and third-person access, by the tie mental qualities have to the perceptible properties that the various mental qualities enable us to discriminate. And once we see how we have third- as well as first- person access to conscious qualitative states, reasoned resistance to the scientific treatment of consciousness dissolves.

There is another reason to reject the idea that qualitative consciousness is accessible only from a first-person point of view. Qualitative character occurs when there is something it's like for one to be in a qualitative state. But qualitative character also occurs without being conscious. Indeed, it's here that some of the most striking empirical findings help. There are experimental paradigms in which subjects are unable to report perceptible stimuli, either because the stimulus is so brief or because it is followed so quickly by another, masking stimulus. Since the stimulus is not reportable, it's not registered consciously. But despite this, the stimulus will in many cases have a robust, testable effect on subjects' subsequent mental processing.[21]

Similarly, blindsight is a condition in which damage to primary

---

[21] Anthony J. Marcel, "Conscious and Unconscious Perception: An Approach to the Relations between Phenomenal Experience and Perceptual Processes," *Cognitive Psychology* 15, 2 (April 1983): 238-300; Bruno G. Breitmeyer and Haluk Ögmen (2006), *Visual Masking: Time Slices through Conscious and Unconscious Vision*, 2nd edn., New York: Oxford University Press; Haluk Ögmen and Bruno G. Breitmeyer, eds. (2006), *The First Half Second: The Microgenesis and Temporal Dynamics of Unconscious And Conscious Visual Processes*, Cambridge, Massachusetts: MIT Press.

visual cortex removes the possibility of conscious visual sensation for a particular area of the visual field. But despite their inability to register consciously any relevant mental qualities, blindsight subjects guess with astonishingly accuracy about perceptible properties, such as color, shape, orientation, and motion. In these cases, individuals with no relevant conscious mental qualities nonetheless evidently sense these distinctively perceptible properties. Experimental work shows that qualitative character sometimes occurs without consciousness, and this in turn constrains how we should think and theorize about qualitative consciousness.

Those who hold that traditional philosophical views must instead constrain the interpretation of empirical findings would dispute this conclusion. They would argue that these priming effects and accurate guessing need not be due to the occurrence of mental qualities. Qualitative character, they would urge, is necessarily conscious; so it must be some nonmental, nonqualitative occurrence that is responsible for these psychological results and abilities in the absence of conscious awareness.

But this line of thought is unconvincing. The effects on subsequent mental processing pertain, in the visual case, to perceptible color, shape, and location. And these are exactly the properties that mental qualities enable us to access in the conscious case. The qualitative similarities and differences in perceptible color, shape, and location are, moreover, registered psychologically, since they play a distinctive, dramatic role in our psychological lives. The best explanation of such registration of qualitative differences is that is is due to differences among the mental qualities that occur without being conscious. To deny that the registration of such qualitative differences involves mental qualities is arbitrary and ad hoc, the denial of an obvious conclusion simply to rescue an outmoded traditional theory.

What are the most important open problems in contemporary philosophy of mind? What are the most promising prospects?

Perhaps the most widely discussed topic in philosophy of mind over the last roughly 30 years is the nature of intentional content. But there has been little agreement among those who write about intentional content as to how to explain its occurrence. Some theorists espouse a holist approach, along lines of a functionalist or conceptual-role theory, whereas others adopt an atomistic theory of such content. Some explain content by appeal to something like biological function, whereas others see content as hinging on a causal or counterfactual connection with the things the content represents. Some see content as in part, at least, a matter of the external physical or social environment, whereas others insist that content supervenes solely on physical states of the organism. Given the lack of convergence on these and related issues, it is natural to see the nature of intentional content as one of the most pressing open problems in contemporary philosophy of mind.

But there is another issue that perhaps cuts more deeply. It is common in philosophy of mind to adapt Kant's well-known distinction between concepts and intuitions to draw a firm distinction between intentional content and qualitative character. Intentional content is characteristic of thoughts, desires, and other purely intentional states, whereas qualitative character distinguishes bodily and perceptual sensations.

This is arguably a good move. It is likely that whatever theoretical treatment succeeds with intentional content, a different account altogether will be needed to explain the nature of mental qualities. For one thing, intentional content occurs in sentence-sized units. Even if sentence-sized content is built up from subsentential pieces, such as concepts, qualitative character never occurs in such sentence-sized units. For another, it's likely that an explanation of mental qualities will have to appeal in part to the differences among sensory modalities, whereas no parallel appeal seems needed, or even possible, in explaining intentional content.

But whatever differences separate intentional content from qualitative character, these mental properties sometimes occur together, as in perceiving and, arguably, the emotions. Perceiving something involves both sensing and conceptualizing that thing, and the conceptual content and mental qualities go together in an especially intimate way. Similarly, if I'm angry, I'm angry that something is so, but my anger also typically has a characteristic qualitative feel, involving bodily sensations.

So if we follow the modern philosophical tradition in drawing a firm divide between intentional content and qualitative character, we must explain how the two fit together in perceiving and the emotions. This is arguably a somewhat neglected question. Some theorists have hoped that so-called nonconceptual content[22] may

---

[22] Gareth Evans, *Varieties of Reference*, ed. John McDowell, Oxford: Clarendon Press, 1982; Christopher Peacocke, *Sense and Content*, Oxford:

help to build something of a bridge between the two as they occur in the perceptual context. But it's unlikely that nonconceptual content will do the job. When we see a rabbit, as such, the qualitative character that pertains to the rabbit must somehow operate in tandem with with the concept of a rabbit. And it's unclear how invoking nonconceptual content can help us understand how this happen.

Representationalist views, such as that of Fred Dretske and Gilbert Harman[23], promise an informational continuity between the conceptual and qualitative in perception. But it is unlikely that representationalist approaches can do justice to the distinctively qualitative character of perceiving. Champions of phenomenal intentionality, who urge that there is something it's like for one to be in intentional states, sometimes regard intentionality as altogether inseparable from phenomenal character.[24] But it's doubtful that intentional content always occurs in connection with conscious qualitative character. And if not, the problem of linking qualitative character with intentional content remains.

Philosophical thinking about the mind has sometimes denied any theoretical discontinuity between the qualitative and the conceptual. Aristotle saw thinking as in the first instance an abstract form of perceiving, and therefore saw the content characteristic of thinking as continuous with the qualitative character of perceiving.[25] And it's arguable that folk attitudes about thinking and sensing more closely resemble Aristotle's in this respect than Kant's. Moreover, the distinction between the conceptual and the sensory is often elided or drawn rather casually in cognitive psychology, suggesting that cognitive psychologists may, like the folk, see continuity instead of a firm divide.

But few today would champion a theoretical account of thinking that is parallel to that of sensing, such as Aristotle's theory of sen-

---

Oxford University Press, 1983, and *A Study of Concepts*, Cambridge, Massachusetts: MIT Press/Bradford Books, 1992.

[23] Fred Dretske, *Naturalizing the Mind*, MIT Press/Bradford Books, 1995; Harman, "The Intrinsic Quality of Experience," *Philosophical Perspectives* IV (1990): 31-52, reprinted in Harman, *Reasoning, Meaning and Mind*, Oxford: Clarendon Press, 1999, pp. 244-261.

[24] E.g., Charles Siewert, *The Significance of Consciousness*, Princeton: Princeton University Press, 1999, esp. ch. 7.

[25] E.g., *Posterior Analytics*, II, 19; *de Anima* III, 6, 8. Cf. Wilfrid Sellars, "Aristotelian Philosophies of Mind," in *Philosophy for the Future*, ed. Roy Wood Sellars, V. J. McGill, and Marvin Farber, New York: The Macmillan Company, 1949, pp. 544-570.

sible and intelligible forms. And if different theoretical treatments are needed for intentional content and qualitative character, we also need an account of how the two figure together in perceiving and the emotions. Like the very nature of intentional content, itself, its connection to the qualitative may well be a major open problem in philosophy of mind.

17
John Searle

Slusser Professor of Philosophy
University of California, Berkeley, USA

Why were you initially drawn to the philosophy of mind?

I think anybody who is interested in philosophy at all must be interested in the philosophy of mind. Not only does it bear on almost all other philosophical issues such as language, knowledge and ethics, but it is also a central part of our lives. There is a sense in which we are our minds. However, I had a special professional reason for wanting to write a book about the philosophy of mind. Previous to my work on intentionality, I had worked almost exclusively in the philosophy of language. When I wrote my book *Speech Acts: An Essay in the Philosophy of Language* (Cambridge 1969), I made free use of such intentionalistic notions as belief, desire and intention. Indeed, the whole idea of the theory of speech acts was to treat speaking as a form of intentional action. The basic idea was that we can analyze such speech acts as stating, questioning, requesting, commanding and promising in terms of constitutive rules and an intentionalistic apparatus that included beliefs, desires and intentions. However, to use this intentionalistic apparatus, to use philosophically puzzling notions without any explanation, was like borrowing money from the bank. I felt eventually I would have to pay back the loan by giving an analysis of intentionality. Oddly enough, though it took me a long time to see it, there was already an implicit theory of intentionality contained in the theory of speech acts. This is not surprising because the speech act is itself an expression of the mental state of the speaker, a statement is an expression of a belief, a promise is an expression of intention, an order is an expression of a desire. Of course there is much more to the speech acts than just the expression of these intentional states, but it is essential to understand that there is an implicit theory of intentionality already contained in my theory of speech acts. It took me many years to see this, and even more years to draw out the conclusions, but eventually I did in my book *Intentionality: An Essay in the Philosophy of Mind* (Cambridge 1983). This book was an attempt to set out a general account of intentionality. It differed from a lot of other such accounts in that there was nothing reductive or eliminative about it. I do not think intentionality can be reduced to something else, and it certainly cannot be eliminated. But it can be *described*, and from a philosophical point of view, it can be *analyzed* into its logical components. This is what I attempted to do in this book.

A second motivation for my work in the philosophy of mind was that when I was working on *Intentionality*, I discovered to my amazement that there were all sorts of breathtakingly implausible views that were not only common, but appeared to be widespread in the philosophy of mind. One way to teach yourself any subject is to teach a course in that subject, so I decided to teach a course in the philosophy of mind and I used certain standard texts for the course. It was when I was teaching this course that I discovered all of these strange views that appeared to be seriously advanced and even commonly held. I am thinking of views like behaviorism and its descendent, functionalism, and its most extreme version computer functionalism, which I later baptized as Strong Artificial Intelligence. Before I taught this course, I assumed that both behaviorism and dualism had been discredited, but I discovered all sorts of variations on them that continued to survive. Functionalism was quite common at the time I was writing, and for all I know, it may still be common. But the most implausible view was one I attacked at some length, and that was that brains don't actually matter; that all that matters is having the right computer program. That is as implausible for mentation as it would be for digestion. Nobody says, "You don't have to worry about the stomach when you consider digestion, just need to understand the computer program that is implemented in the stomach", but people were quite willing to say, "Brains don't actually matter for the mind, you just have to understand the computer program that is implemented in the brain." An equation that was quite common in that era is:

$$\frac{\text{Mind}}{\text{Brain}} = \frac{\text{Program}}{\text{Hardware}}$$

Mind is to brain as program is to hardware.

What do you consider your most important contribution to the field?

What I consider important and what the profession considers important are probably not the same. My most famous argument in the philosophy of mind is probably a refutation of what I call Strong Artificial Intelligence, the view that all that is necessary and sufficient for having a mind just like yours and mine is the implementation of the right computer program with the right inputs and outputs. This is an easy view to refute and I did it with the Chinese Room Argument. This argument is well known, but I will state it briefly here in case some readers are not familiar with it. If Strong AI were true, then I could acquire any cognitive ability simply by implementing the program for having that cognitive ability. Well, let's suppose, as is indeed the case, that I do not know any Chinese. Then if computationalism were right, if Strong AI were the correct view of the mind, then all I would need to do in order to understand Chinese would be to implement the program for giving the right answers to questions posed to me in Chinese. Imagine that I am locked in a room, and that in the room there are several boxes of Chinese symbols. Imagine also that small groups of Chinese symbols are given to me through a slot in the door of the room. I look up in a rulebook written in English what I am supposed to do with these small bunches of Chinese symbols, and by following the rulebook, I give back groups of Chinese symbols through the same slot. Unknown to me, the small groups of symbols that are passed into the room are called "questions", the symbols I give back are called "answers" to the questions. The rulebook is called the "computer program". The boxes of Chinese symbols are called the "database". And I am called the "computer." We will suppose that the people who write the program are so good and I do such a good job of manipulating the symbols that after a while, my answers to the questions are indistinguishable from those of a native Chinese speaker. I pass the Turing test for understanding Chinese. But all the same, I do not understand a word of Chinese. Why not, since I pass the Turing test for understanding Chinese? The answer is quite obvious. I have no way of figuring out what any of these symbols mean. There is no way, in short, to get from the syntax to the semantics. But if I don't understand Chinese on the basis of implementing a computer program for understanding Chinese, then neither does any other digital computer solely on that basis because no digital computer has anything that I don't have.

The proof, and I think it is decisive, rests on two simple principles. First, the *simulation* of understanding is not by itself understanding. That is, *simulation* is not by itself the same as *duplication*. And second, the *syntax* of the computer program is not sufficient for the *semantics* of actual understanding, because syntax is never by itself sufficient for semantics. There have now been literally hundreds of attacks on this argument, but none of them shakes the basic structure of the argument. The bottom line of the argument is that if I don't understand Chinese on the basis of implementing a computer program for understanding Chinese, then neither does any digital computer solely on that basis because no digital computer has anything that I don't have.

Along with all of the attacks on the argument, there were a number of serious misunderstandings, and I can correct a couple of those now. First, I am not arguing that "computers can't think." If anything that can compute is a computer, then we are all computers, and we can all think. So there are a very large number of existing thinking computers, namely all humans and some animals. Second, I am not arguing that it is impossible to build a conscious machine or that only creatures with brains like ours can think. We ought to hear the question, "Can you build a conscious machine?" the way we hear the question, "Can you build an artificial heart that pumps blood?" We know the answer to the second question. We don't know the answer to the first because we don't know how brains do it but we know that the brain is a machine, so in principle at least, it ought to be possible to duplicate and not just simulate the computational powers of the brain.

However, in my own view, the issue about Strong AI is destined to become obsolete as we get a better understanding of how brains cause and realize conscious states. If I am asked what I think my most important contributions to the philosophy of mind are, I would say that the ones I think deal with the most important issues are the following four. First, the analysis of intentionality in the book *Intentionality*, including the analysis of the structure of human action. Second, the analysis of consciousness and in particular the dissolution of the traditional mind-body problem. Third, the explanation of the notion of mental causation. And fourth, my analysis of the notion of the self and especially its relation to rationality.

In the space of this interview I don't really have room to cover all of these topics, and the book *Intentionality* does not admit of a quick summary. So I will confine myself to very brief statements about the other three topics.

Consciousness and the Mind-Body Problem
Basically, there are four principles on which my analysis rests:

1. Consciousness is real and irreducible.
2. It is entirely caused by processes in the brain.
3. It is realized in the brain.
4. It functions causally in our behavior.

I am convinced that these are true. But they seem to run counter to a whole lot of our assumptions about identity, reduction, causation, dualism, etc. What I have done is reject those assumptions. My book *Mind: A Brief Introduction*, as well as other works, is designed to get rid of the set of categories that make it seem impossible to solve the mind-body problem. In particular, I reject both dualism and materialism as they are traditionally conceived. Both are trying to say something true but they end up saying something false. The task is to state the true part without saying the false part. In the end, I hope my most important contribution will be to remove the traditional mind-body problem from philosophical debate. There is an interesting mind-body problem in neurobiology, but in philosophy it is mostly based on a mistake. Once you grant the obvious facts that all of our conscious and intentional states are caused by brain processes, and that they are actually right there realized in the brain, then the problem becomes one for lab scientists, the problem is one of figuring out how brain processes actually cause and realize mental states.

I hope the traditional "mind-body problem" will disappear the way the "mechanism-vitalism problem" has disappeared. It is hard for us today to recover the passion with which the nature of life was disputed. Now that we understand most of the biochemical processes of life, we cannot take that debate seriously. I hope that once we understand how brain processes cause consciousness and intentionality and how they are realized in the brain, the traditional philosohical issues will similarly disappear.

Mental Causation

Once we get a satisfactory account of mind-body relations, then it seems to me the problem of mental causation really falls into place. Mental causation is just a species of higher level physical causation like any other. So for example, we can describe the functioning of my car engine at the level of pistons and cylinders or at the level of the molecules in the metal alloys and the oxidization of hydrocarbons. These are not competing descriptions of two different sorts of phenomena, but they are noncompeting descriptions of the same phenomenon at different levels of description. Now let me go exactly through an account of mental causation that will show how it is like the description of physical causation. I currently have an intention-in-action to raise my arm, and that intention-in-action causes my arm to go up. There isn't really any doubt about that. But we know quite independently that anything that causes my arm to go up in that way must have certain biochemical features. It must, for example, secrete a certain neurotransmitter throughout the motor neurons and it must activate ion channels. But it follows logically then that one and the same phenomenon must have both intentionalistic properties and neurobiological properties. This is not a question of a philosophical mystery. This is just a fact about how nature works. What is interesting about intentional causation is that in addition to its neurobiological features it also has certain logical properties because the intentional content of the intentional state actually functions causally in bringing about its conditions of satisfaction. To use the old time Aristotelian jargon, intentional causation is a form of efficient causation, but it differs from other forms in that there is an intrinsic logical relation between the intentional content that functions in the cause and the conditions of satisfaction which are the effect.

The Self and Rationality

I offer an analysis of the self which grants Hume's skepticism about the self but shows how it can be circumvented by introducing a purely formal notion of the self. Hume argued correctly that we have no experience of the self in addition to all of our other experiences. I agree with that but I argue that all the same, we cannot make sense of our experiences, especially our experiences of rational decision-making, without postulating a formal notion of the self. There are a number of reasons for this, but the character of the postulation is not at all unique in discussing our cognitive apparatus. Just as I cannot make sense of my visual perceptions without postulating a point of view from which I have these perceptions, even though I do not perceive the point of view, so I cannot make sense of my experiences of choosing, deciding, acting, accepting responsibility, etc. without postulating a self which is, so to speak, the point of view from which all of these separate phenomena occur, even though it is not itself experienced as one of these phenomena.

My conception of the self emerged as part of my criticism of contemporary notions of rationality in my book, *Rationality in Action*. In that book I criticize the classical conception of rationality, according to which all rational actions are matters of attempting to maximize the satisfaction of our desires, and that rational actions are caused by beliefs and desires. I think the whole conception is a tissue of confusions and I attempt to expose those confusions.

These four discussions then—intentionality, consciousness and the mind-body problem, mental causation, and the nature of the self and rationality—do not exhaust my discussions in the philosophy of mind, but at least they form a basis for answering the present question.

What is the proper role of philosophy in relation to psychology, artificial intelligence, and the neurosciences?

There are a number of relations between philosophy and these other disciplines. I have already illustrated a couple of them. The single most important contribution of philosophy to the neurosciences is to get the relationships between brain and consciousness stated in such a way that they admit of a scientific solution. I think I have succeeded in doing that, and a lot of researchers are pursuing the kind of research that I am urging.

A second function of philosophy is to give analyses of mental concepts which will enable researchers in the field to pose the empirical questions in a way that makes them subject to laboratory testing. I will give an example of this. On purely philosophical grounds, in *Intentionality* I made a distinction between prior intentions and intentions-in-action. The prior intention is an intention that the agent has prior to performing the action. An intention-in-action is the intention that the agent has while actually performing an intentional action. I make this distinction on purely philosophical grounds, because each has different conditions of satisfaction. However, if I am right about this then there ought to be a neurobiological distinction between prior intentions and intentions-in-action. The closest thing we get in ordinary speech to prior intention is a decision or a plan and the closest thing we get in ordinary speech to intention-in-action is trying. If the distinction is real, then there ought to be some neurobiological correlates. In his excellent book, Marc Jeannerod[1], the French neurobiologist, uses that distinction to investigate a neurobiological basis of human actions. And he does indeed find that there are neuronal correlates for the distinction between prior intentions and intentions in action. This example seems to me to illustrate an ideal partnership between philosophy and neuroscience.

Throughout all of these discussions, I also think philosophy has a critical role to play. It is often said that philosophers should not attempt to criticize scientific research projects. But I do not see why that should be the case. If absurd things are said in artificial intelligence, as indeed they were, I think it is our responsibility philosophically to point out the absurdities. I think some more absurdities have been made about various forms of misapplication of Darwin's results, and I have criticized some of those as well. I am thinking especially of some of the more exaggerated claims made on behalf of sociobiology.

To summarize this part, it seems to me philosophy has two sorts of roles to play. One is an analytic role: that analyzing the concepts and the data allows for empirical testing of what are initially philosophical theories and distinctions. The second is a critical role: people in Artificial Intelligence, neurobiology or psychology sometimes say things that deserve philosophical criticism and analysis, and I think philosophers should provide that criticism and analysis.

However, having said all that, I feel vaguely dissatisfied with it because it suggests that there is a principled distinction between philosophy and other disciplines. I do not really believe that is so. I think I learn a lot from neurobiologists, and I hope some of them learn something from me. I was asked by the *Annual Review of Neuroscience* to write an article discussing consciousness. I assumed they hoped that I would discuss the neurobiological research from a philosophical point of view, and that is exactly what I tried to do. In this way, I was able to state what I thought were some of the philosophically important areas in which progress was being made, but I also saw some philosophical difficulties in current neuroscientific research. I did not regard making these criticisms as in any way hostile or negative. I am not someone *outside* trying to comment on what is going on *inside*, but rather I regard us as all researchers working toward a common goal. We

---

[1] *Motor Cognition*, Published in the Oxford Psychology Series, Oxford University Press, 2006.

are all trying to get the truth about a difficult subject matter and I, with my limited expertise in neurobiology, but my experience in conceptual analysis, hope I can make a contribution. But I do not think that there is any principled distinction between disciplines.

Is a science of consciousness possible?

The question reminds me of a question once put to Doctor Johnson: "Do you believe in Christian baptism?" Johnson's reply was: "Madam, not only do I believe in it. I have seen it done." It is a bit how I feel about this question. It is not only *possible* to have a science of consciousness, but it is *actually* developing as we speak. There are a whole lot of first rate neuroscientists attempting to develop a science of consciousness. The crucial questions we need to answer are the ones I mentioned above. We need to know exactly which processes in the brain cause us to be in which conscious states, exactly how they do it, and exactly how conscious states are realized in the brain. The recent book by Christof Koch, *The Quest for Consciousness*, is an effort to carry out this research project. Christof is not alone. There are lots of other neurobiologists working along the same lines. I think in particular of Gerald Edelman, Guilio Tononi, Antonio Damasio, Rodolfo Llinas, Wolf Singer and Todd Feinberg.

What are the most important open problems in contemporary philosophy of mind? What are the most promising prospects?

I think a lot of progress has been made on some of the most vexing traditional questions. Specifically, the mind-body problem (how exactly do mental states and neurobiological states relate to each other?), mental causation (how exactly can conscious mental states cause bodily movements?), intentionality (how is it possible for the mind to be related to objects outside of itself?), and the nature and character of consciousness. I think a lot of progress has been made on these issues, and you can see my book *Mind: A Brief Introduction* for a summary of at least some of those areas of progress. However, there is one area that seems to me is still pressing, where we have not made much progress, and that is the problem of the freedom of the will. On the one hand, we are unable to abandon the presupposition of the freedom of the will. But at the same time, we have no idea whether or not we really do have free will. I see this again as a case where we will have to get the problem into the kind of shape that admits of a neurobiological solution, and then wait on the neurobiological results. I try to do part of that in my book *Freedom and Neurobiology* (Columbia University Press, 2007). I think the most promising prospects are to pursue the line of investigation that I have called Biological Naturalism. We have to treat mind and consciousness as part of the natural world like digestion and photosynthesis, and at the same time we have to recognize that the right level for discussing these in a scientific way is the level of biology as opposed to, for example, the level of atomic physics or sociology.

18
Stephen Stich

Professor of Philosophy and Cognitive Science
Rutgers, the State University of New Jersey, USA

Why were you initially drawn to philosophy of mind?

I began the Ph.D. program in Philosophy at Princeton in the Fall of 1964, thinking that I would probably focus on philosophy of science. Carl Hempel was one of the best known people in the Princeton Philosophy Department at that time, and as an undergraduate I had been much impressed by his work and the work of other logical positivists (or "logical empiricists," to use the term that Hempel preferred). During the spring of my first year at Princeton, I was invited to attend a series of six lectures—the Christian Gauss Lectures—by Noam Chomsky. Why I was invited has long been something of a puzzle to me, since I knew next to nothing about linguistics. Perhaps the invitation was just a clerical error. If so, it was an error that refocused my intellectual life.

Though Chomsky covered a lot of ground in the Gauss lectures, it was his discussion of rationalism and empiricism that I found most remarkable. There is no philosophical topic more venerable than the debate over the existence and nature of innate ideas and innate knowledge. And in those days, at least at Princeton, it was widely assumed that the empiricists had won the debate. Rationalism, we all believed, was a quaint and implausible view that was of interest only to those who studied the history of philosophy. However, Chomsky maintained that the philosophical arguments advanced in favor of the empiricist account of the mind were unconvincing, and that the issue could be settled by appeal to empirical evidence about the nature of natural languages and the limited data available to children who mastered them. Moreover, he argued that this evidence strongly favored a *rationalist* account of the mind, an account which posited a rich store of innate ideas and innate knowledge. It was a truly extraordinary performance. Chomsky's understated, matter-of-fact style contrasted sharply with his radical conclusions, and the revolutionary empirical methodology he was using to tackle a problem that had been at the center of philosophical discussion since Plato.

I was hooked! *That* was the way I wanted to do philosophy. And since the questions that could be most readily addressed with Chomsky's trail blazing methodology were questions about the nature of language and the nature of the mind, those were the issues on which I decided to focus. I abandoned any thought of writing my thesis on a traditional issue in the philosophy of science like confirmation or explanation, and decided to focus instead on clarifying the methodology of was then called "transformational grammar."[1] The term "cognitive science" had not yet been invented when I began work on my thesis. But about a dozen years later, when I was on the faculty at the University of Michigan, I briefly posted a sign on my office door that said "Ten years ago I couldn't even spell 'cognitive scientist' and now I are one."

What is the proper role of philosophy in relation to psychology, artificial intelligence, and the neurosciences?

Chomsky's work on the rationalism *vs.* empiricism debate provided the model for how I wanted to do philosophy, and the existence proof that empirically engaged work of this sort could be exiting and productive. But was it really *philosophy*? The question was of more than theoretical interest, as I learned at my first job talk. "That's all very interesting, Mr. Stich," the first questioner said in an annoyed tone of voice, "but what does it have to do with philosophy?" Fortunately, by then I had read Quine and he had quickly become a second major influence on my early career. Quine provides what I thought—and still think—is exactly the right way to respond to questions about the relation between philosophy and the sciences.

To explain Quine's answer, and mine, I'll begin with a bit of background. One of the main themes of logical positivism, which emerged in the politically and socially tumultuous period between the two World Wars, was that things had gone very wrong in many parts of the intellectual world. Many philosophers, psychol-

---

[1] The thesis, submitted in 1968, was called "Grammars, Psychological Theories and Turing Machines." Stich (1972) is a revised version of one chapter.

ogists, theologians and political theorists were talking nonsense, and far too often it was dangerous nonsense. To expose and undercut this nonsense the positivists proposed an account of meaningfulness: To be meaningful a sentence had to be analytic (or contradictory), like the sentences in math and logic, or verifiable by experience, like the sentences in well-behaved empirical sciences such as physics and chemistry. Everything else was nonsense—"*metaphysical nonsense*" as undergraduates of my generation often said dismissively.

But there was an obvious embarrassment for philosophers who advocated this doctrine—it threatened to undermine their own livelihood. Since only a few philosophers proved theorems and fewer still did experiments or gathered empirical facts, how could they avoid the accusation that they themselves were talking nonsense? The solution, for much of the English speaking philosophical world, was to locate legitimate philosophy squarely on the analytic side of the positivist dichotomy. Meaningful philosophy was analytic, and the principle job of philosophers was conceptual analysis.

Now, famously, Quine's critique of analyticity and sentence by sentence reductionism helped to demolish the verificationist account of meaningfulness. But unlike many other critics of verificationism, Quine also offered a new job description for philosophy— a new vision of the honest work that philosophers could do in a post-positivist world where the analytic/synthetic distinction (and thus analytic conceptual analysis) could no longer be taken seriously. Philosophy, Quine maintained, was *continuous* with the sciences. What philosophers could contribute to the sciences was typically toward the more theoretical or conceptual end of the scientific spectrum. And philosophers, more often than their colleagues in science departments, could afford the luxury of taking a broader view and reflecting on how theories in different disciplines fit together. But while the emphasis and the level of theoretical abstraction might distinguish this sort of philosophical work from the work typically produced by scientists, there was no difference in status between the sciences and this kind of philosophy; philosophy, done well, Quine insisted, just *is* science.[2]

Some philosophers, I am sure, found this to be a threaten-

---

[2] Though I enthusiastically endorse the central idea in Quine's account of the relation between philosophy and the sciences, I do have some concerns about the details. For more on this, see Stich (1993).

ing idea; many still do. For if philosophy is continuous with the more theoretical reaches of the sciences, if there is nothing special and distinctive for philosophers to do, then philosophy as an autonomous discipline disappears. But others found this idea wonderfully liberating and exhilarating. And out of that sense of exhilaration a new way of being a philosopher has gradually emerged.

In looking at the sciences, philosophers in the Quinean tradition did not have to restrict themselves to clarifying concepts or evaluating arguments or working out the logic of confirmation—though all of these are worthwhile endeavors that Quine took to be part of science broadly construed. Rather, they could develop new concepts and new theories—empirical theories—and test these theories in just the way that scientists themselves did, by seeing how well they comport with the empirical facts that other researchers have reported.

During the last forty years, the sort of naturalistic, scientifically engaged approach that Quine advocated has had a profound impact in many areas of philosophy, including the philosophy of physics, the philosophy of language and linguistics and the philosophy of biology. But nowhere has Quine's vision of philosophy made more of an impact than in the philosophy of psychology and the philosophy of mind. In that area people who took up Quine's call to integrate philosophy into the sciences—people like Jerry Fodor and Dan Dennett—have inspired a whole generation of younger philosophers whose work is so thoroughly interdisciplinary that they collaborate comfortably with colleagues in science departments and publish their work in science journals, or in the new genre of "interdisciplinary" journals like *Mind and Language, Behavioral and Brain Sciences,* and *Cognition.* The existence of this work, and the existence of the journals that publish it, are an extraordinary testament to Quine's vision.

Of course Quine realized that this "new" way of being a philosopher is actually a very *old* way that had simply been pushed out of the main stream by the logical positivists and the practitioners of "ordinary language" philosophy, with a little help from Kant. Descartes was an important contributor to the scientific debates of his day, Berkeley made important contributions to what today would be called perceptual psychology, and William James was simultaneously one of America's greatest philosophers and one of the most important figures in the history of psychology.

On my view there are some notable (and ironic) parallels between Quine and Descartes. Both of them played an important role in changing the way philosophy was done; both of them attempted to contribute to the sciences and—here is the irony—both of them bet on the wrong horse in the scientific sweepstakes of their day. Quine's contributions to psychology and psycholinguistics, in *Word and Object* and elsewhere, were very much embedded in the behaviorist tradition, and that tradition, it has become increasingly clear, is not a productive one. In some distant possible world in which Quine would agree with what I have just written, he would, no doubt, also remind us that betting on the wrong horse is always a risk in doing science. And that risk is one of the things that makes doing philosophy in Quine's way both challenging and exciting.

A few years ago, the photographer Steve Pyke asked me for a brief statement of my view of philosophy to accompany one of his famously edgy photos.[3] The paragraph I wrote will serve as a summary of my Quinean answer to the question about the relation between philosophy and the sciences.

> The idea that philosophy could be kept apart from the sciences would have been dismissed out of hand by most of the great philosophers of the 17th and 18th centuries. But many contemporary philosophers believe they can practice their craft without knowing what is going on in the natural and social sciences. If facts are needed, they rely on their "intuition", or they simply invent them. The results of philosophy done in this way are typically sterile and often silly. There are no proprietary philosophical questions that are worth answering, nor is there any productive philosophical method that does not engage the sciences. But there are lots of deeply important (and fascinating and frustrating) questions about minds, morals, language, culture and more. To make progress on them we need to use anything that science can tell us, and any method that works.

What do you consider your most important contributions to the field?

---

[3] That photo, and many other examples of Pyke's remarkable work, are available on line at: http://www.pyke-eye.com/philosophers_II.html .

For much of my academic career, I have been singularly fortunate in having the opportunity to work with exceptionally gifted and enthusiastic young philosophers. Most of them were graduate students at the universities where I taught; others were visiting students or visiting scholars at my university or at nearby schools. In each case, I learned at least as much from them as they learned from me. But in one respect my relationships with these young philosophers could not be reciprocal. While I had a good job at a good university, they were just launching their careers and were in need of advice and support of various kinds. Mentoring these younger philosophers was a great privilege, and a responsibility I took very seriously. Since almost all of the people I worked with shared my Quinean conviction that philosophy done well is continuous with science, helping them launch their careers was often quite a challenge. Much of the mainstream philosophical world was skeptical about our empirically engaged approach to philosophy, and more than a few people were (and are) openly hostile to it. So I spent countless hours helping my students sharpen their arguments and shape their projects to make clear why their work was relevant to traditional philosophical concerns. I also invested a great deal of time trying to prepare students for the job market by being sure they had engaging, highly polished job talks and well practiced strategies for dealing with the inevitable barbed questions about their empirically oriented approach. Whenever possible, I tried to send them out into the job market with several publications already in the pipeline. The process always required hard work and long hours from both me and the students. (In one memorable case, I did about a dozen mock interviews with a student about to go on the market!) But I am delighted to say that we were always successful. I have never had a student who didn't get a good job, and all of them who have reached the appropriate stage in their careers now have tenure. By far my most important contribution to the field has been the help I provided in launching the careers of these remarkable young scholars.

From the late 1960s until the closing years of the 20th century, philosophers who adopted an empirically engaged approach to philosophy were almost always *consumers* of empirical research. We read the work of our colleagues in science departments and tried to draw out the implications of that work for issues that were important in philosophy. But as the 20th century drew to a close, some philosophers, including me and a number of my former students, became impatient with this approach. There are a number of disciplines that produce evidence relevant to issues in the philosophy of mind, including psychology, linguistics, neuroscience, anthropology and evolutionary biology. But each of these disciplines has a life of its own—a history and sociology that influences the questions researchers are most likely to ask and the studies they are inclined to undertake. Sometimes the findings of those studies are just what philosophers need; but sometimes they aren't. Rather than waiting around for the data that philosophers need, or trying to cajole our empirical colleagues to run the relevant experiments, my former students and I, along with a growing group of other philosophers, decided to take matters in our own hands—learning the relevant methods and running the experiments ourselves. This gave rise to a loosely knit new movement that has become known as *experimental philosophy*. Some, including my collaborators and I, have used the techniques of experimental social psychology to explore cross-cultural differences in philosophically important intuitions or to probe the processes underlying judgments about morality, intention, free will and consciousness.[4] Others, most notably Joshua Greene and his associates, have used fMRI technology to study the processes underlying moral judgment.[5] And as I write this, a team of experimentally inclined anthropologists, organized by philosopher Stephen Laurence, are heading to research sites all over the globe to perform a battery of studies on folk psychology and folk epistemology designed in collaboration with philosophers and psychologists.[6] It remains to be seen how much of an impact this work will have on more mainstream discussions in the philosophy of mind and in other areas of philosophy. But if the passionate debates in the blogosphere—and in more and more mainline journals—is any indication, the experimental philosophy movement will have an important influence on the way philosophy is done in the 21st century. My role in the movement has been relatively modest. I've helped to design and run some studies and have co-authored a handful of papers. I've also had a hand in organizing a number of interdisciplinary groups and projects. But mostly I've been a mentor, facilitator and gadfly.

---

[4] For an excellent collection of papers, see Knobe and Nichols (2008).
[5] The pioneering paper is Greene et al. (2001). That paper and many more recent studies are available on line at: http://www.wjh.harvard.edu/~jgreene/ .
[6] The Culture and the Mind Project that Laurence directs maintains a useful and informative website: http://www.philosophy.dept.shef.ac.uk/culture&mind/ .

If thing go as I predict they will, this too may be reckoned as a valuable contribution.

Is a science of consciousness possible?

Yes. Not a terribly informative answer, I realize, but I have done no significant work on consciousness. The arguments I've seen aimed at showing that a science of consciousness is *not* possible strike me as unconvincing.

What are the most important open problems in contemporary philosophy of mind? What are the most promising prospects?

Since I don't think there is any interesting or principled distinction to be drawn between philosophy of mind and cognitive science, I couldn't possibly answer these questions in a few paragraphs. There are scores of important open problems in the cognitive sciences and dozens of promising prospects. What I'll do instead is focus on one area where I think remarkable progress has been made in the last decade—that area is moral psychology.

Moral psychology has been a central part of moral theory since antiquity, and moral theorists have made claims about a wide range of psychological issues including:

- the role of character in fostering moral behavior
- the role of reason in moral judgment
- the role of emotion in moral judgment
- the nature of moral motivation
- the sources of moral disagreement, and the prospects for resolving moral disagreement
- the extent to which moral knowledge is innate
- the extent to which genuinely altruistic behavior is possible

and a host of others. In support of these claims, the great moral theorists of the past used the only sources of evidence available to them: introspection, history and careful observation of human behavior. But, not surprisingly, these sources of evidence were not adequate to establish or refute the claims made in moral psychology, and thus most debates over issues in moral psychology remained unresolved.

In the late 19th & early 20th century, psychology became an experimental science, and by the last decade of the 20th century, experimental psychology and the various branches of neuroscience had developed quite sophisticated techniques for testing hypotheses about the mind. But, as late as 1990, this work had made almost no impact on moral theory. The reasons for this are many and complex. One important factor was the behaviorist orientation of much experimental psychology until the early 1970s. Since talk about mental states was taboo in the behaviorist literature, philosophers could find little in this literature that addressed the questions they were interested in. Also playing a role were views and arguments, variously attributed to Kant, Frege, G.E. Moore, logical positivism, and even Hume, which suggested that moral theory, or philosophy more generally, is (or should be) an a priori discipline that is independent of the sciences.[7] In my darker moments, I suspect that philosophers' arrogance and laziness also played an important role. But arrogance and laziness are traditional character traits, and John Doris and Gil Harman have argued that there are no traditional character traits. So my darker suspicions must be mistaken. It is also the case that some of the most visible psychologists, biologists, anthropologists and neuroscientists who have written about morality have had only the most superficial understanding of the philosophical issues about which they were writing. So it is hardly surprising that moral philosophers who dipped into that literature decided it could safely be ignored.

All this began to change in the 1990s when a small, but growing group of psychologically sophisticated philosophers and philosophically sophisticated psychologists began to use the data and the methods of experimental psychology, neuroscience, cognitive anthropology and evolutionary biology in an attempt to sharpen and resolve traditional issues in moral philosophy.[8] This work has led to renewed interest, lively debate and, I would argue, remarkable progress on just about every issue that I listed at the beginning

---

[7] For a useful discussion, see Rachels, (2000).

[8] In 2003, I played a role in organizing the Moral Psychology Research Group (http://www.moralpsychology.net/group/). Meetings of the group have become an important venue for interdisciplinary discussions in this area.

of this section.[9] No doubt there are many philosophers would disagree with this sanguine assessment, and even among those who think that substantial progress has been made, opinions will differ on where we have made the most progress. My favorite candidate is work aimed at resolving the debate between psychological egoism and psychological altruism, a debate which has played an important role in moral philosophy since Hobbes—some would say since Plato. The social psychologist, Daniel Batson, is one of the real pioneers in philosophically sophisticated empirically driven moral psychology, and Batson is a conspicuous exception to my suggestion, at the beginning of this paragraph, that this sort of work began in the 1990s. Since the late 1970s, he has been exploring the case for psychological altruism in a series of carefully designed experiments, though it was only in the 1990s that philosophers began paying careful attention to his work. This is not the place to attempt a review of Batson's achievement. However, in a long paper in which we try to provide an overview and assessment of Batson's work, Doris, Roedder and I conclude that "Batson and his associates have made more progress in the last three decades than philosophers using the traditional philosophical methodology of a priori arguments buttressed by anecdote and intuition have made in the previous two millennia."[10]

At this point, I can imagine someone who tuned in late protesting that I haven't answered the questions posed at the beginning of this section, because this work, whatever it's virtues, isn't philosophy of mind at all. Anyone inclined to raise *that* objection should go back and read my responses to the first two questions.

References

Batson, C. D. (1991). *The Altruism Question: Toward a Social-Psychological Answer*. Hillsdale, NJ: Lawrence Erlbaum Associates.

Batson, C.D.. (1998). Altruism and prosocial behavior. In D.T. Gilbert & S.T. Fiske (eds.), *The Handbook of Social Psychology*, Vol. 2. Boston: McGraw-Hill. 282-316.

Greene, J.D., Sommerville, R.B., Nystrom, L.E., Darley, J.M., & Cohen, J.D. (2001). "An fMRI Investigation of Emotional En-

---

[9] For an excellent sampling of this work see Sinnott-Armstrong (2008).
[10] Stich, Doris and Roedder (forthcoming). Good summaries of Batson's work are available in Batson (1991) and (1998).

gagement in Moral Judgment." *Science*, Vol. 293, Sept. 14, 2001, 2105-2108.

Knobe, J. and Nichols, S. (2008). *Experimental Philosophy*. Oxford: Oxford University Press.

Rachels, J. (2000). "Naturalism." In H. LaFollette (ed.), *The Blackwell Guide to Ethical Theory*. Oxford: Blackwell Publishing. 74-91.

Sinnott-Armstrong, W. (2008). *Moral Psychology*. Volume 1: *The Evolution of Morality: Adaptations and Innateness*; Volume 2: *The Cognitive Science of Morality: Intuition and Diversity;* Volume 3: *The Neuroscience of Morality: Emotion, Brain Disorders, and Development*. Cambridge, MA: MIT Press.

Stich, S. (1972). "Grammar, Psychology and Indeterminacy," *Journal of Philosophy*, LXIX, 22, 799-818.

Stich, S. (1993). "Naturalizing Epistemology: Quine, Simon and the Prospects for Pragmatism," in C. Hookway & D. Peterson, eds., *Philosophy and Cognitive Science*, Royal Institute of Philosophy, Supplement no. 34. Cambridge: Cambridge University Press. Pp. 1-17.

Stich, S., Doris, J. and Roedder, E. (forthcoming). "Altruism," to appear in *Oxford Handbook of Moral Psychology* ed. by the Moral Psychology Research Group. Oxford: Oxford University Press.

19
Galen Strawson

Professor of Philosophy
City University of New York Graduate Center, USA
University of Reading, UK

Why were you initially drawn to philosophy of mind?

The philosophy of mind is central to philosophy, because the philosophy of mind is the heart of the study of the human being, and the study of the human being is the heart of philosophy; at least for us. The Buddha stressed the point that the attempt to understand things has to begin with a study of the human mental apparatus long before Kant made it central to his *Critique of Pure Reason* (1781). Hume put it by saying that 'all the sciences have a relation, greater or less, to human nature', and that 'however wide any of them may seem to run from it, they still return back by one passage or another.[1] I came into the philosophy of mind through two problems—the problems of free will and the relation between consciousness and matter—but every philosopher must come there in one way or another.

What do you consider your most important contribution to the field?

---

[1] 'Even *Mathematics, Natural Philosophy, and Natural Religion*', he continued, 'are in some measure dependent on the science of MAN; since they lie under the cognizance of men, and are judged of by their powers and faculties' (1739-40: 4/xv). Hume's two great general (non-ethical) works are 'Of the *Understanding*' (part 1 of his 'Treatise of *Human Nature*'), and 'An Enquiry Concerning *Human Understanding*', Locke's main work is 'An Essay Concerning *Human Understanding*', Berkeley's 'A Treatise Concerning the Principles of *Human Knowledge*'. Reid's are an 'Inquiry into the *Human Mind*','Essays on the *Intellectual Powers of Man*', and 'Essays on the *Active Powers of Man*'.

Putting aside work on free will and on the self, which falls under the heading of general metaphysics as much as under the heading of philosophy of mind, I've tried to encourage discussion of the real consciousness-matter problem, the real mind-body problem. By this I mean the problem evaded or ignored by all reductionists, all those who seek somehow to reduce the mental to the non-mental: behaviourists, functionalists, 'strong' representationalists or whatever.

I've advanced a set of connected ideas. The first is that of *real materialism*, by which I simply mean materialism (or physicalism) that is fully realist about consciousness, conscious experience, experiential 'what-it's-likeness', or as I will simply call it *experience*.[2]

What do I mean by 'experience'? Basic examples will do—pain, seeing the colour blue, tasting bananas. What is it to be a realist about experience, where by 'realist about experience' I mean a *real realist* about experience? One way to convey it to those who claim not to know is to say that it's to continue to take experience—e.g. colour experience, pain experience, sound experience—to be what one took (knew) it to be, quite unreflectively, before one did any philosophy, e.g. when one was five years old. One doesn't need to attribute a general conception of experience to five-year olds to make the point (though one shouldn't underestimate five-year olds). However many new and surprising facts real realists learn about experience from scientists—facts about the 'filling-in' that characterizes visual experience, for example, or about 'change blindness' or 'inattentional blindness'[3]— their fundamental general understanding of what experience is remains the same as it was before they did any philosophy. It remains, in other words, correct. This way of specifying what I mean by 'experience' guarantees that anyone who claims not to know what I mean is being disingenuous.

Real materialism incorporates real realism about experience. It accepts that all mental goings on, including crucially all experiential goings on, are wholly physical goings on, but doesn't take it to follow, reductively, that there must somehow be less to experience than we thought before we did philosophy. Rather, it concludes that there must be more to matter than we thought before we did philosophy—given that we then took matter to be

---

[2] See e.g. Strawson 1994: chs. 3 and 4, 1999, 2003.
[3] See e.g. Pessoa & de Weerd 2003, Simons & Levin 1997, Chun & Marois 2002.

something essentially non-experiential in nature. Real materialism is not *reductive* but *adductive*: if materialism is true, there must be more to the physical than we thought, for experience is real and must be wholly physical if materialism is true. Real materialists don't set up 'mental' and 'physical' in opposition to each other, except when talking loosely, because they hold that everything that concretely exists is physical. Instead they oppose the mental physical and the non-mental physical, the experiential physical and the non-experiential physical; for everything that exists, on their view, and once again, is physical.

All this is part of *real naturalism* (see e.g. Strawson 2005), for real naturalism starts out from the fundamental natural fact, the most certainly known natural fact. What fact is that? It's the fact of experience, the fact of the existence of experience. It then adds a commitment to materialism, and this delivers real materialism as just defined. Real naturalism, genuine naturalism, is in direct conflict with the doctrine now commonly known as 'naturalism', which characteristically denies the existence of experience (real experience).

It's bewildering to find philosophers arguing from materialism or naturalism to the non-existence of experience, for the boot, in fact, is on the other foot. If we call experience 'E', the correct argument is as follows.

[1] If there exists something other than E that we as naturalists take to be a natural phenomenon, e.g. physical-stuff-conceived-as-something-that-is-in-its-intrinsic-nature-wholly-non-experiential (call it 'NE'), and which is such that we find it hard to understand how E exists as it does if NE exists, then NE must be a problem for naturalism; but not E.

We are in this case in no position to say, as naturalists,

[2] NE certainly exists, as a matter of natural fact, and it's most unclear, given NE and the evidently intensely intimate relation between NE and E, how E is possible (and perhaps E is not possible).

We are in a position to say

[3] *If* NE exists, as a matter of natural fact, then it is most unclear how E is possible, given the intensely intimate relation between NE and E.

But then we must contrapose (roughly speaking) and go on to say

> [4] Well, E certainly exists, as matter of certain natural fact, so it is most unclear how NE is possible, given the intensely intimate relation between NE and E; and we have in fact no good reason to believe NE is actual.

It's impossible to imagine a more anti-naturalist doctrine than naturalism as now standardly defined in philosophy, for it denies the existence of the fundamentally given natural fact: experience.

Some define naturalism primarily in a methodological way, as the doctrine that all valid enquiry into the nature of things must proceed in accord with the methods of the natural sciences, and believe that they can extract the conclusion that naturalism can take no account of experience (although it is the fundamental given natural fact), and indeed that experience doesn't exist. They need to be reminded that many experimental psychologists deal in the phenomena of experience in a fully realist manner. If, ignoring this, they take physics as their fundamental model of a natural science, they need to think through the 'structuralist' point that was so familiar in the 1920s but is now severely underappreciated. This is the point that there is a fundamental sense in which physics offers us nothing—absolutely nothing—but numbers and equations.[4] Apart from describing the structure of physical systems in mathematical terms, physics tells us nothing about the intrinsic nature of the physical. In particular, it gives us no reason to think that the physical is non-experiential, rather than experiential, in its fundamental nature. And since we know (more certainly than anything else) that experience is real, and is therefore wholly physical, if materialism is true, we have strong reason, as materialists, to think that experientiality is a fundamental feature of the physical. One reason for this is that we are, otherwise, obliged to believe that experientiality, real experientiality, can be a wholly naturally emergent feature of stuff that is in its fundamental nature, and through and through, wholly and utterly non-experiential in nature. This, however, involves committing oneself to belief in a radical or 'spooky' form of emergence that is wildly at odds with the principles of any research program that can claim to

---

[4]See e.g. Russell 1948: 240-7, Eddington 1928: 258-60, Chomsky 1968: 6-8, 98, Lockwood 1989: ch. 10, Strawson 2003. The point is now regaining currency.

be naturalistic. The point can be summarily expressed by saying that it is diagnostic of any genuinely naturalistic, parsimonious, plausible and indeed 'hard-nosed' materialist position that it takes seriously the possibility that *panpsychism* or equivalently *panexperientialism*—the view that everything has mental or experiential being, whatever other being it has—may be true.[5] Panpsychism allows that everything also has non-mental, non-experiential being, but pure panpsychism, which does not allow this, is the more parsimonious theory.[6]

The fact that 'naturalism' in the philosophy of mind is the name of a position that denies a fundamental natural fact about mind— the fact of experience—shows that analytic philosophy of mind is in a poor state. The structuralist point mentioned above is just one version of a crucial general point about our ignorance of the non-mental. This was most powerfully expressed by Locke, and also by many others in the seventeenth and eighteenth centuries, when all the essential issues were clearly in play, and the general debate was in much better shape. The dispute between *a priori* physicalists and *a posteriori* physicalists, for example, was admirably set out, and every collection of readings in the philosophy of mind should include paragraph 4.3.6 of Locke's *Essay*.[7] An amazing amount of time could be saved in this way.

The third connected idea that I've advocated is that of *cognitive phenomenology*.[8] Many—perhaps most—analytic philosophers still think that phenomenology is restricted to the study of sensory experiences (including 'mental images' of certain sorts) and feelings, including moods and emotions (considered, so far as they can be) just in respect of their entirely non-cognitive felt character. Phenomenology, on this view, is confined to sensation-mood-emotion-image-feeling phenomena, all of which I will here bring under the general heading of *sense-feeling experience*.

Phenomenology, however, is the general study of the character of experience, and the character of experience is as much cognitive as it is sensory. There is more to the overall character of our expe-

---

[5] I argue for this in Strawson 2006a and 2006b.
[6] See e.g. Russell 1948: 246-7.
[7] 1689-1700: 4.3.6; see also 2.23.28-32. On Regius's 1647 endorsement of the *a posteriori* physicalist position, in opposition to Descartes, see Strawson 2006b.
[8] I first adopted this term when considering the complexities of what it is like to experience oneself as a free or truly responsible agent; see Strawson 1986 (e.g. pp. v, 30, 55, 96).

rience than sense-feeling experience. There is also *cognitive experience*—the name is exact. Only analytic philosophers, perhaps, have ever doubted this, but they have done so with some pride, so let me briefly demonstrate the reality of cognitive experience—of cognitive-experiential mental content, cognitive-phenomenological mental content.

Note, first, that I'm using the expression 'mental content' ('content', for short) in the old, natural, currently occluded *internalist* way, according to which the content of one's current experience (the experiential content of one's current experience) can be exactly as it is even if, to take one example, there's no external world as there seems to be. In terms of a familiar thought-experiment: my 'brain-in-a-vat Twin' and I, in having experience that is ex hypothesi qualitatively indistinguishable, have experience that has exactly the same content, although mine is experience of concrete things—birds, say, and the river Cherwell—that his is not experience of.

With this in hand, consider the experience of consciously entertaining and understanding specific propositional contents. I'll call this form of cognitive experience 'propositional meaning-experience'. It's a rather special case of cognitive experience, in fact, because almost all if not all our actual daily experience essentially involves cognitive-experiential content in a larger sense, whether we're birdwatching or cooking or climbing. It's integral to our seeing trees, chairs and so on specifically as trees, chairs and so on. I doubt that we're capable of significant stretches of experience that involve no cognitive-experiential content. But I'm going to put this point aside, in order to focus on the particular case of propositional meaning-experience. More narrowly still, I'm going to focus on the case of propositional meaning-experience involving linguistic representation, because it's a salient example and has been specifically resisted, in the wake of Ryle and Wittgenstein, among others.[9]

Consider, then, your reading and understanding this sentence and the next. This comprehending reading—it's going on at this very moment—is part of the course of your experience. More specifically: the content of the sentences, including this one, is playing a large part in determining the overall character, the over-

---

[9] Here I draw on Strawson 1994: 5-13, and 2005: §6. There's a brilliant discussion of certain aspects of propositional meaning-experience in James 1890: vol. 1 ch. 9. See also Ayers 1991 (vol. 1 ch. 31), Pitt 2004.

all qualitative character, of this particular stretch of the course of your experience, although you're also aware of the page and the print, rain on the window, birdsong, traffic noise, or whatever it may be.

The word 'qualitative' is redundant in the last sentence. It adds nothing to 'character'. I use it for emphasis because one considerable difficulty people have with the notion of cognitive experience or cognitive phenomenology is with the idea that, like sense-feeling experience, sense-feeling phenomenology, it too is ultimately and wholly a matter—to repeat the pleonasm—of the *qualitative* character of experience. In order to stay clear about this, after a conventional training in analytic philosophy, one needs to keep a firm grip on the distinction between [1] cognitive-experiential content and [2] cognitive content *externalistically* understood. Once again, my brain-in-a-vat Twin, or, as a variation, my Twin on Perfect Twin Earth—where water is H_2O, but the Nelson Mandela I know is not to be found—suffices to illustrate the distinction. For although my Twin and I are cognitive-experientially identical in respect of our as-of-Mandela thought-experiences, our as-of-Mandela thought-experiences have quite different cognitive content externalistically understood.

The best way to present the phenomena of cognitive phenomenology at a general theoretical level, perhaps, is to pass beyond the familiar notion of a sensory modality and introduce the more general notion of an *experiential modality*, which we may define by saying that one experiential modality is distinguished from another by the fact that the experiential-qualitative character of experiences available in the first experiential modality is different in type from the experiential-qualitative character of experiences available in the second. With this general notion in hand we can say that all the sensory or sense-feeling modalities (however we count them) are experiential modalities, and ask whether, conversely, all experiential modalities are sensory or sense-feeling modalities.

I'll return to this. First I want to go back to the example of your comprehending of this very sentence. The claim is that the content of your comprehending is something that has to be adverted to in a full account of the character of your current experience in the last few seconds. The content of your comprehending features in, as a part of, the overall character of your experience now.

This is obvious to unprejudiced reflection, but has become obscure to some. One reason for this, perhaps, is that it's very hard to pin down the contribution to the overall character of your experience that is being made by the content of a sentence in such a way as to be able to take it as the object of reflective thought (it seems far easier to do this in the case of the phenomenological character of an experience of green). When it comes to the attempt to figure to oneself the phenomenological character of understanding a sentence like 'Consider, then, your reading and understanding this very sentence' it seems that all one can usefully do is rethink the sentence as a whole, comprehendingly; and the trouble with doing this is that it seems to leave one with no mental room to stand back in such a way as to be able to take the experiential character of one's understanding of the sentence, redelivered to one by this rethinking, as the principal object of one's attention. One's mind is taken up with the sense of the thought in such a way that it is very hard to think about the character of the experience of having the thought.

True, but this doesn't put the reality of meaning-experience in doubt. The reality of the phenomenon can be sufficiently indicated by pointing out that the experiential difference between the event of your hearing and understanding the sentence 'the mass of the moon is just over one per cent that of the earth' and the event of your hearing and understanding the sentence 'This sentence is a sentence of English' is not just a matter of the different auditory experiences you have in the two cases. Nor is it, in the reading case, just a matter of the different shapes and/or silently entertained sounds of the words. It is also, and much more importantly, a matter of their cognitive-experiential content.[10]

Suppose we want to give a truly compendious description of the character of the course of your experience, your lived experience, during a ten-second period of time during which (among many other things) you comprehendingly entertain the thought that no one could possibly have had different parents. The claim is that we won't be able to give anything resembling a compendious description of the character of your experience over that time without citing the thought that no one could possibly have had different parents. And by 'the character of the course of your experience' I mean, of course, and pleonastically, the overall *experiential*—

---

[10] It's not as if we can reduce the experiential difference to the above mentioned auditory/visual differences *plus* non-experiential differences in the ways in which exposure to the two sentences alters your behavioural dispositional set (see Strawson 1994: 5-13).

qualitative—character of the course of your experience. We have to acknowledge the existence of cognitive-experiential qualitative content in addition to sense-feeling experiential qualitative content.

I use undramatic sentences to make the point, rather than sentences like 'The bullfrogs wore green pyjamas'. This is important, because in talking of cognitive experience, and more particularly propositional meaning-experience, and in focusing on the linguistic case, I'm not concerned in any way with any of the many imagistic or emotional or mood-tone experiences that can accompany the understanding of certain words—often in such a way that they can seem to be integral to the semantic understanding. My aim is to damp down all such accompaniments as far as possible, in order to highlight what is then left over, something that is equally real and definite although it can seem troublesomely intangible when we try to reflect on it: that is, the experience that is standardly involved in the mere comprehending of words (read, thought, or heard), where this comprehending is considered completely independently of any imagistic or emotional accompaniments.

I don't know what more to do to avert misunderstanding on this point. Suppose I say 'This sentence has five words', or 'To study is to love, and there is no relief in love'. Suppose you're attending. Your experience has a certain overall character between the time I start and the time I finish. It involves some sensory awareness of your surroundings and bodily state. It also involves hearing sounds like the sounds produced when someone with a voice like mine says 'This sentence has five words', or 'To study is to love, and there is no relief in love'. But there's more: there is the way your experience is specifically in virtue of the fact that you understand what is said.[11] Consider the difference between my saying 'I'm reading *War and Peace*' and my saying 'barath abalori trafalon'.

You have at some time read a book or listened to words (perhaps on the radio) because the content conveyed by them was fascinating. The question is: Why did you continue to read or listen? What was it about the character of your experience that made you continue? Was it merely the sensory content of the visual or auditory goings on? Obviously not. It was the cognitive-experiential

---

[11] Slightly more precisely: there is the way your experience is specifically in virtue of the fact that you automatically (and involuntarily) experience the sounds you hear as representing that p, for some proposition p. For the point that misunderstanding is as much a matter of cognitive experience as understanding, see Strawson 1994: 7.

content of your experience.[12]

Perhaps you have various imagistic and bodily-feeling accompaniments as you listen or read, and you want them to continue. The question is: what's causing them? Is it merely the visual and acoustic properties of the marks or sounds? If so, then the same sounds or marks could presumably have the same effect on someone who is (somehow) just as familiar as you are with the sounds or marks considered just as such, but doesn't experience them as meaning anything in particular.

The difficulty is plain. If one wants to give anything like a full account of the qualitative character of our experience in merely sense-feeling terms, one has to be able to explain in those terms alone how the experience of looking at a piece of paper with a few marks on it, or of hearing three small sounds, can make someone collapse in a dead faint. One has to be able to look at a class of motionless children listening raptly to a story and give a full explanation of the exceptional physiological condition into which the story has put them by reference to nothing more than the auditory experience of the spoken words. The alternative is to say that it has absolutely nothing to do with anything they actually experience.

It can't be done (all the examples make the same point). To introduce theoretical order, I think we need something like the idea introduced earlier—that of an experiential modality. All the sense-feeling modalities (however we count them) can then be filed neatly under the general category *experiential modality*, while space is left for other possible experiential modalities, and, in particular, for the experiential modality of conscious thought, in which we have cognitive experience.

How many experiential modalities are there? One can individuate them as finely as one likes. (If one wants, one can say that every qualitatively different colour experience involves a different experiential modality!) When it comes to counting sensory modal-

---

[12] Why not say 'conceptual content'? This would require one to give an internalist account of concepts according to which a concept is a distinct element in a mental economy that can be individuated as the element it is independently of reference to any non-mental reality (consider the concepts or 'concepts' giraffe and banana as possessed by my brain-in-a-vat Twin). Even if such an account were given, misunderstanding would be likely, because the current understanding of 'concept' in analytic philosophy makes the word seem conceptually inseparable from its externalist interpretation. I consider these complications in Strawson 2005.

ities, however, the best thing to do for most theoretical purposes is to focus on general differences of experiential type of the kind that we mark by sorting experiences into tactile, aural, olfactory, gustatory, visual, visceral, vestibular, musculoskeletal, kinaesthetic, etc. It's a general difference of type that is in question when it comes to the proposal that we need to add the general experiential modality of conscious thought to whatever set of experiential modalities we distinguish under the heading of sense-feeling modalities.

'The experiential modality of conscious thought'. Words like these trigger reflexes of suspicion, at least in members of my generation and its successor. To assert the existence of such a thing is still to make a radical claim in the current analytic-philosophical discussion of experience, especially given all the input from psychology and neuropsychology, which strongly constrains people to think that all experience *must* be somehow sensory.

What's the remedy? It's very important to be clear on the point that there isn't any difficulty at all, let alone any special difficulty, in the idea that the particular form of the experiential modality of conscious thought that is found in creatures like ourselves is wholly a product of a process of evolution by natural selection, just as the particular forms of the sensory modalities that are found in creatures like ourselves are wholly a product of a process of evolution by natural selection. Any real (realistic) materialist who believes in the theory of evolution must believe that this has happened, because the existence of the experiential modality of conscious thought—of cognitive experience—is an evident fact. It's one of the first pieces of data that any credible naturalism must accommodate.

It may be that nothing like the fully developed human form of the experiential modality of conscious thought can evolve until sense-feeling modalities like ours are already well evolved (it's possible that cognitive experience is principally located in early sensory areas of the brain). It may be that the former grows out of the latter, or on top of them, in some way. Perhaps the former can't exist in nature independently of the latter. Perhaps the latter are in Kant's phrase 'always already' seeded with the former in some way.[13] Questions about these matters are as old as they are

---

[13] 1781-7: A346/B404. There are old and obvious reasons to be suspicious of the idea of pure or mere sensation, given the entanglement of sensation and cognition in perception. One can register this point while agreeing with Fodor's rejection (in 'Observation Reconsidered') of the idea that there is no theory-independent observation, and before one considers the 'conceptualist'

important. They are, however, questions of detail, relative to the present concern, and none of them touch the central point that the existence of the experiential modality of conscious thought is an unbudgeable natural fact. *The mass of the moon is just over one percent that of the earth.* Nor do they cast any doubt on the idea that the experiential modality of conscious thought is a distinct experiential modality, as distinct from each of the sensory modalities as they are from each other. The Buddha puts the point very clearly when he distinguishes six principal 'senses', seeing, hearing, smelling, tasting, touching and thinking, the last of which is a matter of 'non-sensory mental activity'.[14]

What is the proper role of philosophy in relation to psychology, artificial intelligence, and the neurosciences?

Is a science of consciousness possible?

What are the most important open problems in contemporary philosophy of mind? What are the most promising prospects?

I think that the main problems in the philosophy of mind lie in its conduct, in its scholasticism and scientism, and in the massive irrelevance (failure to focus on the real issues) that stems from failure to grasp the proper place, in the philosophy of mind, of results from experimental psychology, artificial intelligence, and the neurosciences. There's a matching failure to grasp the distinctive and central rôle of *a priori* investigation in the philosophy of mind, and to understand that the philosophy of mind is a key part of the science of mind, including of course the science of consciousness.

The central problems in the philosophy of mind remain what they have always been just as many of the central problems in science remain what they always have been (e.g. what is the nature of matter?). It's a familiar point that we have to rework and develop our treatment of them from generation to generation. The most promising—if unlikely—prospect is that the views of the great

---

view, advanced paradigmatically in McDowell's *Mind and World*, that there is no non-conceptual content.

[14] Hamilton 2001: 53. I propose that 'experiential modalities' ('modes of experiencing') is an exact translation of Buddha's word 'âyatana', which is usually translated by 'senses' in spite of the fact that one of the senses is then said to be a matter of non-sensory activity. For further discussion see e.g. Strawson 1994: 196, 2009: §2.8.

philosophers of the past will be reintroduced into the the present day discussion, since the best of these views are superior to the views in favour today, and much better expressed.

References

Ayers, M. R. (1992) *Locke* (London: Routledge).

Chomsky, N. (1968) *Language and Mind* (New York: Harcourt, Brace & World).

Chun, M. & Marois, R. (2002) 'The dark side of visual attention' *Current Opinion in Neurobiology* **12**: 184-9.

Eddington, A. (1928) *The Nature of the Physical World* (New York: Macmillan).

Fodor, J. (1984) 'Observation Reconsidered' *Philosophy of Science* 51.1: 23-43.

James, W. (1890/1950) *The Principles of Psychology*, 2 volumes (New York: Dover).

Kant, I. (1781-7/1933) *Critique of Pure Reason*, translated by N. Kemp Smith (London: Macmillan).

Locke, J. (1690-1700/1975) *An Essay Concerning Human Understanding*, edited by P. Nidditch (Oxford: Clarendon Press).

Lockwood, M. (1989) *Mind, Brain, and the Quantum*. Oxford: Blackwell.

McDowell, J. (1994) *Mind and World* (Cambridge, MA: Harvard University Press).

Pessoa, L., & De Weerd. P. (2003) *Filling-In: From Perceptual Completion to Cortical Reorganization* (Oxford: Oxford University Press).

Simons, D.J., & Levin D.T. (1997) 'Change blindness' *Trends in Cognitive Sciences* 1: 261–267.

Pitt, D. (2004) 'The Phenomenology of Cognition, or What is it like to think that *p*?', *Philosophy and Phenomenological Research*.

Regius (1647) *An Account of the Human Mind...* in *The Philosophical Writings of Descartes*, Volume 1, translated by J. Cottingham et al. (Cambridge: Cambridge University Press).

Russell, B. (1948/1992) *Human Knowledge: Its Scope And Limits* (London: Routledge).

Strawson, G. (1986, reprinted with corrections 1991) *Freedom and Belief* (Oxford: Clarendon Press).

Strawson, G. (1994) *Mental Reality* (Cambridge, MA: MIT Press).

Strawson, G. (1999) 'Realistic Materialist Monism' in *Towards a Science of Consciousness III*, edited by S. Hameroff, A. Kaszniak & D. Chalmers (Cambridge, MA: MIT Press), pp 23-32.

Strawson, G. (2003) 'Real materialism' in *Chomsky and his Critics*, edited by L. Antony and N. Hornstein (Oxford: Blackwell).

Strawson, G. (2005) 'Intentionality, terminology and experience' in *Phenomenology and Philosophy of Mind*, edited by D. Smith and A. Thomasson (Oxford and New York: Oxford University Press).

Strawson, G. (2006a) 'Realistic monism: why physicalism entails panpsychism' in *Consciousness and its place in nature* edited by A. Freeman (Thorverton: Imprint Academic) pp. 3-31 (in RMAOE).

Strawson, G. (2006b) 'Panpsychism? Reply to commentators, with a celebration of Descartes' in *Consciousness and its place in nature* edited by A. Freeman (Thorverton: Imprint Academic) pp. 184-280.

Strawson, G. (2008) *Real Materialism and Other Essays* (Oxford: Clarendon Press).

Strawson, G. (2009) *Selves: An essay in revisionary metaphysics* (Oxford: Oxford University Press).

20
Michael Tye

Professor of Philosophy
University of Texas at Austin, USA

I went up to Oxford as an undergraduate to study physics. I chose Oxford over Cambridge at the urging of my school physics teacher who was an Oxford man. When I arrived, I found out that, as a physics student, I was expected to spend one day a week in the laboratory. This seemed to me extremely unappealing not only because it would interfere with my social life but also because the practical side of physics was, to my mind, deadly dull. Happily, I discovered that there was a new undergraduate degree—physics and philosophy—that combined theoretical physics with philosophical issues in the foundations of physics as well as pure philosophy. For this degree no practical work was required.

I asked to transfer into physics and philosophy and, in response to my request, I was told to go away and write an essay on truth with particular reference to the Austin/Strawson debate on the topic. I had never heard of Austin or Strawson at the time, but this I duly did with the help of the college library and, presumably after having not embarrassed myself too badly, I was admitted into the physics and philosophy degree program.

I did not find myself especially interested in the philosophical half of the degree until late in my final undergraduate year. This was due largely to the fact that my college philosophy tutor, who shall remain nameless here, chose not to speak during our tutorials except in the most perfunctory way, preferring instead to stare into the fireplace while puffing on a cigar. (To my knowledge, during his entire career he published just a single essay—on the location of sounds.) I recall his intense dislike of things American. "'Functionalism'," he would later say to me in an exaggerated, slow and disdainful manner, wrinkling his nose as he did so, "I suppose that is an American word."

20. Michael Tye

What lured me into philosophy was the sense-datum theory. I did not believe the theory but I found myself very intrigued by it and largely as a result of the writings of Ayer and Austin, I decided to rethink my original plan, which was to do a theoretical physics doctorate. Mark Platts, who was several years ahead of me at Oxford, advised me that, for graduate work in philosophy, I should go to the United States, the job situation in the UK being dire, and thinking that my best shot for acceptance would be in the philosophy of physics, on the advice of Rom Harre, I wrote in June to Indiana, Pittsburgh and Buffalo. Indiana and Pittsburgh told me that their money was already allocated for Fall graduate admissions but that they would admit me with money a year later. Buffalo gave me funding right away and off I went to Buffalo, not realizing until after I arrived just how mediocre the Buffalo program was. (The Leiter report, alas, was not yet available.)

My graduate career at Buffalo was saved by Frank Jackson who was visiting at the time. Frank would come into class each day armed with arguments from the recent journals on topics in the philosophy of mind (largely on perception). He would write them on the board and he would demolish them one by one. I was impressed, and this is how I was drawn away from the philosophy of physics and into the philosophy of mind. My first article was written in response to Frank; and it appeared, while I was still a graduate student, with an essay of his and an essay by Wilfrid Sellars, all on the adverbial theory of visual experience.

It was not until some seven or eight years later that I got drawn into the topic of consciousness, again via the work of Frank Jackson. I was then visiting Oxford and I worked very hard on an essay, subsequently published in *Mind*, defending materialism against Frank's knowledge argument. I remember meeting with a student in a pub while I was writing the essay and disturbing him with the intensity and irritability of my demeanor, itself a direct result of how much effort had gone into my reflections on Mary.

I then uncritically accepted the view of "qualia freaks" that the subjective phenomenology of an experience (more on this below) is a matter of intrinsic qualities possessed by the experience. It was not until some years later that I came to think that this was wrongheaded: the only qualities of which we aware introspectively, when, for example, we are undergoing a visual experience of something red and round are qualities that, if they are qualities of anything, are qualities of the experienced thing, qualities such as redness and roundness. These are not qualities of the experience; for the experience itself is neither red nor round.

I defended this view in a paper entitled "Visual Qualia and Visual Content," published in a collection of essays (*The Contents of Experience*) edited by Tim Crane in 1992. The essays for the volume were originally delivered at a conference arranged by Tim at King's College, London in 1990. My contribution to the conference was notable for two reasons. First, I managed to lose my paper on the way to my session and so I had to deliver my talk without paper (or notes for that matter). Second, I don't think that anyone else in the room believed anything I was saying. Happily, the reaction today is considerably more sympathetic.

The view I was then starting to develop came to fruition with the publication of my book, *Ten Problems of Consciousness*, in 1995. I suppose I think that the view contained therein, and elaborated further in *Consciousness, Color and Content* (2000), is the most important contribution in my published work so far. Those books offer an intentionalist or representationalist theory of phenomenal consciousness. Let me say a few words next about how I am using the term "phenomenal consciousness."

Of our conscious mental states, some are inherently conscious. That is to say, some of our mental states cannot *fail* to be conscious. For each such mental state, there is a *subjective* perspective that goes along with it. This perspective is conferred upon the subject simply by his or her undergoing the mental state. It is captured in everyday language by talk of 'what it is like'. There is something it is like subjectively to feel pain, to smell vomit, to taste chocolate, to feel elated. Furthermore, what it is like to undergo one inherently conscious mental state can be compared with what it is like to undergo another. For example, what it is like to experience bright red is subjectively more similar to what it is like to experience bright orange than to what it is like to experience dark green.

Mental states that are inherently conscious are standardly said to be phenomenally conscious by philosophers. 'Phenomenal consciousness', then, as I use the term, is a feature of mental states. As to which mental states are phenomenally conscious, one not very informative answer is that they are experiences. More helpfully, we can classify the relevant states into at least the following categories: (1) Perceptual experiences, for example, experiences of the sort involved in seeing green, hearing loud trumpets, tasting liquorice, smelling the sea air, running one's fingers over sandpaper. (2) Bodily sensations, for example, feeling a twinge of pain, feeling an itch, feeling hungry, having a stomach ache, feeling hot, feeling dizzy. Think here also of experiences such as those present during orgasm or while running flat-out. (3) Felt reactions or passions or emotions, for example, feeling delight, lust, fear, love, feeling grief, jealousy, regret. (4) Felt moods, for example, feeling happy, depressed, calm, bored, tense, miserable.

The basic idea of the representationalist view of phenomenal consciousness has two parts: a) all experiences have representational content; that is, each experience has associated with it accuracy or correctness conditions. b) the phenomenal character of an experience—what it is like subjectively to undergo it—either is identical with or at least supervenes on its representational content. In the two books mentioned above, I defend a version of strong representationalism. I claim that the phenomenal character of an experience is one and the same as a representational content the experience has that meets certain further conditions. The relevant content must be poised to bring about a certain range of cognitive responses; it must be abstract or general; and it must be nonconceptual. This view I called the "PANIC (*p*oised, *a*bstract, *n*onconceptual, *i*ntentional *c*ontent) theory of phenomenal consciousness."

The view seems most natural perhaps in application to perceptual experiences, but I argue that it can be applied to experiences generally. In forthcoming work (2008), I should note, I take back some of these claims. I continue to hold that all experiences have representational content but I deny that the content of a veridical perceptual experience is the same as the content of a hallucinatory experience with the same phenomenal character. So, I no longer identify the phenomenal character of an experience with its representational content, preferring instead to identify it with the complex of qualities contained within the content.[1]

As to the proper role of philosophy in relation to psychology, artificial intelligence, and the neurosciences, I do not think that philosophy should be in the business of legislating to the sciences or revising scientific views. I take philosophers to ask very general questions about the world and ourselves, and also about our relationship to the world and one another through our senses and

---

[1] This complex is the phenomenal character only if it meets certain further conditions just as Benjamin Franklin is the actual inventor of bifocals only if he meets the condition of being the unique inventor of bifocals in the actual world. For more, see my forthcoming 2008 book mentioned below.

our social interactions. Philosophers, in my view, should develop their theories in such a way as to respect as much as possible both the latest and best scientific theorizing about the world as well as the vast store of wisdom contained in what might be called our "commonsense, everyday theory of things" (dubbed by Sellars the "manifest image").

One way to capture what philosophers of mind, as opposed to scientists interested in the mind, are (or at least should be) trying to do is as follows. Scientists focused on the mind ask: How does this mental faculty work? How does memory work, for example? How are mental images generated? How does shape recognition take place? These questions are 'how' questions. They pertain to actual creatures of one sort or another (for example, human beings). They do not pertain to non-actual, possible creatures. And they can be understood, in different instances, to ask for the neurophysiological underpinnings of the appropriate mental faculty or for the computational underpinnings or simply for the more basic psychological components that generate the faculty in the relevant range of creatures.

Philosophers of mind ask: What is such-and such a mental faculty or state? What is it to remember something, for example? What is it to recognize a shape? What is pain? These 'what' questions should be understood to ask what is common to all *actual and possible* creatures that have the relevant mental property or state (remembering something, recognizing a shape, etc) in virtue of which they have the property or state. In this way, they are asking about the general nature of the faculty or state.

So, neurophysiology, scientific psychology and artificial intelligence do not directly offer answers to the questions philosophy of mind asks. The philosopher of mind should respect the answers given by scientists to the appropriate 'how' questions while insisting that 'what' questions remain about which there can be reasonable disagreement—questions whose answers require theorizing at a more general level than is found in the individual sciences. Of course with the appropriate theorizing, it may be concluded that one of the sciences in particular—for example, neurophysiology—not only provides an account of how the given mental faculties or states are generated in actual creatures (of their *realization* in those creatures) but also can supply an account of the general nature of the faculties or states. However, this conclusion is not one that the neurophysiologist, qua neurophysiologist, is in any position to reach. It is not shown to be true directly by neurophysiology and it may reasonably be denied while accepting all that the neurophysiogical account has to say.

Is, then, a science of consciousness possible? My answer is that science alone cannot tell us the nature of consciousness. It can only tell us how consciousness is realized in actual organisms. Still, science together with the appropriate philosophical theorizing can reveal the nature of consciousness—at least in principle. I add "in principle" here since there remains the possibility, not to be ruled out a priori, that consciousness has a nature that is describable fully in some scientific theory, though not one that it is within our power, as human beings, to comprehend. I reject this deeply pessimistic view, but I see no incoherence in the idea that human minds, being the product of a particular evolutionary niche, are not suited to discover the nature of consciousness.

My own 1995 PANIC theory of consciousness claims that the phenomenal character of an experience is a representational content that (among other things) is suitably poised for cognitive responses. This proposal, and in particular its 'poised' component, can be fleshed out further via the global workspace view of consciousness elaborated by some psychologists. As such, its further development may be seen as drawing in a straightforward way on scientific claims.

Those who deny that a science of consciousness is possible either must deny that there is a hidden nature to consciousness, holding instead that conscious properties and states are 'given' to us introspectively and that there is no further story to be told about their subjective character, or else they must insist that a priori analysis of our ordinary concepts can tell us what consciousness essentially is (and likewise for such specific conscious states as the feeling of pain, the felt character of anger, and so on) just as a priori analysis of the concept *triangle* can tell us that what it is for a figure to be triangular. The latter view (held by a priori functionalists about consciousness) seems deeply implausible; the former is based upon a number of famous philosophical arguments (perhaps the best known being Jackson's knowledge argument and the appeal to the possibility of zombies). In my view, none of these arguments are compelling.

It has to be admitted that there is not much agreement among philosophers as to the best account of consciousness. Physicalists about consciousness have generally accepted that the right way to handle the arguments just mentioned against physicalism is to suppose that we possess a range of special, perspectival concepts for conceiving of our phenomenal states via introspection (concepts we acquire as we undergo the relevant experiences and attend to their phenomenal character). These concepts, physicalists have held, can easily mislead us into supposing that the states we are conceiving are themselves special. Unfortunately, no physicalist has yet told an acceptable story about the supposed special nature of these concepts and my current view is that even this (usual) point of agreement among physicalists is misplaced. In forthcoming work (*Consciousness Revisited: Materialism without Phenomenal Concepts*, MIT Press, 2008), I claim there are no special, *phenomenal* concepts (as they are often called) and that a new strategy is needed by the physicalist.

One important open problem, then, is to come to a better understanding of the concepts that enable us directly to form beliefs about our experiences. Another open problem, of course, is to come to a better understanding of consciousness itself. A third huge problem in the philosophy of mind is to articulate a satisfactory theory of the nature of mental content.

I continue to think that these problems are connected and that some version of representationalism is the right way to go in trying to understand phenomenal consciousness. I also now think that physicalist theories of consciousness would do well to pay more attention to the distinction between what Russell called "knowledge by acquaintance" and "knowledge by description." The prospects for handling some of the traditional puzzles of consciousness in part by means of an appeal to this distinction now seems to me more promising than any other approach.

One topic which has not received much attention in philosophy of mind is that of attention. The relationship of attention to consciousness is one that psychologists are now beginning to address and I speculate that it will be studied intensively in philosophy in coming years. This may be instrumental in coming to a better understanding of consciousness itself and the role it plays in the functional architecture of the mind.

About the Editor

Patrick Grim is Distinguished Teaching Professor at the State University of New York at Stony Brook, author of *The Incomplete Universe*, co-author of *The Philosophical Computer*, and founding co-editor of over twenty volumes of *The Philosopher's Annual*. He has released a series of lectures as *Philosophy of Mind: Brains, Consciousness, and Thinking Machines*. Grim has published widely not only in philosophy but in other fields as well: theoretical biology, linguistics, decision theory, computer science and artificial intelligence.

Index

a priori, 19, 47, 109, 116, 125, 154, 189, 190, 197, 204, 214
action, 19, 56–58, 113, 132, 171, 174, 176–178
analytic/synthetic distinction, 183
Aristotle, 133, 163, 168
Armstrong, D. M., 72, 107, 108, 123, 158
artificial intelligence/AI, iii, 6, 13, 16, 18, 35, 51, 53, 80, 105, 110, 111, 125, 147, 173, 174, 178, 204, 212, 213, 217

behaviorism, 39, 40, 145, 172
belief, 1, 2, 31, 32, 49, 72, 77, 84, 109, 111, 113–116, 126, 129, 132, 162, 163, 171, 196
blindsight, 17, 35, 54, 126, 161, 165, 166
Block, Ned, 119, 124, 147–151
brain, 2–5, 11, 21, 22, 25, 28, 30, 35, 37, 42, 43, 45, 46, 56, 60–65, 67, 69, 71, 75–77, 79, 81–86, 89, 91–93, 95, 97, 99–101, 107, 108, 117, 119, 127–129, 132, 136, 142, 143, 146, 152, 154, 172, 174, 175, 177, 179, 198, 199, 203

change blindness, 17, 126, 194
chinese room argument, 80
Chomsky, Noam, 29, 48, 181, 182, 206, 207
Churchland, Paul & Patricia, 157
cognitive science, 12–14, 27, 51, 54, 59–61, 66, 80, 118, 137, 182, 188
cognitivism, 39
color, 35, 126, 127, 140, 149, 166
compatibilism, 18
concepts, 5, 23, 29, 30, 32, 37, 54, 66, 89, 91, 95, 102, 109, 111, 129, 146, 167, 177, 178, 184, 214, 215
consciousness, iii, 7, 8, 11–15, 17, 18, 21–24, 26, 28, 29, 34–36, 40–46, 55–61, 65, 66, 76, 77, 79, 80, 92, 102, 105, 109–112, 118, 119, 121, 125–129, 131, 135–140, 142, 143, 147, 157, 158, 160, 161, 164–166, 174, 175, 177–180, 187, 188, 193, 194, 204, 207, 210–212, 214, 215

Darwin, Charles, 42, 178

Davidson, Donald, 48, 49, 70, 73, 74, 117, 132
Dennett, Daniel, 11, 42, 59, 102, 123, 127, 129, 132, 164, 184
Descartes, 25, 121, 128, 163, 184, 206, 207
dreams, 40, 41, 43, 83, 84, 90, 93
Dretske, Fred, 31–33, 35, 37, 38, 124, 147, 150, 168
Dualism, 14, 18, 25, 46, 71, 73, 107, 127, 145, 172, 175
Dummett, Michael, 12, 48

eliminativism, 1
emergence, 46, 86, 118, 196
emotions, 61, 118, 167, 169, 197, 212
epistemology, 16, 24, 31, 32, 40, 43, 48, 76, 117, 132, 187
ethics, 7, 16, 30, 171
evolution, 6, 29, 92, 203
experimental philosophy, 187
externalism, 1, 5, 18, 32, 33

filling in, 127
Fodor, Jerry, 17, 50, 123, 128, 130, 132, 133, 184, 206
folk psychology, 30, 47, 187
free will, 18, 26, 80, 180, 187, 193, 194
Frege, 48, 189
functionalism, 42, 72, 123, 124, 145, 146, 152, 154, 172, 209

Gödel, 11, 28, 59, 86–89, 91, 92, 98, 102
Gibson, J. J., 70, 151

hallucinations, 148, 152–154
hardware, 172
Hempel, Carl, 117, 181
Hume, 176, 189, 193

innate ideas, 181, 182
inner theater, 147
intentional content, 34, 152, 153, 156, 161, 166–169, 176
intentionalism, 147–151, 153
intentionality, 16, 18, 23–25, 33, 105, 106, 121, 124, 128, 129, 132, 138, 150, 155–157, 159, 160, 168, 171, 172, 174, 175, 177, 179, 207
interdisciplinary, 16, 21, 26, 50, 53, 60, 66, 67, 139, 184, 187
internalism, 18
inverted spectrum, 80

Jackson, Frank, 145, 210, 214

Kant, 17, 117, 121, 163, 167, 168, 184, 189, 193, 203, 206
knowledge argument, 108, 109, 145, 147, 210, 214
Kripke, Saul, 47, 147

language, 4, 5, 7, 14–16, 22, 24, 28–30, 36, 47–50, 52–54, 80–83, 85, 90, 94, 96, 98, 100, 102, 108, 110, 135, 141, 157, 171, 182, 184, 185, 206, 211
Locke, 48, 77, 125, 158, 197, 206
logical positivism, 182, 189

McDowell, 48, 147, 149, 154, 206
meaning, 16, 37, 46, 48, 49, 79, 98, 141, 146, 198, 200–202
mental causation, 18, 23, 70, 71, 76, 78, 118, 121, 174–177, 179
Merleau-Ponty, M., 141
metaphor, 50, 52, 95, 97, 139, 140
metaphysics, 1, 2, 5, 6, 14–16, 22, 24, 43, 47, 48, 70, 71, 108, 117, 118, 163, 194, 207
mind, 172
mind-body problem, 15, 71, 118, 174, 175, 177, 179, 194
mind-brain identity theory, 11, 107, 108, 117
monism, 23, 73, 74, 207
moral psychology, 76, 132, 188–190
multiple realizability, 72, 73

Nagel, Ernest, 86, 87, 89
Nagel, Tom, 145
naturalism, 46, 180, 195–197, 203
neuroethics, 67
neuroscience, 18, 21, 24, 30, 35, 40–43, 51, 56, 59–61, 66, 67, 111, 118, 141, 147, 162, 163, 178, 187, 189
Nozick, Robert, 149, 152

panpsychism, 197, 207
Peacocke, Christopher, 125, 131
perception, 18, 23, 31, 32, 35, 54, 56–58, 70, 89, 91, 92, 94, 113, 114, 118, 127, 131, 137, 138, 141, 147–153, 161, 168, 210
phenomenal consciousness, 7, 42, 211, 212, 215
phenomenology, 40, 41, 43, 106, 131, 139, 141, 148, 197, 199, 206, 207, 210
philosophy of language, 14–16, 24, 47–49, 171, 184
physicalism, 108, 111, 194, 207, 214
propositional attitudes, 31, 32, 51, 129, 132
psychoanalysis, 6, 39
psychology, iii, 6, 7, 18, 21, 30, 35, 39–41, 43, 46, 47, 50, 51, 53, 59, 60, 67, 69, 70, 72, 76, 80, 105, 110, 111, 119, 125, 128, 132, 140, 147, 162, 163, 168, 178, 184, 185, 187–191, 203, 204, 206, 212, 213
psychophysics, 163

qualia, 25, 32, 34, 80, 124, 128, 129, 133, 149–151, 210, 211
Quine, W. V. O., 39, 43, 48, 51, 52, 74, 162, 182–185, 191

realism, 5, 148, 149, 194
reduction, 21, 60, 73, 118, 175
reductionism, 1, 183
reference, 1, 16, 21, 50–52, 86–89, 93, 98, 102, 111,

124, 137, 138, 146,
161, 202, 209
Reichenbach, Hans, 146, 148
representation, 17, 33, 34, 61,
90, 114, 128, 129, 131,
133, 150, 198
representationalism, 212, 215
Ryle, Gilbert, 138, 198

Searle, John, 61
strong AI, 173, 174
supervenience, 46, 73, 105, 118

teleology, 79, 123, 124

Wittgenstein, 69, 123, 131, 135,
141, 198

zombie argument, 25, 147

www.ingramcontent.com/pod-product-compliance
Lightning Source LLC
Chambersburg PA
CBHW031253230426
43670CB00005B/160